THEORY OF LITERATURE AND OTHER CRITICAL WRITINGS

WEATHERHEAD BOOKS ON ASIA

WEATHERHEAD EAST ASIAN INSTITUTE, COLUMBIA UNIVERSITY

Theory of Literature and Other Critical Writings

NATSUME SŌSEKI

EDITED BY

Michael K. Bourdaghs, Atsuko Ueda, and Joseph A. Murphy

COLUMBIA UNIVERSITY PRESS

NEW YORK

This publication has been supported by the Richard W. Weatherhead Publication Fund
of the Weatherhead East Asian Institute, Columbia University.
Columbia University Press wishes to express its appreciation for assistance given
by the Pushkin Fund toward the cost of publishing this book.

COLUMBIA UNIVERSITY PRESS

PUBLISHERS SINCE 1893

NEW YORK   CHICHESTER, WEST SUSSEX

Library of Congress Cataloging-in-Publication Data
Natsume, Soseki, 1867–1916.
Theory of literature and other critical writings / Natsume Soseki ; edited by
Michael K. Bourdaghs, Atsuko Ueda, and Joseph A. Murphy.
p.   cm.   (Weatherhead books on Asia)
Includes bibliographical references and index.
ISBN 978-0-231-14656-2 (cloth : alk. paper) — ISBN 978-0-231-51831-4 (electronic)
1. Literature.   I. Bourdaghs, Michael K.   II. Ueda, Atsuko.   III. Murphy,
Joseph A. (Joseph Anthony), 1961–   IV. Title.   V. Series.
PN45.N356   2009
801—dc22   2008010468

Columbia University Press books are printed on permanent and durable
acid-free paper.
This book is printed on paper with recycled content.
Printed in the United States of America

c 10 9 8 7 6 5 4 3 2 1

References to Internet Web sites (URLs) were accurate at the time of writing. Neither
the author nor Columbia University Press is responsible for URLs that may have expired
or changed since the manuscript was prepared.

To Brett de Bary
from her students, direct and indirect

CONTENTS

PART TWO

Other Writings on Literary Theory, 1907–14

ACKNOWLEDGMENTS

Many scholars contributed to the effort that led to this volume. The editors would like to thank Rachael Hutchinson, Jay Rubin, and Keith Vincent for contributing translations to this project. We would also like to thank Ayako Kano and Thomas LaMarre for their generous help in untangling many of the intellectual and linguistic puzzles that we encountered in Sōseki's theories. Suggestions from two anonymous readers helped make this a better book. We wish to express our gratitude to Jennifer Crewe and her colleagues at Columbia University Press for their patience and support. Jay Rubin's translation of "My Individualism" is reprinted here by kind permission of *Monumenta Nipponica*, the Pacific Basin Institute at Pomona College, and the translator.

This book is the end product of a series of workshops and conferences organized by the editors over the course of several years. We would like to express our gratitude to all who participated in those events, in particular: Mark Anderson, Anna-Marie Farrier, Norman Holland, Iida Yūko, Karatani Kōjin, Komori Yōichi, Tom Looser, Masumitsu Keiko, Richard Okada, Dan O'Neill, Vincent Pecora, Atsuko Sakaki, Ann Sherif, and, finally, Brett de Bary, to whom we dedicate this volume.

THEORY OF LITERATURE AND OTHER CRITICAL WRITINGS

Natsume Sōseki and the Ten-Year Project

Michael K. Bourdaghs, Joseph A. Murphy, and Atsuko Ueda

Natsume Sōseki

For university students majoring in literature today, one of the first lessons in literary theory involves studying the history of shifting definitions of the term "literature" and its counterparts in other languages. We are often under the impression that this questioning is a recent development, that only sophisticated postmoderns would consider suspect a term that previous generations no doubt considered natural and universal.

In fact, probing the instabilities that haunt the category of "literature" is not a new activity. The eponymous hero of Natsume Sōseki's 1908 novel *Sanshirō*, a student newly arrived in metropolitan Tokyo from rural Kyushu, attends his first day of classes at Tokyo Imperial University. His second class of the day is a lecture course on literary theory (*bungakuron*).

The professor entered the classroom and paused to look at the blackboard, where someone had written "*Geschehen*" and "*Nachbild*." "Hm, German," he said and, laughing, proceeded to rub them out with great vigor. This destroyed for Sanshirō some of the respect with which he had until then regarded the German language. The professor went on to list twenty definitions of literature that had been formulated by men of letters down through the ages. These, too, Sanshirō recorded carefully in his notebook.[1]

As he grows savvier, Sanshirō will also lose his respectful habit of taking careful notes and even of attending class. He learns from classmates that lectures today are not up to the standards of earlier professors, such as Lafcadio Hearn. In turn, Sanshirō becomes embroiled in university politics, including a campaign by students to replace foreign professors of literature with native Japanese scholars.

Readers of the novel familiar with the author's personal history (as most readers during its initial serialization in the *Asahi* newspaper would have been) cannot help but smile at the sly self-references set in play here. For starters, the university professor in question is clearly modeled after Natsume Sōseki himself, whose *Theory of Literature (Bungakuron)* had been delivered as a series of lectures at Tokyo Imperial University from 1903 to 1905 and subsequently revised and published in book form the year before *Sanshirō* appeared. Moreover, Sōseki was one of the professors hired at the university as part of its campaign to replace foreign scholars with Japanese natives—and the foreign professor whom Sōseki replaced (much to the consternation of many students, who found Sōseki's lectures too dry) was none other than Lafcadio Hearn.

While Sōseki is remembered today as modern Japan's greatest novelist, one who enjoys a rare combination of popular and critical acclaim, these passages remind us that Sōseki started out as a scholar of English literature and as a literary theorist. Sōseki would later look back on his *Theory of Literature* as an immature and unfinished work, as "not so much a memorial to my projected 'life's work' as its corpse—and a deformed corpse, at that." (This quote is from the 1914 lecture "My Individualism" [Watakushi no kojinshugi], included in this volume.) In fact, the work remains of tremendous interest and importance. For example, here Sōseki insists that literary taste is socially and historically determined, a position that allows him to challenge any notion that Western literature might be superior to Japanese or Chinese literature. Moreover, he insists that his theory of literature is scientific—even as a crucial aspect of his project is to theorize the distinction between literature and science. Scholars looking at *Theory of Literature* today see in it a foreshadowing of later developments in literary theory, such as formalism, structuralism, reader-response theory, cognitive science, and postcolonialism. The work remains both intriguing and frustrating because it appears to resemble all of these later schools and yet is nothing like them—in part because Sōseki was struggling to express ideas and concepts for which no vocabulary existed in 1907.

In short, *Theory of Literature* is an astonishing and unprecedented work of literary theory, unmistakably modern yet also clearly (and self-consciously) non-Western even as it insists on its own universal applicability. It would subsequently be joined by a series of lectures and essays in which Sōseki continued to develop his theory in the years leading up to his death.

But why was Sōseki able to launch this unprecedented—and in many ways still unique—theoretical project? In part, this is no doubt due to the circumstances of his life and the concrete historical situation in which he lived. He was born Natsume Kinnosuke in 1867, the last year of the old shogun's regime, in the city that was still known as Edo (it would shortly be renamed Tokyo).[2] As the eighth child born to a once prosperous merchant family in a culture that practiced rigid primogeniture, he was utterly superfluous and was quickly sent out to a foster family. He was subsequently brought back almost immediately when an older sister discovered that he was being neglected. The following year he was legally adopted into yet another family, becoming Shiobara Kinnosuke, the name he would retain for more than a decade even after he returned to his birth family in 1876, following the dissolution of the Shiobara's marriage. According to Sōseki, upon returning to his birth family, he wasn't even sure which of his adult relatives were his own father and mother until a maid surreptitiously informed him that the couple he believed to be his grandparents were, in fact, his parents.

This turbulent childhood would leave its traces in Sōseki's later fiction. Perhaps more relevant to our concerns here, is its historical timing. Born before the Meiji Restoration of 1868, Sōseki belonged to the last generation of Japanese who could remember the old Edo culture that existed prior to the radical changes that were carried out as Japan transformed itself into a modern imperial power in the 1870s, 1880s and 1890s. This meant not only that Sōseki acquired a familiarity with such longstanding Japanese literary practices as Noh chanting and haiku composition but also that he—like virtually all male Japanese pupils of his generation—received his primary education in the Chinese classical tradition, learning at a young age to recite from memory the works of Confucius, Mencius, and other canonical sages. Moreover, in 1881–82 Sōseki enrolled as a student at Nishō Gakusha, a Tokyo academy that specialized in classical Chinese learning. Sōseki would continue to compose classical Chinese poetry (*kanshi*) until his death and would write a significant essay on Lao Tzu while at the university. A number of the literary examples cited in *Theory of Literature* are derived from the classical Chinese canon.

All of which is to say that Sōseki's education left him with the ability to relativize the supposedly universal intellectual systems of Western modernity he would encounter as a student and teacher in the new modern educational system set up by the Meiji state. He was able, that is, "to point out that universality was not a priori, but historical" in origin.[3] In 1888, while a student in the First Higher School, Sōseki at first hesitated before choosing to major in English literature (he had briefly considered architecture, among other alternatives). In 1890 he enrolled in the English literature department at Tokyo Imperial University, where he would study until his graduation in 1893. At the university he was exposed to recent trends in philosophy, literary theory, psychology, and sociology, and he began to help edit the *Journal of Philosophy* (*Tetsugaku zasshi*), an important scholarly journal. After graduating, he began teaching at Tokyo Higher Normal School. In 1895 he took up another post at Matsuyama Middle School in Ehime Prefecture. The following year he married Nakane Kyōko and accepted another position as an English teacher at the Fifth Higher School in Kumamoto, on the island of Shikoku, which was even farther from the cultural center of Tokyo.

In 1900 his career underwent an unexpected—and largely unwelcome—change of direction. He was ordered by the Japanese government to travel to England as an official overseas exchange student, part of a rapid expansion of the Japanese higher education system, which was largely financed by war reparations from China following Japan's victory in the 1894–95 Sino-Japanese War. (Another part of Japan's war spoils was the island of Taiwan, its first overseas colony.) The war reparations essentially bankrupted the Chinese government, hastening the downfall of the Qing Dynasty and the Sino-centric order in Asian culture—in other words, the world that had produced the scholarship underlying Sōseki's primary education. Sōseki's journey to London—metropole of the British Empire—was part and parcel of the geopolitical rise of one empire and the fall of another. If his subsequent theory in some ways represented a postcolonial deconstruction of the pretensions to universality of Western literary theory, it was also a new form of imperial knowledge produced by an official of a newly rising empire.[4]

The two years he spent in London were perhaps the hardest period in Sōseki's life. He suffered a nervous breakdown and largely isolated himself from both the British and his fellow Japanese. It was also in London that Sōseki launched into his project to theorize literature. Upon returning to Japan in early 1903, Sōseki took up positions as lecturer in English literature at both Tokyo Imperial University and the First Higher School. In early 1905 his life took another unexpected turn. He published his first two pieces of fiction in literary journals, the short stories "Tower of London" (London Tō) and "I Am a Cat" (Wagahai wa neko de aru). The latter story proved so popular that Sōseki ended up continuing its narrative, writing a total of eleven installments that were collected and published in book form in 1906. A number of stories and novellas followed, including *Botchan* (1906) and *Grass Pillow* (translated as *The Three-Cornered World*; *Kusamakura*, 1906). While continuing to teach at the university, Sōseki became increasingly well known as one of Japan's most talented novelists.

In March 1907 Sōseki shocked the scholarly establishment when he announced that he was resigning his prestigious position at Tokyo Imperial University—the pinnacle of the Japanese educational and scholarly world— to accept a position as an employee of the *Asahi* newspaper in an age when newspaper journalism was still considered a vulgar profession. (Sōseki's response, his celebrated "Statement on Joining the *Asahi*," is included in this volume.) Sōseki's contract with the *Asahi* promised him a monthly salary of two hundred yen, allowed him to retain all of his own copyrights, and permitted him to publish his nonliterary writings (e.g., *Theory of Literature*) wherever he wished. All he was required to do was serialize his fictional works in the *Asahi*—with no specifications as to number of works, their length, or deadlines. The remarkably favorable terms of the contract were a sign not only of Sōseki's growing popularity but also of his rapid mastery of the new practices of intellectual property and royalty systems, which were undergoing rapid changes as a result of the industrialization of the publishing industry and following Japan's adoption in 1899 of its first modern copyright law.

In June 1907 Sōseki began serializing *The Poppy* (*Gubijinsō*), his first newspaper novel, in the *Asahi*. All ten of his full-length novels (including *Light and Darkness* [*Meian*], left unfinished at Sōseki's death in 1916) would first be published in the form of daily installments in that newspaper. All are available in English translation. Together with the short stories and poetry that Sōseki continued to write during this period, they comprise a remarkable body of work, clearly establishing Sōseki as one of the most important authors of the twentieth century—whether of Japanese or world literature. That Sōseki was frequently in ill health throughout this period only adds to our astonishment at his achievement.

Many of the novels bear clear connections to Sōseki's work as a literary theorist. There are, for example, the discussions of the differences between science and literature that take place in *Sanshirō*, the radical cut-up strategy for reading the pages of a novel out of sequence presented in *Grass Pillow*, and the dark exploration of the conflict between cultural and market value in *Autumn Storm* (*Nowaki*, 1907). However, our purpose in this volume is not to introduce Sōseki the novelist—who is already fairly well known outside of Japan—but rather to introduce Sōseki the theorist. With that in mind, we will now examine in greater depth his *Theory of Literature* and other related essays and lectures. (MKB)

Theory of Literature and the Larger Project

That Sōseki *had* a theoretical project in addition to his practical exercises in fiction writing there can be no doubt. He was originally a professor of literature and shared the ethos of the university as a site for the advancement of substantive knowledge claims, which he glosses as "cosmopolitan," versus the local particularity of his starting point in English literature. This is made explicit in a letter written from London in September 1901 to Terada Torahiko, in which Sōseki describes his feelings upon seeing an account of the newly ascendant atomic hypothesis by Arthur W. Rücker in his inaugural address as president of the British Association for the Advancement of Science.[5] During the course of his undergraduate studies at Tokyo Imperial University, Sōseki consistently recognizes this "cosmopolitan" nature in the advancements of science and seeks to apply it to the study of literature. This is the purport of his resolution, arrived at while in London, to "put away my books of literature in a wicker trunk" and seek the cosmopolitan—that is to say, both the universal and comprehensive—nature of the problem of literature in order to find a site over which to reconcile the incommensurably intuitive nature of his experience of the Chinese classics (which young men whose elementary schooling preceded the establishment of the Meiji educational system studied from childhood) and the distance he felt from English literature.

Sōseki's theoretical project, conceived very early in his career, is to bring the study of literature in line with the study of the physical world as a cosmopolitan project. The task here is to make the case for the consistency and weight of that theoretical project, such that it appears not as a mistake or an optional appendage or footnote to Sōseki's celebrated identity as a novelist but rather as an essential part of his oeuvre, such that consideration of his novels without taking into account his theoretical project seems a truncation or an impoverishment. The following four points can be adduced to strengthen the case that Sōseki's theoretical project needs to be considered in conjunction with his novelistic production: (1) Sōseki's theoretical project brackets his fiction writing; (2) it also informs his fiction writing; (3) it was conceived complete and executed according to his original conception; and (4) it derives its power by interfacing with other areas of knowledge, particularly the empirical and social sciences. These four points will next be considered in turn.

The first point in arguing for the importance of considering Sōseki as a theorist, in addition to his reputation as a popular novelist, is the fact that Sōseki's theoretical project *brackets* his fiction writing. That is to say, it is not a stage he moves beyond. This is, first of all, a matter of fact. Sōseki began conceiving and preparing for this project while residing in London in 1901–2 and delivered its initial phase in the form of lectures at Tokyo Imperial University from 1903 to 1905. His career in fiction writing began with the publication of *Tower of London* and *I Am a Cat* in 1905. Furthermore, after a stint as a successful novelist for the *Asahi* newspaper, Sōseki *rejoined* this project with the publication of a series of lectures on literature, philosophy, and the nature of civilization, including "Philosophical Foundations of the Literary Arts" (Bungei no tetsugakuteki kiso, 1907; included in this volume), but especially "The Civilization of Modern-Day Japan" (Gendai Nihon no kaika, 1911)[6] and "My Individualism." Sōseki's theoretical work precedes his fictional work and brackets a significant portion of his fictional oeuvre. The lectures of 1911–14 are justly famous on their own terms, but it is in the context of the trajectory from *Theory of Literature* in 1903–5 that their full significance emerges. Had Sōseki done this work while an academic at Tokyo Imperial University and then abandoned it upon achieving success as a novelist, one might dismiss this as a transitory step—even a misstep—prior to finding the right path. Returning to it after a substantial period of fiction writing bespeaks a continuing importance for this project aside from the practical pursuit of fiction.

In addition to its being as important as his achievements as a creative writer, Sōseki's theoretical work informs his fiction writing during this same period. Important novels, such as *Sanshirō* and *Grass On the Wayside* (*Michikusa*, 1915), are set in an academic environment and treat thematically the period of his life when he was producing *Theory of Literature*. They provide a rich repository of images reflecting the conflict he had with his students, his family life, and the existential stress of the academic, at two o'clock in the morning, trying to reconcile an intensely held intellectual position with the demands of a student body invested in a different relation to the subject. These thematic references are sustained and significant in themselves and point to this period as one to which he continually returned in his intellectual life.

In addition to thematic treatment, however, it is possible to trace many points in his work where he is formally trying out specific parts of his theory in practice. For example, book 2 (in an excerpt included in this volume) discusses the use of scientific theories as literary material. Scientific theories carry no affective charge and hence are not literary material. Affect (small f) attaches in two ways: at the moment of discovery, as a form of pleasure, and among the general populace as the theory begins circulating in adulterated and popularized form. In its actual, intellectually consistent form, no small f whatsoever attaches. In the opening pages of his final unfinished novel *Light and Darkness*, the protagonist Tsuda is informed by his doctor of the ulcer that is eating away at his gastrointestinal tract. On the way home he engages in a dizzying reflection on the ceaseless change and transformation of the train he is on, his sequence of thought, and then the physical changes occurring "inside his own body." He then places in the mouth of a friend an explanation of the French mathematician Poincaré's theories of randomness and complexity in the most inadequate and superficial manner. As a technique of parody this recalls the bluster and posturing by which the academic and literati types in *I Am a Cat* try to bluff one another with respect to their acquaintance with the most up-to-date European theories. However, according to Nagayama Yasuo, Sōseki typically brings a very keen understanding of the fundamentals of scientific issues to his writing, from atomic theory to thermodynamics. "Unlike the scholars of literature that appear in his novels, such as Prof. Kushami and Sanshirō, Sōseki himself had an unusually keen interest in the sciences and was also aware of its monstrous ability to intervene in social affairs outside its status as thought."[7] When one considers that his pupil and close confidante, physicist Terada Torahiko, had from 1908 onward shifted the focus of his research to the behavior of complex systems and had cited Poincaré, it is doubtful that this cavalier bluff in *Light and Darkness* represents the state of Sōseki's knowledge of the subject. In juxtaposing the protagonist's legitimate horror of the entropy attending changes in the body with the pretentious and inadequate characterization of the physics, one sees not a miscalculation by Sōseki but rather the implications of this section of *Theory of Literature* being worked out and experimented with in practice. As Nagayama points out, a similar difference is effected in *Sanshirō*, in a discussion of radiation or "light pressure," between Nonomiya's precise explanation and Sanshirō's inability to grasp the practical import. Beyond this type of episodic incorporation, Sōseki's theoretical apparatus can be found to structure entire works. Joseph Murphy develops in detail the argument that the impressionistic quality of Sōseki's *Tower of London* is a direct experimental embodiment of the wave model of consciousness worked out in *Theory of Literature* that he was delivering at the same time in his lectures.[8] The level of detail at which the comparison can be made further suggests that this is not an intuitive but a conscious elaboration of the theoretical architecture. At the most general level, it is clear in the discussion of realism and Jane Austen in chapter 7 of book 4 (included here in its entirety) that Sōseki is laying the groundwork for the method of his own novels, the situation of a genuinely tragic form in the life and problems of the middle class.

These examples show that from the very beginning to the end of his creative career, specific parts of the theoretical apparatus conceived in London in 1901–2 continue to inform Sōseki's novels; it remains one of the most important neglected tasks in Sōseki criticism to identify and interpret these points in every novel. The fact that thematic references to the period when Sōseki was conceiving this project—for example, in *I Am a Cat, Sanshirō*, and *Grass By the Wayside*—also occur at the beginning and end of Sōseki's career as a novelist further strengthens the idea that his identity as a theorist is inseparable from his accomplishment as a novelist.

Beyond the evidence that his theoretical work was of continuing importance to Sōseki and informed his creative writing, the question arises as to the quality and interest of his theoretical work outside the circle of Sōseki specialists. The first point to be adduced as evidence of a quality and power in Sōseki's thinking that might claim the attention of scholars aside from Sōseki specialists and the narrow field of Japanese studies is that the overall project was conceived *complete*, in a fever, as an unfolding ten-year plan and executed according to his original conception. This is an unusual intellectual feat. Karatani Kōjin stresses that *Theory of Literature* as we have it was originally part of a much more ambitious ten-year project to situate the convergence of historically distinct senses of literature in the context of modern civilization.[9] *Theory of Literature* seems to have been intended as a first step, designed to rescue Sōseki from the disciplinary strictures of literature as he encountered them in England.

> Over the course of my study abroad I gradually came to dislike literature. Whenever I would read Western poetry, etc., I felt nothing. Trying to pretend that I was enjoying this would be like a person pretending to have wings and trying to fly, or a person with no money walking around trying to look prosperous. About that time Ikeda Kikunae came in from Germany and stayed at my lodgings. Ikeda is a chemist, but when I talked to him a bit, I was surprised to find that he's quite an impressive philosopher. I remember him besting me in arguments on a number of occasions. It was to my great profit that I met him in London. Thanks to him I was able to quit the spectral literature and resolved to pursue a more systematic and substantial line of research.[10]

Letters to his family dating from 1901–2 show the work in genesis. In a letter to his father-in-law dated March 15, 1902, Sōseki describes himself being seized by a new project, "reading day and night, taking notes and little by little formulating my thoughts and advancing the enterprise. If I put out the usual sort of book, it's going to look like table scraps from the Europeans, so I'm working diligently to produce something I won't have to be ashamed to show to people."[11] The preface describes the process of assembling books and materials for the project and the famous decision to "shut away all books of literature in my wicker trunk," the notion of trying to discern the fundamental nature of literature by reading literature being for the Sōseki of this period akin to "trying to wash blood with blood." Sōseki reports achieving a rare level of concentration during this period, though his friends were worried about his health, and he was reprimanded by the Ministry of Education for failing to file necessary interim reports. According to the plan he formulated, *Theory of Literature* was to take two to three years. The ultimate goal of the project, for which he put his literature books away, was not a theory of literature but a step-by-step triangulation of a number of disciplines to situate literature in a comprehensive theory of human experience:

I know this is like baptizing and making a fuss over a child before it is
born, but what I intend to do is the following: Beginning with the question of how it is that we perceive the physical world, I'll move from there
to the question of how to interpret human existence, and from there to
the question of the significance and objective of human life and its
principles of movement. This will lead to dissection of the various elements structuring civilization, and discourse on its nature, as well as
the influence the tendency of these associated developments exerts on
literature. Given the vastness of the problem, this is likely to reach into
the realm of philosophy, history, politics, psychology, physiology, and
the theory of evolution.[12]

Sōseki admits that, though shocked at the scope of the problem, he nevertheless resolves to pursue it to its conclusion irrespective of the cost in
time and resources. At this time Sōseki was still considering whether to
continue as an English instructor upon returning to Japan and could not
have foreseen the trajectory of his career, from holding the prestigious
chair in English literature at Tokyo Imperial University to becoming a
highly successful novelist. Were these the fevered imaginings of a young
scholar far from home? The surprising thing, in this regard, is that this is
exactly what he would do in the lectures of 1911–14, setting in place the
model of civilization as a set of drives in tension, the philosophical under-
pinnings of literature, and the place of the individual as the center of this
open-ended, chaotic system.

If the standard intellectual procedure in Japanese scholarly practice is
to distinguish between early, middle, and late periods in a thinker's career, this practice points up the striking continuity in Sōseki's career,
marking him as an architectonic rather than organic intellectual. Sōseki's
project is also unusual in its contact with other parts of the field of
knowledge, particularly the empirical and social sciences. In the conclusion to his study of funding trends in the academic humanities in the
United States, former NEH chair John D'Arms argues that in their defen-
sive denigration of scientific objectivity the "postmodern" (i.e., post–
1960s) humanities have effectively dealt themselves out of a number of
questions with the most profound consequences, including that of "the
causal relation between neurobiological processes and conscious experience." These questions are currently being pursued outside humanistic
fields by biologists, neurophysiologists, and cognitive scientists. Such

"fresh disciplinary combinations of investigators in these areas are offering accounts of their subject matter that are changing the world as we once understood it."[13] Letters to Terada at the time reveal Sōseki reading intensely in the sciences, and notes to *Theory of Literature* show that his intention was to ground the project in an engagement with the most up-to-date theories of cognition and memory, an effort that resulted in the famous wave diagrams and equations for consciousness in the first chapter.[14] The contemporary climate of suspicion in the humanities regarding the instrumental sciences was foreign to Sōseki and his generation of literary scholars, for whom science was neither an object of excessive admiration nor compensatory fear but merely another field in the production of knowledge, to be evaluated like any other in terms of its rigor, persuasiveness, and ability to constitute and grasp its object.[15] To accomplish the larger task he set himself of situating the individual consciousness in the open-ended, whirling development of physical and social processes—in preparation for which he hid his literature books in a trunk—this meant reading in empirical psychology and sociology. For Sōseki it was unthinkable that one could talk about the effect of literature on the reader without access to the sciences, which deal with psychological processes and consciousness, of the situation of individual experience in aggregate social wholes without sociology, or the circulation of energies on the globe without thermodynamics. This interdisciplinary willingness to grant science respect in its own domains, and to open the study of literature where they cross, still seems fresh today.

Although Sōseki's accomplishments as a novelist typically eclipse his identity as a theorist for the four reasons previously mentioned—namely, that his theoretical project *brackets* his career as a novelist, *informs* his novel writing from first to last, is *coherent* and *complete* in relation to its original conception, and is *interesting* as an experiment in interdisciplinary study—we would like to argue here that any consideration of his novels that fails to take into account his theoretical project misses, in several important respects, what Sōseki was trying to accomplish through both and leaves layers of significance unexamined. The inspiration Sōseki received from contemporary physics as it closed in on the work that would lead to a revolution in our understanding of the fundamental nature of matter is clear. Sōseki seeks for literature an account that is universal but also one that is comprehensive and fundamental. (JAM)

Sōseki and Social Theory

In his ten-year project, Sōseki was determined to theorize literature in part as a social phenomenon, one that must be studied from the perspective of the social sciences.[16] In the preparatory work he carried out for *Theory of Literature*, he surveyed recent work in sociology and related disciplines. As with his study of psychology and the natural sciences (see later discussion), works from "The Contemporary Science Series," edited by Havelock Ellis, provided the core of his study, although Sōseki read widely in the fields of sociology, anthropology, political science, and social philosophy. Sōseki owned works by such authors as John Beattie Crozier, Henri Bergson, Franklin Giddings, Benjamin Kidd, L. T. Hobhouse, Lester F. Ward, and Charles Letourneau. He also owned a copy of Marx's *Capital* in an English translation, and although that book shows no signs of having been read carefully (there is an absence of underlines or marginal comments), in his letters and other writings Sōseki demonstrates a fair acquaintance with the basic tenets of Marxist perspectives on society.[17]

Not surprisingly, it was works in the English tradition that formed the bulk of Sōseki's reading in sociology—and of the sociology taught in Japan following the 1893 appointment of Toyama Masakazu as the first chair in the discipline at Tokyo Imperial University.[18] Although there are surprisingly few works by Herbert Spencer in Sōseki's personal library, the sociology-related texts he did own are dominated by the schools arising from Spencer and Mill. English sociology, which mixed together classical liberalism, utilitarianism, and Social Darwinism, naturally contained a diverse range of positions. If it can be said to have a shared assumption, it was that society consisted of an aggregation of distinct individuals, and that its essence was thus rooted in the natural essence of the individual. It also tended to use evolutionary schemas to describe the progressive development of society, with contemporary Europe, not surprisingly, often posited as representing the highest stage of development yet achieved by any human society.

How did Sōseki react to what was then one of the rising new modern disciplines? As a Japanese, Sōseki was forced to take up an ambiguous stance toward the discipline. He launched into his studies of sociology in order to transform himself into a knowing subject who operated within that discipline. Yet from the standpoint of Western sociology Japan and its society were more properly positioned as the *objects* of knowledge. Japan's turn to the West "coincided almost exactly with the period when scientific racism dominated the natural and social sciences in Europe and the United States," so that for intellectuals like Sōseki "the very process of Westernization involved being told that the racial inferiority of the Japanese was empirically verifiable," leaving them in an "awkward position."[19] Given the instability of his position, it would not be surprising if Sōseki began to harbor doubts about the form of knowledge he was pursuing.

In works where European sociologists turned their gaze on Asia, we find hints of Sōseki's reaction to the discipline. When, for example, Charles Letourneau discusses the history of property in Japan and claims that feudal structures of land ownership remain unchanged to the present day and that first daughters have the same rights of primogeniture as first sons, Sōseki writes "false" (*uso*) in the margin next to each claim.[20] In his copy of another work by Letourneau Sōseki writes: "Can such a thing be? How foolish!" (*Konna koto ga aru ka. Baka wo ie*) next to a passage mistakenly describing Japanese marriage practices.[21] Likewise, when John Beattie Crozier claims that Buddhism is inferior to Christianity because its disinterest in the material realm hindered the rise of modern science in Asia, Sōseki's copy contains several skeptical marginal comments jotted down in English. One such remark declares the argument a "specimen of sophistry & inaccurate reasoning. It is not Buddhism that has promoted science but neither can it be said of Christianity that it has helped in any way the advancement of science. On the contrary history shows that it has been a great obstacle in the evolution of it. If they at present utilise the results of science for the welfare of people, why should not the Buddhists?"[22]

In sum, as Sōseki sought to theorize literature using Western sociology, he repeatedly encountered the problematic ways in which that discipline objectified Japan as belonging to an inferior stage of civilization. He was, in other words, forced into an awareness of the politics of sociological knowledge.

In many sections, however, *Theory of Literature* reflects the influence of English sociology. In revising his original lecture notes prior to their publication in book form, the social side of literature is one of the topics to which he devoted particular care, rewriting his original lecture notes extensively.[23] A number of the sociological studies Sōseki relied on were acquired following his return to Japan from London—yet another indication of his continuing interest in this field during the years he was writing *Theory of Literature*. In particular, we see the impact of English sociology in book 5, "Group F," in which Sōseki explores the mechanisms of collective consciousness and its transformations through time. For example, Sōseki argues that social collective consciousness consists of the aggregation of individual consciousnesses, so that the nature of society derives from the prior nature of the individuals who compose it. Moreover, despite the outbursts described earlier, he at times also shows a strong tendency to accept the views of Social Darwinism and even Max Nordau's quasi-scientific theory of degeneration. As Mark Anderson has argued, Sōseki strategically attempts to avoid the racializing power relationships that were inherent in much of the aesthetic and literary theory current in his day. However, his use of social evolutionary theory to guide that escape meant that he was implicitly reproducing much of the intellectual framework that was being invoked to legitimize those imperialist hierarchies.[24]

But we also find instances where Sōseki's theory seems to counter English sociology. While collective consciousness is grounded in the consciousnesses of the individuals who make up that social body, Sōseki also clearly argues that these individual consciousnesses, in turn, are historically determined. As Thomas Lamarre's has noted, a tense relationship is set up between the two terms: "Significantly, the individual is not in opposition to society, nor is it subsumed."[25] Our ordinary consciousness is shaped by our historical and cultural environments; we mimic the actions and thoughts of those around us. Echoing William James and others, Sōseki stresses the importance of an innate disposition for imitation that serves as a kind of glue holding societies together. Sōseki argues that this compulsion to imitation is natural and necessary in the struggle for survival, yet his stance here resonates more clearly with Max Weber's "spirit" and Emile Durkheim's "morality" than with a Hobbesean belief in an inherently acquisitive human nature. Although Sōseki did not have the opportunity to read the new continental sociology that arose in the early twentieth century—one that was often quite critical of its English predecessors—it appears that he may have been groping for ways to conceptualize the nature of society that bore some resemblance to the contemporary work of Durkheim, Mauss, Simmel, and Weber.

Sōseki argues that the key sociological aspect of literature is its historical fluidity. Our shared literary tastes are constantly shifting, so that someday perhaps even Shakespeare will be forgotten—a remarkable statement for 1907, given the canonical status that the bard held in both the West and Japan at the time. Sōseki argues that, unlike scientific truth, which is permanent and universal, literary truth is historical and relative. The meanings and values of literary works, in other words, are not *properties* that *belong* to those texts but rather temporary outcomes of the fluid processes that occur when a reader's consciousness, shaped by that reader's cultural and historical environment, brings that text into focus. This view, in turn, allows Sōseki to challenge the authority of English literary critics— taste being relative, the literary criticism of a Japanese, even of an English poem, is as valid as that of an Englishman—a position he would expound again in his 1914 lecture "My Individualism."

More crucially, Sōseki insists that while biological organisms, sense perception, society, and scientific knowledge may all undergo progressive evolution into superior forms, such is not the case for literature and literary taste. He argues that there is constant shifting in the focal point F of our collective consciousness toward literature due to the discomfort caused by the boredom or stress that arises when any given focal point stays in place for too long. But the fluctuations that result are in no way arranged in a progressive form. Literature may evolve through history, but it does not follow the sort of developmental model of civilization and enlightenment that held sway in English sociology.

In other words, while relying on English sociology to construct his theory of literature, Sōseki also attempts to carve out a realm for literature that is relatively exempt from the laws that the discipline argued were fundamental to social existence. It is also striking that Sōseki uses literary figures—specifically the catalog of rhetorical devices that he expounds on at length in book 4—as his primary device for explaining social change. It was this originality that led one Japanese sociologist to propose a revision of the basic structure of his discipline to one based on the forms of sociality depicted in literature—including, most notably, the novels of Natsume Sōseki.[26]

Nonetheless, the sociological aspects of *Theory of Literature* remain one of its least satisfying elements. Beyond supplying visual graphs that attempt to depict the problem in geometric form, Sōseki makes no attempt to explain how or why individual consciousnesses would form a shared societal consciousness in aggregate. He here seems to accept rather naively the notion of zeitgeist invoked by Hippolyte Taine and others (we will return to this point shortly). However, as the ten-year project unfolded, in later years Sōseki would return to the issue of society and its constituent elements with a new set of concepts appropriated from the natural sciences rather than sociology. In that sense it marks a further development of the line of thought that sought to ground the theory of literature in the empirical science of psychology during the initial phase of the project. (MKB)

Sōseki and the Natural Sciences

While references to sociology are important and consistent in *Theory of Literature*, in some ways the most striking interdisciplinary aspect of Sōseki's work is the interplay with the natural sciences. Looking at his overall project, it would seem that Sōseki seeks to bring the study of literature in line with physics as cosmopolitan, that is to say, universal (applicable in all contexts) and comprehensive (characterized by iterable procedures that continue to account for new phenomena). Hence, there is a logic to choosing psychology—the study of individual, finite minds—and sociology—the study of aggregates of experience—to move from the question of literary experience to a dissection of the elements of civilization and "discourse on its nature." However, there is a dissymmetry in *Theory of Literature* between his engagement with psychology and his engagement with sociology, both in terms of quantity and contemporary significance. According to surveys of his library, in addition to volumes in Havelock Ellis's "Contemporary Science Series," works from this period tended toward science and psychology. According to Terada Torahiko, he maintained this interest in the sciences and read widely in specialized journals to the end of his career. For example, the discussion of the "pressure of light" in *Sanshirō* was based on work by Lebedev in 1901 and was only available in professional journals of physics. Terada states that Sōseki "was deeply interested in general science and took particular pleasure in discussions on the question of scientific methodology. If one looks at his critical essays, notes, and the like, one can see that the big theme of the question of scientific research applied to literature reverberated ceaselessly inside his head."[27]

By comparison, the books he consulted in so-called sociology were written in the tradition of Herbert Spencer's Social Darwinism.[28] In studying abroad Sōseki, like Ōgai before him, prized above all the opportunity to assemble books, foregoing the usual dissipating pleasures in London to conserve funds, and lamenting that he could set himself up for life if he only had a thousand yen to buy books. However, if we accept Miyake Yūjirō's account in *Fifty Years of New Japan* (1909), there was no need to go to England to get Spencer-influenced books on sociology. Beginning with the lectures of E. S. Morse in the mid-1870s at the precursor to Tokyo Imperial University, "Spencer was supreme" in Japanese letters. "Together with Darwin's 'Descent of Man,' Spencer's theory of evolution . . . and his principles of sociology appear to have been employed to interpret all social phenomena."[29] Sōseki's use of Spencer partook of long-established interpretive schemes in Japan and did not carry the same intellectual tension as the use of William James or Théodule-Armand Ribot. Hence, not only was Sōseki's engagement with the science of psychology more serious than his involvement with sociology, but by "psychology" he appears to mean something recognizable to the contemporary discipline, whereas for Spencer "sociology" represented a very broad field barely distinguishable from history and philosophy. We will next consider this relation to the natural sciences, including Sōseki's itinerary in relation to the sciences, why the psychology Sōseki uses might be considered a natural science, and his displacement of sociology by thermodynamics in his final statement on the nature of civilization in his later lectures.

Sōseki's fundamental interdisciplinary move in *Theory of Literature* is to hide all his books of literature in a wicker trunk and borrow from psychology. But there are many different types of psychology, and the question of whether in the 1900s he meant by *shinrigaku* something similar to what is meant by psychology today needs to be resolved. Looking first at his cited authorities, the first chapter incorporates contemporary experimental psychological accounts of consciousness from Lloyd Morgan's *Introduction to Comparative Psychology* (1896) and E. W. Scripture's *New Psychology* (1897) as a wavelike movement, where the top of the wave is what the mind is focused on at a given point. In assembling his model of the moment-to-moment experience of literature, Sōseki further refers to figures such as Ribot, Morgan, and Edward Groos. With the complicated exception of Ribot, these are not major figures in the history of psychology and remain unknown to specialists in the field today. However, all are involved in clinical or experimental psychology and acknowledge their debt to William James, whose *Principles of Psychology* (1890) is also mentioned in *Theory of Literature* and who established the concept of "stream of consciousness." Sōseki indicates this empirical commitment when, after explicating the movement of objects from the peripheries of consciousness to the center and back through the process of focus or attention, he comments: "This is not just something you know from your daily experience, it has been established by precise scientific experiment" (book 1).

Masumitsu Keiko has established that as early as 1890 Sōseki took a course in "mental physics" at Tokyo Imperial University taught by Motora Yūjirō, who published the first book in Japanese on the modern discipline of psychology. Motora studied at Johns Hopkins in the 1880s under G. Stanley Hall, a student of William James, and is said to have met James personally while in the United States.[30] As Masumitsu establishes, Sōseki read James's work in the original and made copious marginal notes. Furthermore, James was in Glasgow in 1901 to deliver the lectures that would comprise his *Varieties of Religious Experience*. Sōseki owned personal copies of that work, as well as of James's *Pluralistic Universe* (1909). Hence, if one wishes to gain an idea of what psychology means in the context of *Theory of Literature*, both in terms of Sōseki's personal academic itinerary and cited authorities in the text, one is led to William James, a central figure in defining the modern discipline of psychology and differentiating it from philosophical and metaphysical questions.

In a section of *Principles of Psychology* (1890) entitled "Psychology Is a Natural Science," James writes: "That is, the mind which the psychologist studies is the mind of distinct individuals inhabiting definite portions of a real space and a real time. With any other sort of a mind, absolute intelligence, mind unattached to a particular body, the psychologist has nothing to do. . . . It is highly important that this natural-science point of view should be understood at the outset. Otherwise more may be demanded of the psychologist than he ought to be expected to perform."[31]

Further, psychology for James is a reductive science: "Psychology, the science of finite individual minds, assumes as its data (1) *thoughts and feelings*, and (2) *a physical world* in time and space with which they coexist and which (3) *they know*. Of course these data themselves are discussable; but the discussion of them is called metaphysics and falls outside the province of this book. . . . [W]hen [psychology] has ascertained the empirical correlation of the various sorts of thought or feeling with definite conditions of the brain, it can go no farther."[32] And this science has a method, when the "various sorts of thought or feeling" go beyond reflex and attention to higher processes: "Introspective observation is what we have to rely on first and foremost and always."[33]

Sōseki shares with James the commitment to scientific study of the mind, as well as the idea of consciousness as a flow or stream of instantaneous moments, which is the most famous theme in the *Principles of Psychology*, though Sōseki cites secondary figures rather than James. Hence, at the stage of conceiving the basis of his theory in the experience of literature, Sōseki chose a natural scientific model. As to the question of what it would *mean* for Sōseki to adopt a natural scientific approach to the experience of literature, this would entail (1) putting the experience of literature in definite relation to processes in the brain, and (2) making statements verifiable in principle by experience, whether in the form of clinical experiment, or by the method of introspection, presented to the assembled lecture hall for verification.

There are reasons both internal and external to this early work to suspect that Sōseki may have had in mind a scientific theory when conceiving the ten-year project to grasp the nature of civilization and dissection of its elements. First, there is the formula (F+f), introduced in the first pages as descriptive of the form of literary experience and used consistently throughout the book, which, with the addition of an equal sign, suggests the possibility of using the relations of mathematics for prediction. Second, there is the move in book 2 to the question of quantification (*bungaku no sūryōteki henka*), which confirms the purport of the (F+f) formula and gives the theory a clear technical sense. Third, there is the general systematicity of the work itself. *Theory of Literature* opens with the construction of a model for the phenomenon in the initial section. Then it steps sequentially through each of the six bodily sense modalities and a taxonomy of simple emotions. With these elements in place, it moves to questions of quantification, composite perceptions, and emotions, the aggregate F, and the definition of literary truth, consistently returning to the (F+f) notation in considering individual cases. This systematicity, testifying to the power of Sōseki's conception, lends itself to elaboration through an experimental program but could also be indicative of the generation of a rhetoric. Considered collectively, these points suggest that Sōseki's ambitions for his theory are in some sense scientific.

It may be taken as an objection to this when Sōseki discusses the two types of truth in book 3, "Scientific Truth versus Literary Truth," and declares them to be different. However, in these passages Sōseki is dealing with "literary truth," that is, the *object* of his theory, not literary critical truth, the *method* of his theory. It is possible to argue that a good deal of the contemporary difficulty in understanding the relation of literature to science in the academy involves a slippage between *literature* and *literary criticism* as intelligent activities. However, Sōseki seems to have held the distinction in mind. As he wrote in the "Preface" to *Literary Criticism* (*Bungaku Hyōron*; included in this volume):

Given the preoccupation with the designation "literature," it is assumed that everything related to literature is independent of science. This is a misunderstanding that must be corrected. Leaving the definition of literature aside, when asked what literature is, we most likely refer to literary products, that is, to the literary works themselves. Now, if we take up the process through which a given work is produced, it is (generally) different from science. However, literary works are, of course, not the same as their criticism or history. What distinguishes history and criticism is our stance [*taido*] vis-à-vis the finished work; since we are not approaching a work with the perspective of creating a verse or prose, we treat it as a material of objective research. As such, our stance can be equated with that of a scientist who takes a natural phenomenon as his research material. Because we see literary works as a given phenomenon, our stance differs greatly from that when we produce literary works.

There are also reasons extrinsic to *Theory of Literature* to suggest that Sōseki may have intended to produce a scientific theory. First, Sōseki is in constant contact with top scientists during the genesis of the project, from the course in psychology with Motora, to his conversations with the chemist Ikeda Kikunae while in London (cited earlier), to his correspondence with protégé Terada Torahiko, who became a world-class physicist in the 1910s. According to Komiya Toyotaka, the encounter with Ikeda in 1901 marked the genesis of *Theory of Literature*. Throughout his life Sōseki maintained a close relationship with Terada, who served as the model for the young physicist Mizushima Kangetsu in *I Am a Cat*.[34] Sōseki's subsequent development of the ten-year project continues to use natural scientific models, ending with a model based on thermodynamics and entropy in the 1911 lecture "The Civilization of Modern-Day Japan." Hence, from his initial, curious, "shopping around" phase as a student in 1890, through his stay in London in 1900–1902, to the completion of his project with his later lectures, his reference points for the production of theory are

consistently the natural sciences, specifically physics, chemistry, thermodynamics, and physiology. The reference to a soon-to-be superseded
atomic hypothesis, and final settling on thermodynamics—the nineteenth-
century science par excellence—as an explanatory model might seem to
impart an antiquarian cast to Sōseki's science. Although this conclusion is
partially correct, it overlooks an important point. While the classical
atomic theory Sōseki alludes to in his letter to Terada in 1901 was still innocent of postclassical quantum and statistical accounts, thermodynamics, by contrast, is a science that has never been amenable to classical accounts. For example, there is today still no classical way to describe
turbulent flow, which is statistical, nonreversible, and unpredictable. It is
not that it is too complex—scientists do not even know where to start.[35] In
this sense, thermodynamics is the one traditional science that seems to
foreshadow these developments precisely (quantum statistical accounts
and complexity). On the one hand, it might be said that Sōseki's engagement with a soon-to-be displaced classical account imparts an antiquarian cast to the project. On the other hand, in an uncanny way he moves in
his later work to the one traditional science that was always postclassical.
That is to say, he spotted the problem. In the same way, his selections from
late-nineteenth-century psychology, though eclipsed for much of the
twentieth century by behaviorist paradigms, end up seeming quite contemporary at the end of the twentieth century.

In fact, *Theory of Literature* abandons this implicit empirical line early
in book 1 and becomes something more like a rational system-building or
a rhetoric. However, ten years later in "The Civilization of Modern-Day
Japan" Sōseki continues to refer to this empirical setup. After reintroduc-
ing his model of consciousness, he writes: "Now let me explain this bit
about the arc, or the curve, or whatever we wish to call it. . . . You'll see
what I mean if you experiment a bit. No, you won't need any apparatus for
this 'experiment.' It's simply a matter of noticing what goes on in your
head. Consider reading, for example. . . ."[36]

This typically ironic reference to the method of introspection indicates
that Sōseki sees the act of comparing the facts of consciousness to be the
laboratory for higher mental processes. However, some of the most interesting evidence that the problem of a natural scientific approach to culture
"moved ceaselessly" inside Sōseki's mind comes from the ultimate answer
to the ten-year project, provided in the same essay, which abandons the
under-theorized extension of a psychological model to long time frames

and social aggregates, and turns to a thermodynamic model to place civilization in a definite relation to material processes *on the earth*, specifically thermodynamic processes relating to the transformation of energy into work and into expenditure, with accompanying waste and entropy.

The choice of a thermodynamic model is a point of the utmost importance in this sense. It both indicates a rethinking of the sociological models Sōseki tried out in *Theory of Literature* and indicates a monistic outlook implicit in James, which viewed human society in communication with the natural world. Shorn of the distractions of the connection between psychology and sociology, one can see overlaid on the ten-year project a movement from empirical, psychological models relating to individual, finite minds, to thermodynamics, relating to statistical relations of work and order in complex, aggregate systems. This in some ways answers the problem of the extension of psychology to social aggregates in *Theory of Literature*. Sōseki has either jettisoned as untenable the Spencer-derived assumptions of the earlier work and taken on a more adequate and appropriate theory for modeling or, as part of the unfolding symmetry of the project, overlaid a procession of scientific models on the movement from individual to social. Whichever is the case, the period from 1907 to 1912 remains a puzzle of great interest. One of the most important benefits of tracking in what way specific literary works experiment with specific aspects of *Theory of Literature* remains locating the change from a sociological to a natural scientific basis for thinking about civilization.

This engagement with thermodynamics—in terms of offering a discourse on the nature of civilization and dissection of its elements—goes beyond a mere authorizing metaphor. Sōseki makes two powerful moves that bespeak a serious engagement with the underlying principles. First, toward the end of the nineteenth century the second law of thermodynamics—which states that the production of work within a system moves the system inexorably toward increasing disorder (entropy) and eventual heat death—was widely held to be a judgment on the Victorian work ethic and to have definite, highly pessimistic implications for the survival of the European imperial project then at its height. This is an obvious case of the attachment of an affect f to an adulterated scientific conception F when it begins to circulate in the popular consciousness. Sōseki, however, correctly discerns—by looking beyond these anxieties about decline and devolution dominant in both the general intellectual context (popularized by Lord Kelvin's lectures), and the specific sources he relies on (Max

Nordau's degeneration)—that civilization, as a manifestation of energies on the globe, relies on an infinite energy source from a separate system and is therefore capable of local exemption from the second law of thermodynamics. This is the purport of his notion of an intertwining series of "labor-saving devices" and "energy-consuming contrivances" that produce a series that *has no limit*.[37] Sōseki is alone, in a Euro-Asian context, in correctly discerning this at the time, prefiguring Bataille's general economy by forty years. Second, in zeroing in on his target from the general to the particular—first defining "civilization" (*kaika*), then "modern-day" (*gendai*), then Japan (*Nihon*)—he places his object in a time frame not of the Meiji period but spanning multiple generations of civilization, enabling statistical regularities that constitute the objects of thermodynamic inquiry. Sōseki does not define the controls that would permit verification through experiment, but the sense of confidence with which he assures his auditors in the audience at Wakayama that he has told them a truth suggests he would be open to that.

Writing in 1961, Takeuchi Yoshimi sees Sōseki as one of two early twentieth-century figures (with the other being John Dewey), who were broadly predictive of the path Japan would take in the twentieth century leading up to defeat and collapse.[38] Takeuchi borrows from "The Civilization of Modern-Day Japan" Sōseki's framework of internal and external motivation for civilization (*naihatsuteki* vs. *gaihatsuteki*) to explain why, in 1961, he sees the future in China rather than Japan. Takeuchi seems to take the defeat in wartime as definitive, and it is difficult to know what he would have made of the reemergence of Japanese power during the ensuing forty years. In some ways he missed the larger point of Sōseki's essay, which is about endlessly proliferating manifestations of energy and which better grasps the broad outlines of the twentieth century. The strength of a scientific model lies in its capacity to account for new circumstances that could not have been foreseen by its author. It is testimony to Sōseki's prescience that he could be transported to present-day Japan or North America and, despite superficial differences, would not be surprised by what he saw. His deceptively simple thermodynamic system of an ungoverned process of technological innovation, and a population driven to ever more frenzied activity by its labor-saving contrivances is predictive of the ability of faxes, e-mail, the Internet, and other aspects of the current telecommunications revolution to divide our time into ever-decreasing units for more effective exploitation in the work arena (the fundamental concern of both

Marxism and thermodynamics). Sōseki could not have foreseen the details, but he grasped the technical mechanism precisely.

Sōseki's commitment throughout his theoretical work to natural scientific models— from the model of literary experience as a wave form to the model of civilization as a manifestation of energies across the globe—makes this work more than just a casual metaphor. Sōseki sought rather deep affinities between the mental and social worlds in which he operated, on the one hand, and the physical world, on the other, and could not make those connections without serious engagement with science. (JAM)

Theory of Literature in the Context of Early Twentieth-Century Literary Theory

Despite Sōseki's claim that he shut away all of his literary works in his wicker trunk and focused on psychological and sociological theories in theorizing literature, his *Theory of Literature* and other critical writings both explicitly and implicitly draw on works of "literature." In order to establish a dialogue between Sōseki's writings and the literary environment of his time, we should first note the general tendency to focus on the individual that arose in the seventeenth and eighteenth centuries in various realms, whether philosophical, scientific, or aesthetic. For example, in the philosophical sphere the line of inquiry, owing in part to the development of Cartesian philosophy, began to shift from the cosmological to the individual. It marked a movement from the abstract to the individual, that is, to the subjective and concrete. Concomitant with it arose the growth of a "historical sense" and an interest in the individual's place in history.[39]

This prompted several crucial changes in how people perceived and addressed language and literature. First and foremost, it affected the study of rhetoric. The latter, of course, has a long history and any attempt at a comprehensive overview is bound to fail. For our purposes, two important trends in the eighteenth-century development of rhetoric ought to be mentioned here. The first may be called the philosophical-psychological vein of rhetoric, in which scholars began to perceive rhetoric as a means to study man's "mental nature." Unraveling rhetoric became a crucial part of unraveling the mystery of the human mind. Inextricably linked to this was the idea that what appeals to the emotions has the most power of persuasion. Drawing on associationist psychology, in such a mode of rhetoric ideas were thought to be held together by laws of association—namely, similarity, contiguity, and contrast—which were used to categorize the figures of speech. This can be seen in works such as Alexander Bain's *English Composition and Rhetoric* (1866), a book that had tremendous impact both in the West and Japan.

The second trend involves the rise of belletristic rhetoric, which closely intersects with literary criticism. Belletristic rhetoric engaged with the ongoing debate that developed throughout the eighteenth century on "taste" as a discriminator of aesthetic judgment, a topic that fascinated such theorists as Addison, Burke, and Hume, whose works had considerable impact on Sōseki. That taste was designated as a basis for aesthetic judgment was also a product of the general focus on the individual, since these theorists defined taste as a faculty inherent in all human beings. However, it is important to note that taste was deemed a faculty that needed to be cultivated. While all human beings possessed the basic faculty, it needed to be developed, and belletristic rhetoric attempted to do just that.

The rise of belletristic rhetoric was also shaped by the appearance of a new reading public that arose as a result of changing economic conditions: for those who were active in the world of commerce, the power of persuasion in English was more valuable than knowledge of Greek or Latin, which for classical rhetoric was a mark of erudition among the upper classes. English studies thus became more central to the study of rhetoric. Interestingly—or perhaps inevitably—belletristic rhetoric developed first in Scotland. It arose there to accommodate the need for formal training in English in order "to promote ethnic English culture among the Scottish middle class."[40] At the request of Lord Kames, Adam Smith, who was among the first to give impetus to the belletristic movement, developed a teaching curriculum of rhetoric at the University of Edinburgh. The lectures were based on literary selections mainly from English literature in order to produce young men with "cultivated English taste." Smith clearly had a moralizing agenda in his lectures, namely, to offset the individualism that modern economic principles promoted. Among other things, he focused on character analysis, both of writers and fictional characters, to promote ethical conduct.[41] In the audience at his lectures was Hugh Blair, perhaps the most famous rhetorician of the eighteenth century whose *Lectures on Rhetoric and Belles Lettres* remained greatly influential in the nineteenth and early twentieth centuries.

Coinciding with these developments in rhetoric was the rise of the modern discipline of literary history, yet another sphere in which the focus on the individual prompted change. The compilers of literary histories accordingly emphasized individual poets and weighed in heavily on the writer's background.[42] The poet became the original creative mind and his mental peculiarities were sought as the origin of expression. As such, biographical readings of poetry became prominent in the eighteenth century, which clearly engaged with a mode of reading that focused on individual character espoused by belletristic rhetoric. Moreover, with the advent of Social Darwinism in the nineteenth century, the focus of literary histories shifted even further to social evolution. In this framework the individual was part of a zeitgeist, with literature deemed an expression of the social, political, and cultural environment of a given work's creation. Perhaps the most influential work in this vein was Hippolyte Taine's *History of English Literature* (1863). Taine, considered to be the founder of the sociological study of literature, introduced the celebrated formula "race-milieu-moment" as the main constituents of literary history and sought to identify the national *Volk* expressed in the texts. According to Taine, "a work of literature is not a mere play of imagination, a solitary caprice of a heated brain, but a transcript of contemporary manners, a type of a certain kind of mind."[43]

In such a model of literary history, moreover, the thoughts and feelings of individuals were sought behind the writings: "It is a mistake to study the document, as if it were isolated. . . . Behind all, we have neither mythology nor languages, but only men, who arrange words and imagery according to the necessities of their organs and the original bent of their intellect."[44] More specifically, historians sought the "soul," a "psychology" seen as "the continuous development and the ever changing succession of the emotions and conceptions out of which the text has sprung."[45] In effect, literature was deemed an expression of inner selves, which were shaped by the social forces of the time.

In the discursive environment that surrounded Sōseki in England, "literature" was a sphere inextricably linked to a form of study in which a gentleman's power of persuasion and refined composition, as well as elegant English expression, were held in high esteem. Constant references were made to nurturing proper "English taste" through literary and rhetorical studies, which served as a means of "internal" education and cultural conversion. In addition, literary history was redefining literature as the "inner" voice of the national people, subjugating literary works to history and social evolution.

Theory of Literature and other critical writings by Sōseki engage with this literary environment both explicitly and implicitly. The internal focus in the realms of "literature" cannot be divorced from Sōseki's shift to psychology in defining literary substance. "Taste"—which occupies an important part of Sōseki's model of literature, being inextricably linked to emotive f, the defining component of literary substance—was also an important faculty integral to rhetoric and literary criticism of the time. Another explicit and obvious link can be seen in book 4 of *Theory of Literature*, where Sōseki discusses "the mutual relations between literary substances" and introduces the figures of speech, which are organized according to the major principles of associationist psychology, thus establishing a clear dialogue with the philosophical-psychological vein of rhetoric.[46] Furthermore, as Tsukamoto Toshiaki notes, there is a striking similarity between the four categories of F in *Theory of Literature* (sensation F, personification F, metaphysical F, and intellectual F) and their relationship to emotive f and George Campbell's theory of vivacity of impression. According to Campbell, there are three mental activities, namely, sensation, memory, and imagination. Vivacity is the strongest in sensation, but as mental activities become more involved, and as they progress through memory and imagination, their corresponding vivacity decreases. This is very much like Sōseki's model in which the strength of emotive f decreases as F becomes more abstract.[47]

Perhaps the more implicit engagement between Sōseki's writings and "literature" is with nationalizing forces inscribed in the literary environment. Sōseki's model offers itself as a critical frame by which to examine the formation of contemporaneous realms of "literature." For example, *Theory of Literature*'s attempt to define literature scientifically and posit literature in universal terms (F+f) erases the national divides that permeate the contemporaneous studies of literature. In Sōseki's model, the formula $(F+f)$ exists in any language.[48] This should not be taken to mean that his universal formula relativizes the national, which evokes the universal/particular dynamic, an understanding that merely reinforces one another. Instead, the formula—the idea of literary substance—gives equal ontological rights to all Fs, all of which do not constitute an additive. In such a model, the category of the nation does not enjoy any special status; the "national F" (*kokumin* F) has the same status as "literary writer

F" (*bungakusha* F) and "individual F." Furthermore, in *On the Form in English Literature* (*Eibungaku keishiki ron*, 1903) and *Literary Criticism* Sōseki continues to search for a realm in taste that is not culturally bound. While contemporaneous literature sought "national taste," he theorized "universal taste."

In his search for universal taste, Sōseki further attempted to reformulate literary criticism, which was dominated by readings that clearly subjugated literature to history. In sharp contrast to the literary histories of the time, Sōseki specifically adopted a formalistic approach to literature. For example, in the "Preface" to *Literary Criticism* he discusses the universality of taste based on order and arrangement of literary materials (as opposed to taste based on the literal materials themselves, which, according to Sōseki, tends to be more culturally bound):

Take Alexander Dumas's *The Black Tulip*, for example. If I say this work is bad—its structure is too contrived, almost like a cheap trick; it may be clever, but it is extremely artificial and unnatural—my taste is not responding to the materials themselves but to their order and arrangement. . . . Here is another example: I take Maupassant's *Une Vie* and say it has no focus. I cannot tell whether the main theme is the relationship between the husband and wife or the affection between a parent and child. They are both independent and do not properly integrate with one another in producing a single work. This is again a criticism that is based not on my taste regarding the materials themselves but regarding the way the materials are arranged.

By distribution and arrangement of materials, Sōseki had in mind unification of plot, narrative configuration, and other structural analysis of narrative. In effect, what he deployed here were the discussions on basic structures of the novel that were common in turn-of-the-century England.[49] Sōseki apparently felt that such approaches to literature had the potential to liberate literature from history. This is not an argument for any sort of aestheticism but rather a criticism of the prevalent literary history, which viewed literary writings primarily as an expression of the historical moment, the zeitgeist. As has been argued elsewhere, this notion of history presents a rather limited view of time.[50] It is not a coincidence that in *Theory of Literature* Sōseki posits three registers of time that undermine the dominance of time presented in literary history, thereby questioning the linearity of time and homogeneity of space and expression. In doing so, he underscores the highly ideological nature of the seamless link between individual, society, and the zeitgeist. Such a resistance to history was not unique to Sōseki in late-nineteenth-century England. For example, George Saintsbury questioned literature's subjugation to history and compiled *A Short History of English Literature* (1898) specifically from a "literary" point of view.[51] Sōseki isolated literary techniques to provide an alternative to such history and culturally driven literary criticism. (AU)

Previous Scholarship on Sōseki's Theoretical Works

While the body of scholarship devoted to Sōseki's fiction is considerably larger, numerous studies have addressed Sōseki's theoretical and critical writings, especially in Japan. Predictably, however, Sōseki's theoretical writings are often considered a mere prelude to his great literary career. Naturally, there are two camps of scholars, namely, those who claim continuity between Sōseki's theoretical endeavors and his fictional works and those who claim discontinuity between them.[52] While the former group attempts to explore the various ways in which Sōseki's theories are actualized in his fictional works, the latter divorces the theoretical endeavors from his illustrious career as a fiction writer, often highlighting Sōseki's failure in writing theory. This latter group follows Sōseki's own claim in "My Individualism," where he characterizes *Theory of Literature*, perhaps the most monumental of his theoretical endeavors, as a "decomposed corpse."

Whichever position they take, scholars have to grapple with Sōseki's position as a *kokumin sakka*, or "national writer," whose popularity even now extends far beyond the scholarly world. The educational arena (particularly at the middle and high school levels) is most responsible for disseminating this image of Sōseki; state-sanctioned textbooks have produced and reproduced Sōseki's image as a moralist, viewing his works as a vehicle for ethical education. Of the fictional works, *Kokoro* has been the most popular and has been used to teach readers about the evil of egoism and the necessity of lofty spirituality.[53] Among nonfiction works, "My Individualism" has been most often quoted and used in a similar manner, emphasizing the section in which Sōseki ostensibly argues for individualism that does not infringe on others.[54]

Not only is Sōseki a national writer, but he is also a literary giant who enjoys a godlike status, an image that still lingers in academia to this day. Author-centered strategies of reading remain strong and, as such, Sōseki's own personal narratives often remain uncontested. In *Theory of Literature* the personalized "Preface" is by far the most famous and oft-quoted section of the monumental treatise. His personal narratives in "My Individualism," which outlined the ten-year project he initially planned, as well as his letters to acquaintances discussing his determination to complete the project, are often taken at face value, as if it were somehow sacrilegious to question them.

Such images of Sōseki have long governed critics' interpretation of self-centeredness (*jiko hon'i*), a term in "My Individualism" that Sōseki uses when discussing his uneasiness in finding how his understanding of English literature "clashed with those of native English critics."

> Whence, indeed, did this clash arise? From differences in habits? Mores? Customs? Surely, if you traced it back far enough, national character was a source. But the usual scholar, confounding literature with science, mistakenly concludes that what pleases country A must of necessity win the admiration of country B. This, I was forced to recognize, was where I had made my mistake. . . . My next step was to strengthen—perhaps I should say to build anew—the foundations on which I stood in my study of literature. For this, I began to read books that had nothing whatever to do with literature. If, before, I had been dependent on others, if I had been other-centered, if occurred to me now that I must become self-centered [*jiko hon'i*].

This stance is further explicated in the "Preface" to *Literary Criticism*: "Somewhere in their minds, Japanese people believe that the English people's evaluation of the work is correct because they are taking up a work produced in England and offering a native evaluation of a native product." Instead, he continues, we must "analyze exactly how we feel about a given work without thinking of the language barrier, without worrying about clarity or ambiguity, without thinking about whether it corresponds with the Westerners' opinion. . . . Just because your criticism contradicts a Westerner's, it does not mean that you are shallow-minded." Sōseki thus argued for the importance of reading from the "Japanese point of view" (*nihonjin no tachiba*), which became a crucial phrase in Sōseki criticism.[55]

As such, *jiko hon'i* and his methodology of reading have often been equated with national pride.

Such reading, however, is symptomatic of scholarship that valorizes Sōseki as a "national writer" by mainly focusing on his personal narratives and disregarding other crucial sections. Recent critics have moved away from such interpretation by arguing that Sōseki's emphasis on universality in theorizing literature is one visible marker that opposes the "Japanese point of view." By exploring the importance of the universality of taste, Takano Mikio argues against previous scholarship that assumed that *Literary Criticism* was written from the "Japanese point of view."[56] Karatani Kōjin argues that *jiko hon'i* is ultimately a position that questions the historicity of "literature," showing that universality of (F+f) is posited against historical particularity.[57] Analyzing the textual placement of *jiko hon'i* in "My Individualism," Komori Yōichi argues that *jiko hon'i* marks an effort to identify the criteria by which the displacement between English and Japanese positions are foregrounded, thus linking *jiko hon'i* and universality.[58] Nakayama Akihiko, in a rigorous analysis of *Theory of Literature* as a narrative, emphasizes the manner in which (F+f) is a regionally neutral substance.[59] Recent scholarship has thus liberated *jiko hon'i* from a specifically "Japanese point of view."

Sōseki, however, is not anti-nationalistic, as this trend in scholarship might suggest. To say so is to go against the foundational principles of *Theory of Literature*, in which all F's claim ontological equivalence with each other. If Sōseki's model looks anti-nationalistic, it is only to the extent that Sōseki criticizes nation F for claiming to take on a higher ontological status than literary writer F or individual F. But this is not to say that nation F should be deprived of its status.

Most recent critics who have focused on the importance of universality (including the editors of this volume) have grounded their scholarship on the link between Sōseki's theoretical works and the sciences, which include works by Spencer, Lombroso, Nordau, William James, Lloyd Morgan, and Ribot, to which Sōseki makes explicit references. The publication in 1972 of *Notes on "Theory of Literature"* (*Bungakuron nōto*), a transcript of notes Sōseki took in England, added critical depth to such a line of inquiry, giving scholars access to the process through which he conceptualized his ten-year project and the works he referenced. Ogura Shūzō has written a book on William James's influences on Sōseki and has continued to examine how Sōseki adopted Morgan's *Comparative Psychology*.[60]

Masumitsu Keiko has also written a book-length study on the ways in which Sōseki conceptualized "consciousness."[61] Shigematsu Yasuo traced the manner in which Sōseki's reception of James changed from *Theory of Literature*, to "The Philosophical Foundation of the Literary Arts," to "The Attitude of a Creative Artist."[62] Komori Yōichi has also worked extensively to determine how Sōseki deploys the sciences in his *Sōseki o yominaosu* (Rereading Sōseki) and elsewhere. Many others have analyzed the link between Sōseki's theoretical writings and Spencer, Nordau, and other psychological and sociological theories.

Though perhaps less naively, an overemphasis on the personal narrative has continued. The emphasis on the preface in Sōseki's *Theory of Literature*, as well as his later speeches, has led critics to focus almost exclusively on psychological and sociological theories as his primary influence. On the one hand, efforts to establish a link between Sōseki's theoretical endeavors and the sciences have contributed greatly to the shift in Sōseki scholarship away from discussions of the "Japanese point of view" as well as the textbook image of Sōseki as moralist. On the other hand, critics have not paid much attention to the "literary works" that Sōseki allegedly "shut away" in his trunk. The trend in Sōseki scholarship that tends to valorize his brilliance and to sustain his image as a literary genius also contributes to the focus on nonliterary studies because it tends to foster the sense that his achievement was beyond that of any literary writer at the time.

Fortunately there are several notable exceptions. Tsukamoto Toshiaki, who has focused on Sōseki's use of theories of rhetoric, has argued that they constitute a crucial component of Sōseki's theoretical paradigm. Rhetoric, especially in the eighteenth and early nineteenth centuries, was a discipline inextricably linked to literature and literary studies. As he notes, book 4 of *Theory of Literature*—which is one of the longer books in the work—clearly shows Sōseki's engagement with rhetoric. Tomiyama Takao, in an essay entitled "The Books Sōseki Didn't Read" (Sōseki no yomanakatta hon) examines the realms of literature—especially English studies—on which Sōseki drew, incisively examining the roles they played in the construction of *Theory of Literature*.[63] Karatani's discussion of the historicity of "literature," as well as his discussion of Sōseki's perception of realism and romanticism should also be mentioned in this context.[64]

We may not have to grapple with the deified image of Sōseki, but English-language scholarship has been governed by a different kind of dynamic. Surprisingly little has been written on Sōseki's theoretical works. Several book-length studies of Sōseki, though valuable, have focused almost exclusively on his fictional works. As Michael Bourdaghs has argued, this is partly a result of the orientalist tendencies that still govern our scholarship. According to such a paradigm, a Japanese writer cannot be the theorizing subject but merely the object of inquiry as a writer of fiction. (The inquiry then is carried out by Western Scholars.)[65] There is a yet another hierarchy implicit in this division of theory and practice: theory must be Western, a means by which the non-Western practice is validated. This is a paradigm that even critics in Japan reinforce today by continuing to focus their discussion on *Theory of Literature* and its link to psychological and sociological theories prevalent in nineteenth-century England primarily in terms of "influence." There is, of course, no way to dissociate Sōseki's works from the place he conceptualized it and the dominant discourses that governed it. However, the danger inherent in such discussion must also be noted.

Here, too, there are exceptions: Jay Rubin's translations and commentaries on "My Individualism" (1979) and "The Civilization of Modern-Day Japan" (1992) represent earlier attempts at breaking this impasse. Murphy has taken up Sōseki's theoretical writings in his book *Metaphorical Circuit*, where he featured the link between science and literature in modern Japanese theorists.[66] Matsui Sakuko has also focused on Sōseki as a critic of English literature.[67] A special issue of the journal *Japan Forum*, guest-edited by the editors of the present volume, included several new essays on Sōseki's theoretical project (material from which has been included in this introduction). (AU)

For reasons both practical and intellectual we have chosen to produce an abridged translation of Sōseki's *Theory of Literature*. We have translated somewhat less than half of the material contained in the original. In part, this was due to space and time restrictions. We also felt that while *Theory of Literature* is an important and fascinating text, it also contains much repetition and involves a fairly mechanical unfolding of different elements of its structure. The cuts and omissions also made it possible for us to include later writings by Soseki, which, when read in conjunction with the passages from the earlier book, provide a better and more comprehensive portrait of the scope of Sōseki's ten-year project—which, as we have argued here, underwent considerable development beyond the form in which it first appeared in 1907.

We firmly believe that *Theory of Literature* is a crucial and unique work in the history of literary theory worldwide. In a 1906 letter to his disciple Morita Sōhei, Sōseki encouraged the frustrated young writer by insisting that the true value of a work is not known until at least a hundred years have passed.[68] The same may be said of his *Theory of Literature*, "a flower that bloomed out of season and therefore left no seed."[69] We believe that its time may finally have arrived.

PART ONE

EXCERPTS FROM *THEORY OF LITERATURE*

(*BUNGAKURON*, 1907)

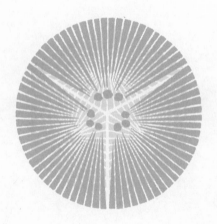

PREFACE

With its personal narrative of the author's experiences in London and its recounting of his
motives in launching the project to construct a scientific theory of literature, the preface is ✓
the best known section of Theory of Literature. *In fact, many scholars seem content to*
read only it, without venturing into the main body of the work. Despite the powerful emo-
tional tone that characterizes much of the preface, it—like the rest of the book—is written ✓
in a formal, scholarly style that partakes of many elements drawn from classical forms of ✓
the Japanese language. It is quite distinct from the genbun'itchi *vernacular writing style*
that Sōseki used in most of his fictional pieces.
   N.B.: We have translated the preface in its entirety.

As I set this work before the public, perhaps I had best recount the original
motive under which it germinated, the motive by which it then became a
series of lectures, and the reasons I am publishing it now.

In Meiji 33 [1900], when I received orders to go to England as an over- ✓
seas student, I was a teacher at the Fifth Higher School. At the time I harbored no particular desire to go abroad, and I believed there were others
much better suited to it than I was. I conveyed these sentiments to the
then current president and head of faculty of the school. The president and
head of faculty replied that whether there were others more qualified was
not a matter for me to concern myself with; the school had nominated me
to the Ministry of Education, the Ministry of Education had approved that
nomination and appointed me to serve as an overseas student, nothing

more, nothing less. If I had a specific objection, that was one thing, but if not, then it would be proper and good for me to obey the order. All I could say was that I harbored no particular desire to go abroad. Having no other reasons for refusing the order, I gave my consent and departed.

The subject I was ordered to study was *English*—not *English literature*. Feeling the need to know better the extent and details of what was expected of me in this, I paid a visit to Ueda Kazutoshi, the then chief of the Specialized Educational Affairs Section at the Ministry of Education, to ask him about this.[1] Ueda replied that there was no particular need to place tight restrictions on this; I should simply specialize in a subject or subjects that were suitable for teaching at the Higher School or University level after I returned to Japan. In this way I confirmed that there was some leeway for modifying, according to my own views, the subject matter of English that I had been assigned. I departed for the West in September of that year and arrived at my destination in November.

Upon arriving, the first thing to decide was where to study. Even in far-off Japan I had heard of Oxford and Cambridge, those august seats of learning. As I was debating in my mind between the two, I was fortunate enough to receive an invitation to Cambridge from an acquaintance there, and so I set off for a visit—partly in order to sightsee.

In addition to the man I visited, I met two or three other Japanese there. They were all the sons of wealthy families who, in their mission to acquire the status of "gentleman," were able to expend thousands of gold pieces year after year. My government stipend was only 1,800 yen per year, a sum that—in a place where the power of money controlled everything— would make it impossible for me to carry on as if I were their equal. Even if I didn't try to keep up and contented myself with merely trying to observe the "gentleman" style from a distance, it still wouldn't suffice: I knew I would be hard pressed to support myself even if I refused all social intercourse and did nothing but sit in on appropriate classes. Even if I used great care and somehow managed to scrape by, I wouldn't be able to buy any books to bring back with me to Japan—one of my goals for the trip. And so I reconsidered. My situation as an overseas student was different from the carefree life of those privileged youths. The gentlemen of England might well be an exemplary collection of model persons, endowed with noble characters and worthy of imitation. But for someone like me, who had spent his youth in the oriental fashion, chasing after much younger English gentlemen and trying to acquire their habits of conduct would be like a fully grown adult whose bones are no longer limber trying to master all the deft techniques of a lion-dance acrobat. No matter how much I might admire them, no matter how much I might worship them, no matter how much I might adore them, this belonged to the realm of impossibility—even if I resolved to cut my daily meals from three to two.

When my companions heard this, they told me they attended one or two hours of lectures in the morning, that they used the two or three hours after lunch in outdoor exercise, that at teatime they paid social calls, and that in the evening they engaged in communal dining at their colleges. I realized that, irrespective of whether it was seen from the perspective of expense, the use of time, or my character, I had no business trying ✓ to acquire the deportment of a gentleman. I permanently abandoned the ✓ notion of settling in there.

I believed the situation at Oxford would be no different from that of Cambridge, and so I did not bother going there. I considered heading north to Scotland or across the sea to Ireland, but I quickly realized that both places were ill-suited for the purpose of practicing *English*. At the same time, I recognized that London was the best place for me in terms of linguistic training. And so I set my bags down there.

In terms of linguistic practice, London was the most expedient choice— for obvious reasons. I believed this to be true then and find no reason to doubt it now. Yet I had not come to England solely for the purpose of im- ✓ proving my language skills. Orders were orders, but I had my own agenda ✓ as well. I was free to satisfy my own desires insofar as I respected the broad outlines that Ueda had suggested. I believed that carrying out research in literature in addition to acquiring linguistic proficiency was not merely a matter of following my own curiosity but, in fact, was also one way of obeying his instructions.

There is one thing I should note here to avoid any misunderstanding. The reason I chose not to devote my two years wholly to the study of lan- ✓ guage was not that I look down on linguistic ability or think it unworthy of study. Rather, it was the result of my taking it all too seriously. Two ✓ years was hardly sufficient time for acquiring proficiency even in one branch of language training—be it pronunciation, conversation, or written expression—much less to attempt to master the whole discipline! I counted on my fingers the length of time allotted for my overseas studies, considered my own lack of talent, and set to thinking about how much I might really be able to develop within the time limits I faced. After giving this careful thought, I came to the realization that it would be difficult if not impossible to produce the good results I hoped for in the short time available. Given my situation, it was unavoidable that my research agenda deviate at least partly from the terms of my orders from the Ministry of Education.

The next problem to arise was how one might go about studying literature. What specialty should one master in order to learn it?[2] Looking back now, I regret that I was unable to reach any conclusion regarding the naive and ill-formed question I had set myself. As a result, I ended up following a rather mechanical course of action. I headed for the university and audited lectures on contemporary literary history. Moreover, I availed myself of one other convenience: I sought out a private tutor with whom I could consult on matters that were unclear.

I gave up on the university lectures after three or four months. They were neither as interesting nor as informative as I had hoped. As for my private tutor, I recall that I saw him for about one year. During this period, I read every work related to English literature that I could get my hands on. Of course, I had no notion then of using these as materials for an essay, or of using them in a university lecture course after returning to Japan. I was merely flipping randomly through as many pages as possible. To be honest, I was not very knowledgeable about this field—certainly not knowledgeable enough to deserve selection for the honor of overseas study, as might befit the bachelor of arts in English literature that I was supposed to be. Following my graduation, I was forced to move repeatedly, meaning I daily grew estranged from the main literary circles [in Tokyo]. Not only that, but due to my personal and family circumstances, I did not have the opportunity to read as widely as I would have liked, and as a result even the famous classics that were on everybody's lips were in the main known to me only by their titles; it was my constant regret that I had not passed my eyes over sixty or seventy percent of them. As a result, I could not think of a better policy for using this opportunity than to read through as many books as possible. After using up more than one year in this pursuit, I compared the number of books I had managed to read with the number I still needed to read—and was shocked at how little progress I had made. I came to the realization that to spend my remaining year in the same fashion would be utterly foolish. I needed to make a drastic change in my approach to studying.

(A note to young students: Some in your situation, with their whole lives still in front of them, believe that before they can make some original contribution to their field of scholarship, they must first make an exhaustive survey of the field. They therefore resolve to read through the entire canon of relevant literature, new and old, high and low, accumulated over the millennia. Should you resolve to follow this course, know that even when your hair has turned white with age, you will still not have completed your exhaustive survey. As a specialist in English literature, I have yet to make a complete survey of the canon in my field. I doubt very much that this will change even after another twenty or thirty years.)

As I increasingly felt the pressure of time constraints, there were other factors that caused me to depart from this course of action—in addition to the fact that my utterly undisciplined method of reading was leaving me in somewhat of a daze. In my childhood I was very fond of studying the Chinese classics. Despite my having studied them for only a short while, I nonetheless acquired from the Four Histories[3] the vague notion that they defined what literature was supposed to be. I then simply assumed that English literature must be of a similar nature and, if that were so, I believed it was a subject that one could devote one's life to studying without regret. The decision I made on my own to enter the English literature department, which was hardly fashionable at the time, was based entirely on this childish, simplistic reasoning. But the three years I stayed at the university were largely spent being tormented by Latin, overwhelmed by German, and acquiring only the shakiest acquaintance with French—all of which eluded my grasp, but thanks to them I had almost no time left for reading the works of what was supposed to by my area of specialization. At the time I graduated and received the lofty title of bachelor of arts, my heart was assailed by a terribly desolate feeling.

Since then I have watched ten springs and autumns slip past. I cannot claim that I had no spare time for studying; all I can do is lament my failure to study more thoroughly. Moreover, when I graduated I was bothered by a notion that lingered at the back of my mind—that somehow I had been cheated by English literature. Still harboring that troubling notion, I headed west for Matsuyama, and a year later headed farther west for Kumamoto.[4] After several years in Kumamoto, that troubling notion had still not dissipated—at which time I traveled to London. If I could not resolve this troubling notion even after coming to London, there was little hope that I could fulfill the main task for which I had been ordered overseas. But could I, in the coming year, conquer the doubt I had been unable to resolve over the preceding decade? If not completely impossible, this was at least highly unlikely.

√   Having abandoned my reading, I considered what lay before me. It was quite regrettable that, given my innate stupidity and lack of scholarly ability, I had not attained any mastery of foreign literature, my supposed specialty. Given my past record, it seemed unlikely that my scholarly abilities would improve much in the future. Faced with these poor prospects, it seemed that I must develop some other means besides scholarly ability if I wanted to enhance my appreciation. But I was finally unable to discover any such method. In reflecting on my own past, moreover, I realized that, despite lacking a solid scholarly foundation in classical Chinese, I nonetheless believed myself able to appreciate fully the Confucian classics. Of course, my knowledge of English was not particularly deep, but I did not believe it to be inferior to my knowledge of classical Chinese. For my sense of like and dislike between the two to be so widely divergent despite my having roughly equal scholarly abilities must mean that the two were of utterly different

√ natures. In other words, what is called "literature" in the realm of the Chinese classics and what is called "literature" in English must belong to different categories and cannot be subsumed under a single definition.

In sum, it was not until I sat under the solitary lamp in my London room, years after my graduation from the university, that my intellectual worldview first encountered its home territory [*kyokusho*]. It may well be that others would call this childish. I myself think it childish. That I only stumbled upon this far too obvious question after traveling all the way to London was something of an embarrassment for this overseas student. But facts are facts: it may be shameful that I only then first became aware

√ of this issue, but it is also true. Facing this situation, I decided that I must, first of all, resolve the more essential question: What is literature? At the

√ same time, I made up my mind to use my remaining year as a first stage in carrying out research on this problem.

√   I closeted myself in my room. Furthermore, I shut away all books of

√ literature in my wicker trunk. To read literary works to try to learn what literature was, I believed, was the same as trying to wash blood with

√ blood. I vowed to determine what *psychological* necessity there was for

√ literature— for its emergence, its development, and its decline. I vowed to pursue what *social* necessity there was for literature—for its existence, its rise, and its fall.

Because the problem I had set before me was by its nature so vast in scope—and also so new—I believed it would not lend itself to being solved in a year or two no matter who undertook the effort. I devoted all of my time to it, gathering research materials from the various relevant fields and using as much of my stipend as possible to purchase reference works. The six or seven months that followed this decision were the most ardent and diligent period of study in my entire life. It was also during this time that I received official reprimands from the Ministry of Education for failing to file my regular progress reports.

I devoted all of my energies to my task, reading the books I had acquired one after another, jotting down comments in the margins of what I read and—where necessary—taking extensive notes. After five or six months I began to feel as if I were somehow honing in on the real substance of the matter in the midst of what at first had seemed an amorphous, endless pursuit. At the time I was not a university professor, and so I did not anticipate using these as material for a course of lectures. Nor was there any urgent necessity for me to write my research up in the form of a book. At the time I calculated that it would take ten years of hard ✓ study following my return to Japan to bring this project to proper fruition, and I was prepared to hold off presenting it to the world until that time.

The notebooks I compiled during my overseas stay, written in tiny script the size of a fly's head, amounted to a stack five or six inches tall. These notebooks were the one real asset I brought back with me to Japan. Almost as soon as I had returned to Japan, out of the blue I received an appointment as instructor at Tokyo Imperial University, where I was to lecture on English literature. It was not with this end in mind that I had traveled to the West—nor was it with this end in mind that I had returned to Japan. Not only did I lack the scholarly competence necessary for a university professor in charge of English literature classes, but I was also not pleased to have teaching responsibilities that would interfere with what had now become my real ambition: to complete work on my theory of literature. As a result, I at first thought to decline the appointment, but thanks to the good offices of a friend (Ōtsuka Yasuji), to whom I had by letter divulged my desire to find employment in Tokyo, I found that the arrangements were nearly finalized even prior to my return, and so I ended up accepting the appointment—regardless of my inadequate preparation.[5]

Prior to the beginning of my lecture course, I struggled mightily over the choice of topic. I felt that for today's students specializing in literature, an introduction to my theory of literature would be both interesting and timely. Of course, I was a person who had long served as a teacher in a rural district, after which I had traveled to the West, only then to return to Tokyo [after many years away from the city]— in other words, there was no way that I could know at that time what the current trends were among the literati in the capital. I decided, however, that I could best bring honor to myself by placing before these youths—the future leaders of our cultural progress—the fruits of my efforts, the summit of my scholarly attainments, and so I chose this topic to present to my students, knowing I would receive their critical response.

Unfortunately, given the enormous ten-year project I had in mind for studying the theory of literature—in which my main purpose was to explain the fundamental vital force of literature primarily from the perspective of the disciplines of psychology and sociology—my project was hardly in a form suitable for classroom lectures. Moreover, for a course in literature it seemed to lean too heavily in the direction of abstract logic, deviating too far from the realm of pure literature. As a result, I expended my efforts in two directions. First, using the materials I had accumulated, I tried to bring a certain degree of practical order to my hitherto scattered thoughts. Second, in preparing my lectures I revised my arguments, which had been structured in the form of a logical system, to bring them as close as possible to the realm of pure literature.

Laboring against time limitations as well as those of my physical and mental health, I was unable to achieve either goal satisfactorily. But the actual results of my efforts are attested to by the contents of this volume. I lectured for three hours each week, beginning in September, Meiji 36 [1903], and continuing through June, Meiji 38 [1905], for a total of two academic years. I am afraid, however, that my lectures were not as stimulating for the students as I hoped they would be.

I had planned to continue work on this lecture series for a third academic year, but a variety of circumstances intervened to prevent that. Nor was I able to carry out my intention to rewrite the lectures I had already delivered in order to revise the sections that I found unsatisfactory or lacking. The lecture notes sat untouched at the bottom of my work basket for roughly two years, until I submitted them for publication in response to a publisher's request.

Even after I agreed to publish them, I was completely preoccupied with various personal matters and could not even find the time to produce a clean copy of my old lecture notes. In the end, I was forced to entrust all ✓ preparations of the manuscript—including the arrangement of the notes into chapters and the editing of the table of contents—to my friend, Nakagawa Yoshitarō.[6] Nakagawa, in fact, attended part of the lecture course. Possessed of wide learning and a fine character, of all the people I know he seemed the most suitable for the task of bringing order to my notes. I am deeply grateful for his kindness. I hope that his name will be remembered for as long as this book continues to exist. If not for his good offices, there is little hope that in my present situation I could have brought this book to publication. In future days, when Nakagawa has had the chance to establish his name in literary circles, I suspect that the world will remember this book in association with his name [rather than mine].

As I have described it earlier, this book has come about through my passion-driven labors. However, because I had to contract my ten-year ✓ plan down to two years (and two years in name only: apart from the time spent in making corrections for publication, what I spent on this was actually two summers), and because I had to change its fundamental structure due to its failure to meet the expectations of the students of pure literature, even now it remains an unfinished work—and it cannot but remain incomplete. But the world of academia is a hectic one, and even by the standards of this hectic world my life seems doubly hectic. If I had held off until I had filled in the missing blanks, corrected that which needed correcting, and written additional material where needed, then—barring some radical change in the circumstances of my life—I likely never could have presented it to the world, even if I had vowed to devote all of my remaining days to the task. That is why I have decided to publish it in its unfinished state.

Because this is still an unpolished draft, I have no expectations that it will instruct today's students or provide an answer to the question of what literature is. If those who read this book, upon finishing it, find themselves taking up a related question or entertaining doubts on some issue, if they should perhaps advance a step beyond what is presented in this book or open up a new perspective and thereby point the way forward—if that should happen, I will have fulfilled my purpose. The edifice of learning is not built in a single morning, nor is it the product of any single person. I simply feel as if I have fulfilled my duty in contributing my small share of the labor needed for its construction.

The two years I lived in London were the unhappiest two years of my life. Among the English gentlemen, I was like a lone shaggy dog mixed in with a pack of wolves; I endured a wretched existence. I heard that the population of London is five million. Five million beads of oil and I the sole drop of water: I have no hesitation in asserting that I barely survived! The owner of a freshly laundered white shirt will certainly be displeased if he splashes a drop of ink on it. In London I was that drop of ink, wandering aimlessly like a beggar through Westminster. I feel sorry for the English gentlemen who for two years had to endure my drawing breath from the same thousands of cubic yards of the great city's skies, filled as they were with man-made clouds being emitted from smokestacks. With humility I hereby pronounce the following to those Englishmen who present the model of the proper gentleman: please know that I did not head to London out of curiosity or for fun. I was under the control of a will greater than my own; I am sorry to say that it was not my wish to spend those months and years sharing in the blessing of your bread. When my two years were up, I felt like a goose returning north in spring. During my sojourn I was unable to model myself after you or live up to your expectations. Even today I regret that I am unable to become the model character that you seek among the children of the Orient. But one who goes under official orders is not like one who goes by choice. Were I to have followed my own will, I would never have set foot on English soil my whole life through. As a result, I who received your help then will likely never be in the position to receive that help again. Remembering your kindness, I regret that I will not again have the opportunity to be touched by that kindness.

The three and a half years following my return to Japan were also an unhappy three and a half years. But I am a sovereign subject of the nation of Japan. Simple unhappiness is not a reason for leaving Japan. I, who possess the honors and privileges of a sovereign subject of Japan, inhabit this land together with some fifty million others and desire, at the very least, to uphold my fifty-millionth share of those honors and privileges. If for some reason my share in those honors and privileges should be reduced to something less than a a fifty-millionth portion, this would still not provide sufficient reason for me to deny my existence or leave behind my native land. Rather, I would better labor with all my strength to restore that fifty-millionth share. For me this is not a trifling matter; it is a will [*ishi*] that is more fundamental than my own will [*yo ga ishi ijō no ishi nari*]. Given that it is a will more fundamental than my own, I cannot somehow shape it to suit my own will. This will more fundamental than my own commands me: I must face without shirking whatever measure of unhappiness may prove necessary when it comes to upholding the honors and privileges due a sovereign subject of Japan.

For an author to impose his own emotions on a scholarly work and describe them at length in its preface may seem inappropriate. But when I look back on this scholarly work and remember the unhappy circumstances under which it was first conceived, the unhappy circumstances under which it began to take shape and under which it was then delivered as a lecture and, finally, the unhappy circumstances under which it is now being published, I cannot help but feel a great sense of satisfaction that the task has reached its present state of completion—even if it does not measure up when compared to the works of other scholars. I hope the reader will more or less share in this feeling.

The English people who observed me called me neurasthenic. A certain Japanese person even sent a report back to Japan that I had gone mad. Who am I to question the pronouncements of such wise persons? I only regret that I didn't have my wits about me enough then to express my gratitude to them.

Even after returning to Japan, I apparently remained unchanged—a neurasthenic and a madman. Even my own family accepted this view! Since my own family accepts this view, I am well aware that I, the person in question, have no leave to argue otherwise. But it was thanks to my neurasthenia and to my madness that I was able to compose *Cat*, produce *Drifting in Space*, and publish *Quail Cage*.[7] Thinking about this now, I believe I owe an enormous debt of gratitude to my neurasthenia and madness.

Insofar as there is no drastic change in my personal circumstances, I imagine that my neurasthenia and madness will continue for as long as I live. So long as they persist, I have hopes of publishing any number of *Cats*, *Driftings in Space*, and *Quail Cages*, and so I pray that my neurasthenia and madness never abandon me.

Neurasthenia and madness have spurred me, willingly or not, in the direction of creative writing. As a result, it may well be that in the future I will have neither the time nor the means to indulge myself in writing another scientific treatise along the lines of this *Theory of Literature*. If that turns out to be the case, and this volume turns out to be the sole memento of my attempts at writing [literally staining my fingers (with ink)] a work of this nature, then at least for the author it is a project worthy of the print shop's troubles—even as I acknowledge its meager value. I have tried to explain the reasons for this here.

November, Meiji 39 [1906]

Translated by Michael K. Bourdaghs

BOOK 1

CLASSIFICATION OF LITERARY SUBSTANCE

✓ *All the central problematics of* Theory of Literature *appear in condensed form in the open-*
✓ *ing chapter on the "form" of literary substance. Here Sōseki borrows from current experi-*
mental psychology to produce a model of literary experience based not on the formal proper-
ties of the work, nor on the activities of the writer as individual creative genius, but on the
✓ [*moment-by-moment experience of the reader encountering the text.*] *The model he*
produces—with its famous (F+f) formula and waveform model of consciousness—is highly
original and provides the three basic frames across which the study plays out. The model of ✓
consciousness as a standing waveform—with its dynamic possibilities and direct connection
to contemporary experimental psychology—disappears from the work in the supple, highly
visual presentation of book 1, subsequently appearing only in schematized, tabular form.
✓ *However, the (F+f) model, the second basic frame, is held with great consistency, and in*
✓ *some ways the entire subsequent project is a systematic exploration of F—its different*
sources, types, and possibilities of analysis and combination—and an exploration of what
"truth" is when the definition of the object lies not in judgments about the veracity of F
(concepts and impressions) but in the accompanying f (affect, emotion). The consistency
with which this will be held is glimpsed in chapter 2, where Sōseki begins his analysis by run-
✓ *ning through* [*Groos's six senses*] *(the standard five plus temperature) as source material for F,*
with examples that show them dominant in a passage, and reflecting on their combination
in a long passage from Shelley's Prometheus Unbound. *Following this long exercise, Sōseki*
✓ *succinctly concludes: "Emotion constitutes the single test case for literature, the beginning*
and end of the question. Consequently, for all the F in the myriad of social objects, insofar as
we can attach an f this must be treated as literary substance, and when that is not the case it
must be resolutely excluded from the domain." It is this investigation of F in all its possibili-
ties, and the subsequent rules for qualitatively and quantitatively evaluating the accompa-
nying affective charge, that gives Theory of Literature *its symmetry and form. This shift*

from an initial overture to an experimental theory to an elaborate taxonomy of materials and substances in some ways marks Sōseki as one of the last great rational system makers.

✓   *The third basic frame provided in the compact opening is the extension of concepts drawn from the moment-by-moment experience of literary consciousness by finite, individual minds to longer time spans and social aggregates. The extension of these concepts—authorized by a reading of experimental psychology and always developed first in reference to moment-by-moment experience— is also consistently held throughout the work and is one of the most problematic aspects of his project at this stage. Sōse-*

✓ *ki's commitment to this, driven by the ambitious scope of his ten-year project, at this stage reflects less a reasoned mediation of psychology and sociology than a turn-of-the-*

✳ *century preoccupation with the idea that "ontogeny recapitulates phylogeny," expressed here as the idea that the development of civilization recapitulates the development of the individual. This method of thinking was common with Freud and is traceable to Lombroso and Nordau. In particular, this aspect of* Theory of Literature *requires careful historical contextualization and scrutiny to see its development into the late Meiji lec-*

✓ *tures on civilization and individuality. If one accepts this commitment, however, the architectonic systematicity with which Sōseki works the problem over its several axes is impressive, resulting in interesting insights into literary history, genre, nationalism, the relation of English literature to material social and economic conditions,and so forth, in books 4 and 5.*

N.B.: Chapter 1 has been translated in its entirety, whereas only the opening sections of chapters 2 and 3 have been included.

Chapter 1: The Form of Literary Substance

✓ One can perhaps approach the form of literary substance with the expres-
✓ sion (F+f). F here indicates impressions or ideas at the focal point of con-
✓ sciousness, while f signifies the emotions that attend them. In this case, the formula stated above signifies impressions and ideas in two aspects, that is to say, as a compound of cognitive factor F ("large F"), and the
✓ emotional factor f ("small f"). Thus, the impressions or ideas we experi-
✓ ence in everyday life can be divided into three types:

✓   1. (F) but no (f), that is, cases where the intellectual factor is present but unaccompanied by the emotional factor; for example, when the idea of a triangle is present to consciousness but unaccompanied by any further emotion.

✓   2. (F) gives rise to an accompanying (f), as in the idea of a flower or a star, and so forth.

✓   3. in the case where there is only (f), and one is unable to cognize a corre-
✓ sponding (F), as in "fear of everything and fear of nothing." The sense of

dread with no accompanying object, for example, belongs to this category.
Ribot, in his *Psychology of Emotion* (1896),[1] divides this type further into four
categories, connecting it to the body as follows: "In the emotions we discover
a composite effect of the body's various faculties, that is to say, a pure, moreover autonomous, aspect rooted in the ordinary alteration of sense perception, and undergoing no direction by intellectual activity whatsoever."

Of the three types delineated above, it is case (2) that constitutes the substance of literature, that is to say, experience that takes the form of (F+f).

To give a detailed explanation of case (1), the most appropriate examples
are of the form of the axioms of geometry or Newton's laws of motion: "Every body at rest remains in its state of rest, and every body in motion remains in uniform motion in a straight line, unless it is acted upon by a
force external to it." Here the words activate only our intellect and excite no
emotion whatsoever. Or else they illustrate the principle that underlies the
high degree of emotion experienced by the scientist upon the discovery or
solution of a problem. However, this emotional component clearly relates
to the concept of discovery, to the joy of success derived from the feeling of
pleasure when a law is discerned from general facts or a principle from experiment. The emotional component does not attach to the law or principle
per se. There is in scientific knowledge itself no element that draws forth
emotion, only the pleasure when intellectual activity finds a suitable use.
Hence this class of things cannot be regarded as literary substance.

When we come to case (3), it lacks F from the start, and consequently
has no concept to mediate f. Even if one could bring such a case of dread to
consciousness oneself, it is doubtful that one could distinguish it from
other instances of f. It is worth noting that there are examples where an
overwhelmingly emotive content has been expressed in lyric poetry using
just this kind of form. For example:

> Out of the day and night
> A joy has taken flight;
> Fresh spring, and summer, and winter hoar,
> Move my faint heart with grief, but with delight
> No more—Oh, never more!
> (Shelley, *A Lament*)

This poem tells us nothing whatsoever about the source of the sadness,
and we have no way to judge from whence this emotion springs. It simply

sings of a misery—whether from love, whether from sickness, we have no way to tell. The poet simply transmits by this means the feeling of pathos.

There would seem to be three methods for appreciating this type of poem: (1) The person reading the poem first conjures up an F, thereby supplementing and converting the experience to (F+f) form; or, alternatively, (2) the person recalls the conception of pathos and absorbs sufficiently of its content, thereby providing direction to subsequent reflection; or else (3) some combination of the aforementioned 1 and 2. In this way both 1 and 2 tend to return to the (F+f) form, the only difference being that 1 is composed of source of pathos plus feeling while 2 is composed of the concept of pathos plus feeling. However, in the everyday appreciation of a poem this procedure is carried out almost unconsciously; indeed, if one posited a need to carry this out consciously, poetry would typically become a species of agony.

Previously I defined F to be the impression or concept residing at the focal point of consciousness, but I think there is a need to add a few words about this term "focal" or "focal point" [shōtenteki]. However, in order to provide an explanation of this, we will first have to trace back and begin with the term "consciousness." Specifying exactly what "consciousness" is is no easy task even from the point of view of psychology. If a certain specialist in the field can go so far as to assert that it is not possible to assign a fixed definition, it does not seem necessary in these lectures—which are not a course in psychology—vainly to try to provide a complete definition of this elusive term. If we can just convey some general idea of this object called consciousness, that should suffice. It will be convenient to begin the explanation with the notion of a "wave of consciousness."[2] On this point I will rely mainly on the admirably clear exposition in Lloyd Morgan's *Introduction to Comparative Psychology* (1894).[3]

Now, if one first takes up and examines the smallest unit of consciousness—that is to say, an instant of consciousness—one will see that within this instant are contained numerous relations and transformations. To use Morgan's own words, "In any random instant of consciousness, sundry mental states unceasingly appear, and then are washed away. In this sense, though we call it an instant it is not the case that the contents of that instant are fixed in one place." It is easy to adduce evidence for yourself that this is the case.

Let's say we have a person standing before St. Paul's Cathedral. Suppose that as he gazes upon that splendid architecture, his eyes move gradually from the pillars at the bottom section to the balustrade at the upper portion and finally reach the highest point at the tip of the cupola. At first, while gazing at the pillars, that portion of the structure is the only part perceived clearly and distinctly, while the rest only enters the field of vision indistinctly. However, in the instant the eyes move from the pillars to the balustrade, the perception of the pillars begins to attenuate, and simultaneously the perception of the balustrade gains in clarity and distinctness. The same phenomenon is observed in the movement from the balustrade to the cupola. When one recites a familiar poem or listens to a familiar piece of music, it is the same. That is to say, when one isolates for observation a moment of consciousness from the continuity of a particular conscious state, one can see that the preceding psychological state begins to attenuate, while the portion to follow, by contrast, is gradually raised in distinctness through anticipation. This is not only something we can feel in our daily experience; it has been precisely verified by scientific experiment. (I refer you to chapter 4 of Scripture's *New Psychology* (1897) for a detailed explanation).[4]

The moment-by-moment activity of consciousness takes the shape of a waveform, and if represented by a graph would look like the figure below (see fig. 1). As you can see, the summit of the waveform, that is to say, the focal point is the clearest portion of consciousness, and before and after this point one finds the so-called peripheries or threshold of consciousness. What we call our conscious experience typically takes the form of a continuous series of these psychological waveforms.

Following Morgan, we can represent this series as follows:

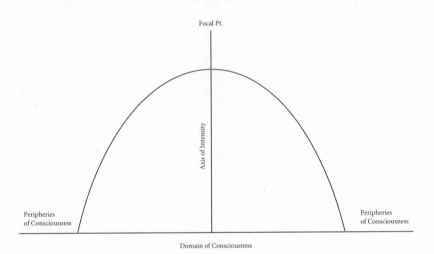

FIGURE 1. Waveform Model of Consciousness

That is to say, when the focal point of consciousness A migrates to position B, A is attenuated to peripheral consciousness a', and when B transfers further to C, a and b take an additional step toward the periphery of consciousness. In this way I hope the reader gains some understanding of the term designated F, how it resides in consciousness, and the relative position it takes.

Reasoning further from the analytical waveform thesis elaborated above, when we expand the domain to which these rules apply, cannot one say that just as in each instant of consciousness there resides a focal point F, so in ten, then twenty successive instants—indeed, in the flow of consciousness for even an hour resides something that lays claim to the same designation F? Let's say we spend an hour reciting the Chinese and Japanese poetry popular these days. It is clear that during that period our consciousness will be passing unceasingly from word a to word b, and on to word c in accordance with the above principles. However, when you recollect the innumerable small waveforms that by turns appeared and passed away during this time, is there not also for that hour a distinct focal point of consciousness, aside from the accumulated set of instantaneous F's (and in opposition to the hours that precede and follow)? Similarly, for a half day there should be a similar F, again for a full day, and, following this conjecture, there should be a focal F that spans a year, then ten years, even a single life span. If we take it as self-evident that, just as there is a focal F running longitudinally through each individual, in the same way there will be a distinct F for a generation and an age. In this broad sense F can be categorized as follows:

1. F in a single instant of consciousness
2. F within a span of time for an individual
3. F within a span of time of a society's evolution

Case (1) should need no further explanation. As for case (2), for example, F during the time of childhood might be toys, dolls, etc.; for a youth wrestling and fighting, adventures, etc.; for a young man this might turn to romantic love, while the primary F for middle age would be the acquisition of money, power, etc.; for an old man thoughts of salvation and redemption for humanity, contemplation of the world to come, etc.—in a never-ending process. To make the case that the same waveform thesis applies to the succession of F when we are dealing with sustained periods of time rather than instants, we might consider the following example. Let's say there is a person who, during a certain period of life, is extremely taken with Chinese poetry and reads it frequently. Then afterward, for a period of several years, he puts poetry aside and does not touch it at all. One day by chance he finds himself picking up the volume again. In that moment, despite the fact that he can decipher the meaning, the impressions and poetic imagery seem vague and unclear, and as a result the interest excited by the poetry is faint. However, as he regains practice in reading, and the poetic imagery works its way into his mind, his pleasure eventually reaches a peak. As this process continues, the pleasure recedes bit by bit, gradually slipping into the domain of indifference. Here we can say consciousness with regard to Chinese poetry ascends from the peripheries of consciousness to the focal point and then descends again to the peripheries. Case (3), F for a generation or an age is called in popular terms the spirit of the times, or zeitgeist, but if we were to find a word closer in the Eastern tradition we might choose the word *ikioi*, "the force of time." *Ikioi* from times past has been identified as heaven and as life.[5] Though some might say that in bringing up *ikioi* we're simply substituting X as an explanation for Y, this single word nicely grasps the broad sense of F I'm trying to convey, so I have no hesitation in using this word. It's possible that what we call the history of past and present is nothing more than the ceaseless transformation of this period-level F.

To take an example close at hand from our own country, the focus of contemporary consciousness during the time of the Restoration forty-odd years ago consisted of the three concepts of "expel the barbarian" (*jōi*), "support the government" (*sabaku*), and "duty to the Emperor" (*kinnō*). Let's say hypothetically that there was a man in that period who surpassed Shakespeare in expressive power; still, this period-level F would have no room to accommodate such a person. Even if a second Matthew Arnold were to appear to elucidate the principles of "Sweetness and Light" (a famous essay advocating literature in education), he would probably be unable to move any of his listeners.[6] The consciousness of the age would not allow for this. That not even a great sage or genius can defy the force of an age [*ikioi*] exemplifies the principle of the focus of consciousness F of a given age.

If we were to illustrate the adaptation of this waveform of consciousness and concept of F, ranging from instantaneous units of consciousness to a wider sense of the collective consciousness of an age, it would look like the diagram below.

/   The little chambers arranged vertically represent the successive transitions of F—from an instant of time in an individual consciousness to one hundred years—and are not meant to imply that F begets F^1, F^1 begets F^2, and so on. F stands for the focal point of consciousness of an instant, F^1 stands for the focal point of an hour's consciousness, and so
/   on. The horizontal rows, then, are the collective consciousness of the people who share a certain era, such that if you link together the fifty-year row you can understand this to be a collection of F of a generation over a fifty-year period. However, one would generally expect
/   this horizontal row of F to coalesce across a certain point, and this

point is what we call the general opinion, the zeitgeist, or, alternatively, the *ikioi* of that fifty-year period.

Chapter 2: The Constituent Elements of Literature

In the last chapter I argued that literary substance is best expressed in the form (F+f). Here I would like to break that down a bit. There are various positions on literature: some see literature as merely a tool for some high-class form of intellectual entertainment, while others see it as a channel for conveying morality, and so forth. I would like to show these as providing an unnecessarily narrow view of the domain of literature.

The first order of business in this research is to stand the object up from the simple perceptual elements that form its basis. We can begin to assemble evidence following the taxonomy of children's play found in Groos's *Spiele der Menschen* (1899).[7] This provides a principle by which we can see the degree to which innate tendencies make their way, under the guise of various forms, into the putatively pure realm of literature and confirm for ourselves the truth of the old saying "Adults are just children advanced in years." However, when we arrive at content of sufficient complexity and find elements that do not correspond to Groos, there we will find the limits of this approach.

1. Touch. Groos first takes up touch and records a number of examples from children's favorite forms of play based in this sense. Following his order of categorization, I will begin by quoting some examples from the domain of literature:

Yet I'll not shed her blood!
Nor scar that whiter skin of hers than snow,
And *smooth as monumental alabaster.*
(*Othello*, act 5, sc. 3, ll. 3–5)

But *O for the touch of a vanish'd hand,*
And the sound of a voice that is still!
(Tennyson, *Break, Break, Break*)

In these simple examples we discover that what seems at first glance unsuitable for literary expression has an unexpected power.

2. Temperature

> St. Agnes' Eve—Ah, bitter chill it was!
> The owl, for all his feathers, was a-cold;
> The hare limp'd trembling through the frozen grass,
> And silent was the flock in woolly fold.
> (Keats, *The Eve of St. Agnes*)

If this were simply a case of supplementing complex scenery by adding information about the temperature this sense of cold wouldn't immediately translate into (F+f), but when these various phrases are arrayed in this manner to excite the sense of cold, there is no question temperature begins to exist as literary substance.

3. Taste. If one imagines that the baser senses, such as appetite, should not intrude on the putatively sublime pleasures of literature, I would offer the following:

> The board was spread with fruits and wine;
> With grapes of gold, like those that shine
> On Casbin's hills;—pomegranates full
> Of melting sweetness, and the pears,
> And sunniest apples that Caubul
> In all its thousand gardens bears;—
> Plantains, the golden and the green,
> Malaya's nectar'd mangosteen;
> Prunes of Bokara, and sweet nuts
> From the far groves of Samarcand.
> And Basra dates, and apricots,
> Seed of the Sun, from Iran's land;—
> With rich conserve of Visna cherries,
> Of orange flowers, and of those berries
> That, wild and fresh, the young gazelles
> Feed on in Erac's rocky dells.
> (Moore, *Lalla Rookh, The Light of the Haram*)

Verse 30 of Keats's *Eve of St. Agnes* moved Winchester to remark, "It relies on pleasurable elements based in the inferior senses a bit too much to be regarded as a first-rank poem."

4. Smell. There would not be space here to enumerate the many instances in which scent figures throughout the history of literature. That in our own country *hana no kaori* ("the flower's fragrance") appears as a fixed rhetorical technique testifies to the generality of this principle.

It was a chosen plott of fertile land,
Emongst wide waves sett, like a little nest,
As if it had by Natures cunning hand
Bene choycely picked out from all the rest,
And laid forth for ensample of the best:
No daintie flowre or herbe that growes on grownd,
No arborett with painted blossomes drest
And smelling sweete, but there it might be fownd
To bud out faire, and throwe her sweete smels al arownd.
(Spenser, *The Faerie Queene*, bk. 2, can. 6, st. 12)

An excellent example also appears in Shakespeare's *Macbeth*. For details please refer to Verplanck's commentary in *New Variorum Shakespeare*, p. 257.

日靜重簾透　　風清一縷長

(The sun quiets slowly, passing through the slats of the blinds
The breeze pure, clean like a thread [alt. through a single thread of incense])

The frequent use of the smoke of incense in Chinese poetry has been frequently remarked.

The morn is up again, the dewy morn
With breath all incense, and with cheek all bloom,
Laughing the clouds away with playful scorn,
And living as if earth contain'd no tomb—

And glowing into day.
(Byron, *Childe Harold*, can. 3, ll. 914–18)

This, of course, is personification. However, it is precisely to the degree that incense carries a pleasurable association that one can say "with breath all incense."

 ✓   5. Hearing. The position this sense occupies in the production of pleasurable aesthetic sensation can be discerned from the fact that music exists ✓ as an independent art form. That sound is stressed and rhythm revered in ✓ poetry is nothing other than an attempt to utilize this sense. The rustling of a garment; the scuttling of fallen leaves in a garden; the sound of wind, rain, thunder, waves; the cry of a bird—there is no limit to the sounds on this earth. At times I believe it is possible to construct quite fine literature simply from this sense of hearing.

> *Duke*: If music be the food of love, play on;
> Give me excess of it, that, surfeiting,
> The appetite may sicken, and so die.
> That strain again! It had a dying fall:
> *O, it came o'er my ear like the sweet sound*
> *That breathes upon a bank of violets,*
> *Stealing and giving odour!*
> (*Twelfth Night*, act 1, sc. 1, ll. 1–7)

> I chatter over stony ways,
> In little sharps and trebles,
> I bubble into eddying bays,
> I babble on the pebbles.
> (Tennyson, *The Brook*)

> I heard the water lapping on the crag,
> And the long ripple washing the reeds.
> (Tennyson, *The Passing of Arthur*)

> Or sweetest Shakespeare, Fancy's child,
> *Warble his native wood-notes wild.*
> (Milton, *L'Allegro*, ll. 133–34)

That Shakespeare would be likened to a bird and his poetry to their sweet song is a testament to how prized the sound of the bird is to people in this world.

> By this the storm grew loud apace,
> The water-wraith was shrieking;
> And in the scowl of heaven each face
> Grew dark as they were speaking.
> (Campbell, *Lord Ullin's Daughter*)

/   6. Sight. As with painting and sculpture, fully realized artistic traditions East and West find their basis in the sense of vision. The range that stretches from simple colors all the way to complex composite figures, such as the human form, provide a quantity of possible F's, with their accompanying f, that is simply incalculable.

/ a. Light

> Sparkling and bright in liquid light
> Does the wine our goblets gleam in;
> With hue as red as the rosy bed
> Which a bee would choose to dream in.
> (Charles Hoffman, *Sparkling and Bright*)

> There shot a golden splendour far and wide,
> Spangling those million poutings of the brine
> With quivering ore.
> (Keats, *Endymion*, bk. 1, ll. 350–52)

> A violet by a mossy stone
> Half-hidden from the eye!
> —*Fair as a star, when only one*
> *Is shining in the sky.*
> (Wordsworth, *She Dwelt among the Untrodden Ways*)

/ b. Color

> I remember, I remember
> The roses, red and white,

The violets, and the lily-cups—
Those flowers made of light!
The lilacs where the robin built,
And where my brother set
The laburnum on his birthday,—
The tree is living yet!
(Hood, *Past and Present*)

The degree to which the impression of this passage is rich with color should be clear after one reading (whether or not the characters for red, white, and green are used).

The leaves dead
Are driven, like ghosts from an enchanter fleeing,
Yellow, and black, and pale, and hectic red,
Pestilence-stricken multitudes.
(Shelley, *Ode to the West Wind*, ll. 2–5)

Within the shadow of the ship
I watched their rich attire:
Blue, glossy green, and velvet black,
They coiled and swam; and every track
Was a flash of golden fire.
(Coleridge, [*The Rime of the*] *Ancient Mariner*, ll. 277–81)

[Next are shape (c), and movement (d), followed by a summary, where Sōseki reads a long passage from Shelley's *Prometheus Unbound* and analyzes the different sense ratios, composed of constituent parts and composite objects.]

Chapter 3: Classification of Literary Substance
and Its Qualitative Equivalence

While only a rough outline, in the preceding chapter we were able to define the domain of objects that can serve as literary substance—that is to say, those that show accompanying emotion—and suggested through examples that this substance could always be described by the (F+f) formula. These examples obviously only scratch the surface of English literature and in some cases have not, I fear, been the most appropriate. In any case, hopefully I have gained the assent of the reader that these various constituent parts all possess the character of existing as literary substance, and that the resulting composite objects need to be treated as literary substance. Of course, this is not to say that since each individual element qualifies, the composite figure will also necessarily qualify. While fish, meat, vegetables, rice, and grain all constitute a part of our diet, the combination of any two of these may well provoke an upset stomach or diarrhea. In the same way we must grant that while each of the substantive parts mentioned above may individually possess literary quality, a particular combination of them may unexpectedly result in failure. However, as a general rule we can expect that this kind of composite figure will usually exhibit an impressive literary substance, just as a full-course meal is better than a single dish. However, criteria for judging the success or failure of the combination—that is to say, the rules of seasoning—require a section unto themselves.[8]

As I've argued above, emotion constitutes the single test case for literature, the beginning and end of the question. Consequently, for all the F in the myriad social objects, insofar as we can attach an f this must be treated as literary substance, and when that is not the case it must resolutely be excluded from the domain. Given this, all objects that can be treated as literary substance, that is, that can be restated in the (F+f) form, can be grouped into four categories, as follows:

1. sensation F
2. personification F
3. metaphysical F
4. intellectual F

with the natural world providing the basis for (1), the human drama (i.e., matters that reflect the variety of emotions) providing the basis for (2), religion providing the basis for (3), and concepts pertaining to the questions of human existence for (4).

The objection might be raised that in addition to this there is also what psychologists would call the aesthetic F. Literature is a type of art; hence the emotions one feels in relation to literature must be aesthetic in nature. If so, what is the reason for not including this in your calculations?

Here is how I would answer. It is an obvious fact that the emotions that arise in response to literature are aesthetic. However, this is simply something that always occurs in conjunction with a given F and is not a feeling that arises in isolation. Hence, if one feels compelled to use a term like "aesthetic feeling," it would suffice to take up any of the examples given above. This is why I do not construct a special category for this. As for the various theories about the origin of this aesthetic feeling, such as Schiller's "Spieltheorie" or Groos's theory of instinct, I do not intend to address them. But it should be pointed out that insofar as the so-called aesthetic sense or feeling is a subjective feeling in response to the beautiful, it is clearly subsumed within the f described above. If, however, we accept that aesthetic feeling is generally thought to be a pleasurable sensation, one has to realize that at times it will correspond to f and at other times it will not.

Now, while it is clear enough that the four types of literary substance are in all cases accompanied by feeling, I have not yet argued as to which brings about the most intense experience of f, that is to say, which is the most appropriate as literary substance.

Milton has argued that poetry should be simple, sensual, and filled with passion. So let us set aside the others for a while and concentrate on sensation F, or what we may call (using some up-to-date terminology) the "concrete element" of sense perception, which, since time immemorial, has always been considered the most essential condition not only for poetry but for all literary expression. If you will take up the first type—the material of sense perception—and examine it, you will see that it is due to this advantage of concreteness that the feelings it evokes in us have a characteristic intensity. When an identical physical object is described both from a purely objective and an internal subjective standpoint, it is quite clear which produces the higher degree of emotional intensity. In reading the poetry of Burns, one feels the hot intensity of the passages, whereas it is difficult to escape the dullness of excitation in the work of Wordsworth, where, despite employing the language of emotion, he tries to grasp a kind of abstract spirit in the natural world. One is direct and arouses the reader's emotions as if it were an electrical flash or an echo of a voice. In the other the reader must first enter a state of contemplation with the poet. Only as a result of this meditation is the reader able to feel the lure of the poem, with the result that it is somewhat lukewarm and indirect in effect. To look at the second type, the

material of human or personal affairs, there is no need for lengthy dis-
putation about whether our hearts are touched more intensely by living
drama accompanied by people's actions than by systematic theories of
personal affairs cut off from living actors, for it is clear that in the end a
dozen treatises on romantic love can't match a single page of a novel describing the instantaneous glance that passes between a man and woman.
It is not all that rare for a person captivated by a beautiful woman to attempt suicide in the throes of agony, whereas I have yet to hear of a case
of a person losing his mind as a result of mature reflection on the abstract essence of "love." It is not difficult to contemplate casting oneself
into the stream for one's parents, or throwing oneself under the horse of
one's lord, precisely because the parents are present as concrete animals
and the lord as a living, functioning human being with eyes and ears.
However, when it comes to sacrificing one's life for one's country, that is
more difficult to conceive of. The nation is vastly inferior to the individual in terms of degree of concreteness. It is too vague a thing to offer
up one's life for. It's not easy to offer up one's life for an abstraction. If it
were, we would spend a great deal more time tilting at windmills. Consequently, people said to be engaged in this are, as a matter of fact, not
dying for an abstract emotion but are always seeking behind it some
kind of vivid, concrete object toward which they can direct their attention as they move forward. However, that is not to say that such suicidal
idealists don't exist. These would be the people who hold in their hearts
feelings for that ridiculous abstract object, the "ruler who enjoys the
mandate of heaven." To die for principles [*michi no tame*] is to attach an
emotion to them without really being conscious of what they are. It is
like the knowledge of the Zen devotee, where one discards all ties and
devotes oneself fully to an investigation of the nature of self, "earnestly
devoted, advancing with fierce spirit, in the myriad positions of daily
life."[9] What he seeks is some heretofore undisclosed law at the bottom of
things, a way to an object that ultimately cannot be grasped or realized.
Prior to enlightenment there is for him neither a guarantee that such a
law exists nor any reason why he should seek it. Nevertheless, for the
sake of this incognizable law and this incognizable way, he stakes his life
without looking back. In this he becomes the true thing, a monster rag-
ing against an incomprehensibility, far from the ordinary person. So
let's accept that this is an exceptional case, something not found in the
average person. Therefore, following our reasoning, we have to accept as

a fact that f continues to vary in direct proportion to the degree of con-
√ creteness of F. And of the four types of content listed above, the ones
relatively abstract and lacking in clarity would obviously be the third
and fourth types. Of course, the substance that defines the fourth type
√ may be concepts, but concepts are abstractions of what was originally
concrete, so irrespective of the case it will not completely lack f, but it is
without doubt that such investment and emotion attach according to the
degree of concreteness.

I have an example. Pope's *Sappho to Phaon* alludes to the same work by
Ovid, and in the final stanza, where Sappho urges Phaon to return home
across the sea:

O launch thy bark, secure of prosp'rous gales;
Cupid for thee shall spread the swelling sails.
(ll. 252–53)

It would really be hard to interpret the second line as abstract, but Bowles[10]
criticizes it as follows: "If we suppose Pope has miscalculated here, it
would have to be in the excessively comprehensive tendency. Given the
well-ordered impression of concreteness one finds in the original, this is
all the more difficult to overlook. If one checks the original for the line:
'Cupid for thee shall spread the swelling sails,' one finds Cupid directs the
ship as the pilot, and with his soft hands spreads the sail. There is absolutely no mistaking the impression given to the reader." One has to grant
the persuasiveness of the interpretation.

Again we find the following in the first verse of Wordsworth's "Ode to
Duty":

Stern Daughter of the Voice of God!
O Duty! If that name thou love
Who art a light to guide, a rod
To check the erring, and reprove;
Thou, who art victory and law
When empty terrors overawe;
From vain temptations dost set free,
And calm'st the weary strife of frail humanity!
(ll. 1–8)

Look at this! This is flavorless, dry as dust. (At least that's my opinion. /
I don't know what a Westerner would say.) Now let's think about the reasons. If we examine this, we find (1) overall there is a preponderance of $\rceil$ /
abstract, conceptual words, and (2) the elements of a picture are almost $\rfloor$
completely lacking; there is no color. (To avoid this—or perhaps to give it
the form of an ode—he has deployed a kind of personification here, but to
little effect.) All one can allow is that there is a faint concreteness to the
line "a light to guide, a rod / To check. . . ." Matthew Arnold reproves
Wordsworth for this tendency to lapse into the trap of reason. I quote:

> The *Excursion* abounds with philosophy and therefore the *Excursion* is
> to the Wordsworthian what it never can be to the disinterested lover of
> poetry,—a satisfactory work. "Duty exists," says Wordsworth, in the
> *Excursion*; and then he proceeds thus—

> . . . Immutably survive,
> For our support, the measures and the forms,
> Which an abstract Intelligence supplies,
> Whose kingdom is, where time and space are not.
> (bk. 4, ll. 73–76)

> And the Wordsworthian is delighted, and thinks that here is a sweet
> union of philosophy and poetry. But the disinterested lover of poetry
> will feel that the lines carry us really not a step farther than the proposi-
> tion which they would interpret; that they are a tissue of elevated but
> abstract verbiage, alien to the very nature of poetry.[11]

The lines in the work that approach poetry most closely are:

> Flowers laugh before thee on their beds, And fragrance in thy footing
>   treads;
> Thou dost preserve the starts from wrong;
> And the most ancient heavens, through Thee, are fresh and strong.
> (ll. 45–48)

If you consider it for a moment, the reason is simply because they are relatively concrete.

What has been said above about poetry also applies to prose. When you take the reduction of concrete elements to the extreme—as in Kant's critiques, the philosophical lectures of Hegel, or Euclid's geometry—you will find that there is no excitation at all. Of course, insofar as these efforts, as Plato put it, "raise order from chaos, recover objects from the boundless waste, draw borders in the borderless, give form to the formless, and represent the things of the world in concepts," you are not likely to remain unmoved, but the content of these discourses themselves admits of no negotiation with emotion. Let's say for the moment that we are not dealing with a philosophical or scientific text circulated among specialists but a text that partakes of literary substance of the fourth type (intellectual F). Unless it touches, to some degree, on an incident of some purport in human affairs, our interest declines and ebbs, becoming like the ripples a light breeze produces on the surface of the water, and it will elicit little more than a smile. Following are a few good examples:

This was the shadowy sentiment that made the wall of division between them. There was no other. Lord Ormont had struck to fragments that barrier of the conventional oath and ceremonial union. He was unjust—he was Injustice. The weak may be wedded, they cannot be married, to Injustice. And if we have the world for the buttress of injustice, then is Nature the flaring rebel; there is no fixed order possible. Laws are necessary instruments of the majority; but when they grind the sane human being to dust for their maintenance, their enthronement is the rule of the savage's old deity, sniffing blood-sacrifice. There cannot be a based society upon such conditions. An immolation of the naturally-constituted individual arrests the general expansion to which we step, decivilizes more, and is more impious to the God in man, than temporary revelries of a licence that Nature soon checks.

{Meredith, *Lord Ormont and His Aminta*, chap. 24)

It's not that this is uninteresting. A person of some cultivation, or a person with some experience of the world, will read this through and feel a slight sense of interest in his heart. It will not, though, be the pleasure of passion, the electric experience, the joy of direct impression. Rather, it will be the calm, cool pleasure in reflection.

"Oh! You may shake your head, but I would rather hear a *rough truth* than the most complimentary evasion."

"How would you define a *rough truth*, Dr. Middleton?" said Mrs. Mount Stuart.

Like the trained warrior who is ready at all hours for the trumpet to arms, Dr. Middleton wakened up for judicial allocution in a trice.

"A *rough truth*, ma'am, that the world is composed of fools, and that the exceptions are knaves," Professor Crooklyn furnished the example avoided by the Rev. Doctor.

"Not to precipitate myself into the jaws of the first definition, which strikes me as being as happy as Jonah's whale, that could carry probably the most learned man of his time inside without the necessity of digesting him," said De Craye, "a *rough truth* is a rather strong charge of universal nature for the firing off of a modicum of personal fact." ✓

"It is a *rough truth* that Plato is Moses atticizing," said Vernon to Dr. Middleton, to keep the diversion alive.

"And that Aristotle had the globe under his cranium," rejoined the Rev. Doctor.

"And that the Moderns live on the Ancients."

"And that not one in ten thousand can refer to the particular treasury he filches."

"The Art of our days is a revel of *rough truth*," remarked Professor Crooklyn.

"And the literature has laboriously mastered the adjective, wherever it may be in relation to the noun," Dr. Middleton added.

"Orson's first appearance at Court was in the figure of a *rough truth*, causing the Maids of Honour, accustomed to Tapestry Adams, astonishment and terror," said De Craye.

That he might not be left out of the sprightly play, Sir Willoughby leveled a lance at the quintain, smiling on laetitia: "In fine, caricature is *rough truth*."

She said: "Is one end of it, and realistic directness is the other."

He bowed: "The palm is yours."

(Meredith, *The Egoist*, chap. 36)

What you all likely feel on first reading this passage is its labored quality. The six or seven people gathered here all compete in cleverness and tact, demonstrating a kind of adroitness and intellectual cultivation. You may well find one in a hundred, or two in a thousand, of this type among the people you daily interact with, but for six or seven to meet accidentally like this, and then for each to demonstrate this kind of clever volubility, is bound to appear a bit unnatural—even if we are talking about the sophisticated West. Hence the feeling that these men and women are the type that regularly displays this type of polished language fades, and you are occupied instead with admiring the technique of the author himself, who, having grasped a "rough truth," unfurls it carelessly and with great style. However, this stops at the point of admiration and does not rise to the level of a general emotion. In other words, it's like the "neither . . . nor" in "it's neither this nor that, neither here nor there," just chatter. It is the literary equivalent of fun and games, like a third-rate dandy showing off by trading quips with a courtesan or a teahouse girl, leaving the others in the room yawning with boredom. In this way the connection with the principal emotions and problems in the course of life is very tenuous, and the f accompanying the central F in this passage correspondingly thin.

It should be clear from the examples above that the intellectual F is from the start not very well suited as literary substance. However, one can be taken aback at times by the fierce emotions reported by scientists in response to works in their field of specialization:

> Descuret introduces an Italian named Mentelli in his book *Care of the Passions*. Mentelli was a linguist and a mathematician, who, without any particular practical goal in mind dedicated his life to pursuit of the pleasures of scholarship and satisfying his intellectual desires. He lived in a low-class lodging house in Paris, however even this was let to him out of charity. He economized in every facet of his life and all expenditures except what was absolutely necessary. Consequently, with the exception of expenditures for books, he was able to limit his living expenses to 7 *sous* per day, with 3 *sous* going to food, and 4 *sous* to fuel. With this arrangement he was able to devote 20 hours out of each day to the continuous study of books, and gained his living expenses by teaching mathematics one day per week. What he needed consisted of water, potatoes (which he cooked over his lamp), oil and brown bread, only these four things. He had a large trunk which he kept in the room, and in the day he would set it up as a desk and keep his legs under

wrapped in a blanket or straw, and at night he would sleep inside. Aside from an old beaten armchair, a small table, a vase and a tin pot and a small concave tin fragment (which he used as a lamp), he had no other accessories. Further, to conserve on laundry fees he never wore underwear, and aside from a military surplus jacket bought second-hand, pants made from Nanking cotton, a fur cap and wooden shoes, owned no other clothes. In 1814 artillery shells from the federated army landed near the lodging house, but he couldn't be bothered to move. When cholera first broke out in Paris, it was said he was ordered to put down his books so his filthy room could be sterilized, but he refused and finally they had to intervene by force. In this way he passed 30 years in intense concentration, without regret or a single day of ill health, but on December 22, 1836, as he approached the Seine to collect some water, he lost his footing and unfortunately fell into the rising water and drowned in the most piteous circumstances. Mentelli published no books in his lifetime, and the results of his many years of study vanished with him.

(Letourneau, *Physiologie des Passions*, p. 23)

This example is actually no example at all. That is to say, it is an exception. Most scholars choose as their object the fame that Milton called "that last infirmity of Noble Mind" and pursue their research with a sort of associated emotion, whereas this fellow's lure, by contrast, was in the research itself.

In any case, seting aside these exceptions, it is clear that in general literary content of the fourth type will not be accompanied by strong emotions.

The third type of substance occurs when a metaphysical object is taken as the material for literature. At times this type of substance can assume an even more abstract form than the fourth type, and while one can say that f attaches to this F in the same way, this new f appears in a much stronger form than in the fourth type. Ancient and modern, East and West, the ferocity of religious emotions is a common trait. If you would like to look further into this, simply consult a religious history or compendium of lives of the saints. For Japanese, who are rather indifferent to religion and unable to discern the nature of God, that ferocity can be difficult to imagine. As to why an F characterized by such a similar degree of abstraction should excite such wildly different f's, that is a topic of considerable interest that we will need to examine for ourselves later in the course.

(For further reference see Lombroso's *Men of Genius* [1864; Eng. trans. 1891], William James's *Varieties of Religious Experience* [1902], and *Lives of Saints.*)

Translation by Joseph A. Murphy

BOOK 2

QUANTITATIVE CHANGE IN LITERARY SUBSTANCE

In Book 2 Sōseki tries to place literary experience on a quantitative basis, prefatory to the
situation of literature vis-à-vis science in the field of knowledge in book 3. According to
Jeremy O'Brien, "All science is founded on measurement, and improvements in precision
have led not just to more detailed knowledge, but also to new fundamental understanding. "[1] Quantification—that is to say, the reduction of phenomena to units capable of increase, decrease and equivalence—is the essential first step in putting scientific issues on
a technical basis, but this is in no way separate from fundamental understanding. This
implies the methodological importance of this step in seeing the systematicity of Sōseki's
project. While quantification is in tension with the differentiation of scientific and literary truth which constitute the subject of book 3, it gets to the core of the question of knowledge. By putting literature on a quantitative basis, Sōseki sharpens the distinctions he
does find relevant in the following book.

If, on the one hand, quantification is a surprising move in an intuitive domain like
literature, then, on the other hand, economic analysis as a methodological assumption is
well established in the human sciences as a way to present a particular aspect of a phenomenon that might well be described in other ways. For example, in The Language of
Psychoanalysis Laplanche and Pontalis distinguish the economic analysis of psychic processes from the topographical and the dynamic. They find the economic hypothesis to be a
permanent feature of Freud's theory, deriving "from a scientific spirit and a conceptual
framework which are shot through with notions of energy."[2] Freud's decision to treat
seemingly ineffable psychic processes in this way, like Sōseki's hydraulic and later thermodynamic models of human processes, is not exceptional. The gesture in book 2 to quantify
is part of a general resistance to the idea that psychic processes operate according to other
than physical principles and prepares the object for comparison with scientific objects in
book 3.

√   *If quantification is itself a methodological issue, then the substantive issue is that the phenomena being subjected to increase, decrease, and equivalence are obviously concepts and impressions (F) and affect (f), in aggregate the substance of literature. Having been*
√   *dissatisfied with his advisers in London, Sōseki is trying to express ideas for which a vocabulary has not yet been invented. This causes problems in interpretation—for example, in sorting out his use of naiyō and zairyō (typically, though not exhaustively, translated as "substance" and "material"). A more difficult point in some ways is the set of terms that translates "small f." We have sometimes translated Sōseki's kanjō as "emotion" and at other times as "affect," as the argument on the processing of literary substance suggests. These terms are also not yet clearly settled in the specialist literature in English.[3] Rather than mechanically translate these terms, we have tried to allow for maximum suggestivity for plugging into a moving field.*
√   *A third point of interest in book 2 is a position on experience suggestively close to the early Schleiermacher's thesis concerning the identity of thought and language. As Sōseki analyzes quantitative changes in F over historical time, it is not the case for him that ancient peoples—or people from another sociolinguistic domain, such as sixteenth-century Europe—have thoughts and feelings just like us but don't have words to express them. In*
√   *fact, there is an identity of thought and language, such that in ancient times when people had few words available to them, they did not have sharply distinct thoughts and emo-*
√   *tions either, leaving open the idea that translation and poetry attempt to introduce new thoughts and emotions into the target domain. This is a highly consistent position and a rejection of the humanist position that deep down people have the same universal human thoughts and emotions.*

   N.B.: We have translated chapters 1–2 of book 2, omitting chapter 3 (on f in cases of fascination or bewitchment) and chapter 4 (on the specific instance of tragedy).

The preceding section differentiated the material that comprises literature into four types and gave an account of their characteristic qualities and
√ mutual interactions. At this point we will shift our sights slightly and raise the question of the principles under which quantitative transformation of
√ these four types of material occurs. To raise the question of quantification
✳ is to ask under what conditions the total quantity of material available as literature is advancing, declining, or in stasis.

Before entering into this problem, it will probably be worthwhile to
√ backtrack a bit and recall what is meant here by literary substance. Around the beginning of these lectures I argued that all literary material was liable to restatement in the form (F + f). Specifying the manner of increase and
√ decrease in literary material will therefore first require that we master the manner of fluctuation of the single element of (F + f)—large F. Once we have in place a means of accounting for the manner of increase and de-

crease in this single element F, we will then proceed to examine the manner of shift of the small f that accompanies this fluctuating large F. In this way, after clearly determining the nature and interaction of these two elements, we will first be able to talk of quantitative changes in the material of literature.

Chapter 1: Change in Large F

What is the manner in which large F changes? If we observe this in terms of the life of an individual—as one passes through infancy to childhood, through adolescence and then youth—change in cognitive capacities reveals two characteristics. First is the increase in the capacity for distinction, and second is increase in the objects to be distinguished. This is not something simply to be said with respect to an individual's life. I believe some similar effect obtains in the history of human development. By development of the capacity for distinction, I mean that in the world of a child, or in a precivilized world, what was initially thought to be the case of a single, unified F is, through the long accumulation of time and experience, gradually discovered to be two or more distinct F's. That is to say, with the development of the capacity for distinction, one reaches the point where an individual F proliferates into F', F'', F''', and so forth. In light of this point, the quantity of F increases as time goes on. The second point— an increase in the number of objects to be distinguished—means that day by day or moment by moment throughout the course of one's life, the opportunity for contact with new objects, or at least indirect knowledge of new objects, is bound to increase. The quantity of information available to a child bears no comparison to that of a person who has reached full adulthood. Similarly, there is no doubt that there is a marked difference between the quantity of F available to people in a primitive state and to people in the modern conditions of today. If we map this twofold manner in which F increases into the four constituent literary elements laid out in book 1, we get something like the following:

(1) material of sensation [*kankakuteki zairyō*] (a) In terms of increase in the capacity for distinction, if the power of judgment of a person who does not recognize a difference between the green of summer grass and the green of a conifer is sharpened only a little, they quickly come to see that a great difference exists between the two. The same goes for wines,

tobacco, perfumes, aloe and so forth. In terms of an individual lifetime, a child lacks the capacity to make fine distinctions, but this ability is gradually developed through the accumulation of experiences, and in this way the data of sensation undergoes a continual, marked increase. Following this line of reasoning, in terms of quantity the constituent data of sensation of humankind today exceeds what was available to the quiescent cultures of ancient peoples due to the accumulation of experience over thousands of years. (b) In terms of the raw increase in objects of knowledge available for distinction, it is probably not necessary to elaborate. The state of affairs in the African desert or deep in the forests of the Americas, the splendor of the Himalayan ranges, the flooding of the Yellow River—in the past these were natural objects known only through direct contact by people living in very confined regions of the world. Today, in the twentieth century, we obtain knowledge of every corner of the world as simple facts.

(2) material of personification [*jinjiteki zairyō*] (a) In archaic times all the different shades from rage to indignation were satisfactorily expressed with the single word "anger" (*ikari*). However the fact that nowadays there are many levels of anger, and that we employ a variety of words to bring out these shades of meaning must be seen as a result of progress in the capacity to distinguish. We express resentment, outrage, exasperation and so forth, the list goes on and on. (b) As our capacity for distinction develops, we take up analytical means, and in human affairs and emotions once thought to be identical begin to recognize a variety of differences as described above. On the other hand, there are all sorts of matters (pertaining to human affairs) unavailable to experience in ancient times of which we have knowledge today. Affects unavailable to large parts of the globe were cognized without problem in other parts existing at the same time. For example in savage peoples the feeling engendered in the face of the natural world was simply fear, whereas a civilized people will look on it with a complex feeling of sublimity. However this notion of sublimity is something that is newly attached through the gradual increase in human capacity.

(3) metaphysical material [*chōshizen*] and (4) intellectual material [*chishiki*], proceed in the same way as described above, developing in terms of two aspects—differentiation and raw increase—with appropriate modifications.

Chapter 2: Change in Small f

The question therefore arises as to what is happening to small f while the large F available to cognition is ceaselessly increasing from the augmentation of distinction and increase in domain. There can be no doubt that in a certain sense this increases as well. At this point we will need to address the question of increase in small f. I would suggest that the increase in small f is governed by the following three principles: (1) the rule of displacement of affect; (2) the rule of expansion of affect; and (3) the rule of persistence of affect.

1. One of the most striking facts uncovered by contemporary psychology is the phenomenon of "displacement of affect," so let's begin with that. Given a certain small f that arises in conjunction with the F of an object A, the principle of displacement indicates the phenomenon whereby the same small f attaches for some reason to another object B. In other words, a certain chain of associations occurs among F and f. To take a simple example, let's say a chicken sees a caterpillar, pecks at it, and flees in surprise. When this chicken encounters the same circumstance again, although it will not repeat the same path, it will reach the same conclusion. That is, the process whereby

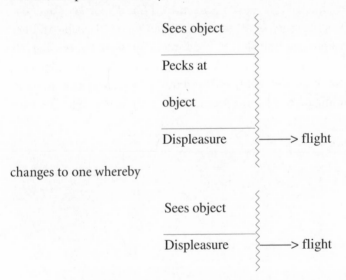

Sees object

Pecks at

object

Displeasure ——> flight

changes to one whereby

Sees object

Displeasure ——> flight

In this way, though the original association was between pecking and displeasure, the association between visual confirmation and displeasure is perfectly established. That is to say, the affect of displeasure has been displaced from pecking to the visual sense. To take another example, it is with the fulfillment of specific desires that humans first experience the sense of satisfaction. However, this sense of satisfaction is displaced from the fulfillment of desires and extended to money, such that if one gets a hold of money, the sense of satisfaction is immediately produced. This is a clear illustration of the principle of displacement of affect. Similarly, "Cockney" is a word used to designate the dialect used by the lower classes in London. However, there is no rationale for assigning a feeling of excellence or inferiority to this dialect itself, it being just a matter of displacing the sense of disgust we feel in relation to the lower classes onto their dialect, and before you know it a sense of displeasure is engendered at simply hearing the accent.

The keepsake of a departed mother or wedding ring is recognized by most people to possess an emotional charge based on this principle. This has nothing to do with the fineness of the piece but is simply a displacement of the emotion felt toward the former possessor. Since this is a seminar in literature, perhaps we should provide a few examples from there. The tragedy of Isabella, from tale 5 of the third day of Boccaccio's *Decameron*, is a veritable discourse on this principle of displacement. In his later years Keats refashioned this into a poem entitled *Isabella*, or *The Pot of Basil* (1818). This is the story of a beautiful woman named Isabella and her ill-fated lover, Lorenzo. Isabella was born into a good family, passing her days peacefully in the company of her two brothers. However, the young maiden has a lover named Lorenzo with whom she is secretly besotted, and the two yearn impatiently for the moment they can be together. The man pines away:

To-morow will I bow to my delight,
To-morrow will I ask my lady's boon
(st. 4)

The woman, for her part, burns with love:

Until sweet Isabella's untouched cheek
Fell sick within the rose's just domain
(st. 5)

But Isabella has a ne'er-do-well brother who refuses to assent to the union of his sister with the likes of Lorenzo. He employs every strategy to keep them apart but finally realizes that the love between these two cannot be vanquished by any ordinary means. He secretly lures Lorenzo deep into the forest and kills him, telling Isabella that Lorenzo has gone off to a foreign country. However, in a chilling scene the murdered Lorenzo appears at Isabella's bedside in a dream and announces:

> I am a shadow now, alas! alas!
> (st. 39)

With this Isabella realizes she has been deceived by her brother. The following morning she ventures out with an elderly nursemaid into the forest she saw in her dreams, discovers the place where her lover has been buried, exhumes the body, severs the head from the corpse, and carries it back home. Upon arriving home, she takes the severed head, arranges its locks with a golden comb, wraps it in fragrant cloth, and buries it in a flowerpot, in which she plants basil.

> And she forgot the stars, the moon, and sun,
> And she forgot the blue above the trees,
> And she forgot the dells where waters run,
> And she forgot the chilly autumn breeze;
> She had no knowledge when the day was done,
> And the new morn she saw not: but in peace
> Hung over her sweet Basil evermore,
> And moisten'd it with tears unto the core.
> (st. 53)

(For those who are interested, there is a depiction of the beautiful Isabella leaning against the flowerpot by the painter Holman Hunt of England's Pre-Raphaelite school.)

In this case the path for the displacement of affect is as follows:

$$(1) \ \frac{\text{Lorenzo}}{f} \ ; \qquad (2) \ \frac{\text{Severed Head}}{f} \ ; \qquad (3) \ \frac{\text{Flower Pot}}{f} \ ;$$

FIGURE 1. Displacement of Affect in Keats's *Isabella*, or *The Pot of Basil*

For another example we can take the following verses from Pope's *Eloisa to Abelard*. Eloisa declares to Abelard:

Soon as thy letters trembling I unclose,
That well-known name awakens all my woes.
Oh name for ever sad! for ever dear!
Still breath'd in sighs, still usher'd with a tear.
(ll. 29–32)

Clearly, as large F accumulates, moving along with the text, small f is transferred from A to B, and then from B to C, without limit according to the rule of displacement. In such a case, the literary substance (F + f) will increase as well.

2. We'll provisionally apply to the second principle the term expansion of affect. In this case, rather than f transferring from A to B, a new small f attaches to a newly realized large F, enriching the literary substance as a result. A point comes up here with regard to the intellectual F, discussed earlier. The peculiar characteristic of intellectual material is its abstract nature. Consequently there is, by definition, little *direct* relation to our daily lives, and as such little expectation of large quantities of sentiment. That is to say, insofar as something has only an attenuated relation with the give-and-take of everyday life, as scientific laws and concepts do for the average person, it is ultimately unable to produce the small f of emotional association. However, even a difficult theory can gradually seep into ordinary people's brains (whether or not it comes to shape or govern our lives), and when this intellectual F is cast into the domain of the common knowledge of the people, the new large F acquires a small f and thereby obtains membership in the category of literary. For example:

So careful of the type she seems,
So careless of the single life.
(Tennyson, *In Memoriam*, st. 55)

This is clearly a distillation of the thesis propounded by the evolutionists. For someone in the seventeenth century, there is not even a large F, hence no need to inquire into the transformation to (F + f). Same thing for the eighteenth century. When we get to the nineteenth century, the thesis of evolution is first broached to the world but only comes to the attention of a limited circle of specialists. Unknown as it is among the general populace, the theory exists as a kind of F, only without the accompanying f. However, in the present day, when this new F has gradually worked its way into the consciousness of the average person, before you know it, it begins to display its own peculiar f.

> Gossip must often have been likened to the winged insect bearing pollen to the flowers; it fertilizes many a vacuous reverie.
> (Meredith, *Lord Ormont and His Aminta*, chap. 7)

It is only when botanical knowledge has advanced to a certain point and been made available to the common person that this becomes constituent material for literature and can flourish in literary circles. The following piece is of the same type:

> Man is that noble endogenous plant which grows, like the palm, from within outward.
> (Emerson, *Representative Men*)

This principle of expansion is not something that applies solely to intellectual material. Death is the point toward which we share the highest aversion. For the sake of continued living we incessantly labor; to prolong our life we fret and fuss. For this reason the large F "death" typically attaches uneasiness and fear as its small f. It is the nature of our sentiment to share this universally. However, with the state of the world at the point it is today, it is no surprise that people appear who rather prize and seek death, that is, assign to death a pleasurable affect. That is to say, depending on time and context, the exact opposite f can attach to the same fact of death. This tendency appears in a variety of forms. Finding life painful, a person may rejoice at the prospect of death; finding life humiliating, a person may attach to the prospect of death; finding life pointless, a person may seek it out. I recall a poem by Swinburne attaching this type of small f to the notion of death.[4] The French writer Balzac composed a short story to this effect called "Doomed to Live." The work is entitled this way because it describes the emotional torment of the one man left behind to serve as second for a disgraced warrior clan, whose other members are pitched headlong toward death to avenge the name of the clan—that is to say, it refers to the idea of the misfortune of life. We find this plot repeatedly visited in the Kabuki tradition of our own country.

There is no displacement involved here, only the attachment of f to a new type of F. Hence I distinguish these as expansion of affect.

3. This is neither displacement nor expansion but what we will provisionally call persistence of affect. Persistence would occur when (a) the large F itself ceases to exist or (b) despite the loss of necessity in attaching small f, as a result of convention it remains customary to attach the same emotion as before.

(a) Consider, for example, the case of a vow. One would expect the emotion born of a vow to be extinguished along with the death of the person to whom the vow was made. However, we find ourselves regarding the vow with the same feeling in life or death. Tradition has it that Ji Zi once pledged to give his sword to a certain person, but on his return he found that person to have passed away.[5] He placed the sword on the person's grave and left. No profit attaches to leaving the sword on the grave. This behavior is merely the result of emotions attaching to the fulfillment of this vow in his friend's death, just as in life. To take another example, consider the case of a woman's chastity. The saying goes that "a chaste wife sees not the second husband." However, it seems clear enough that if the husband dies, the wife's duty to remain faithful disappears as well. However, common opinion esteems the idea that, once married, a wife doesn't take a second husband, and women, too, deem it more honorable this way. This demonstrates nothing other than the continuity of this affect. This is the sense in which I speak of the persistence of affect.

Thackeray's *Vanity Fair* provides a good example of this issue of fidelity. A major point of the plot involves the heroine, Amelia, faithfully guarding her chastity long after the death of her husband, George Osborne, and this elicits great sympathy from the reader. During this time a man named William Dobbin incessantly woos her but is unable to gain Amelia's assent. She rebuffs him in a very moving passage: " 'It is you who are cruel now,' Amelia said with some spirit. 'George is my husband, here and in heaven. How could I love any other but him? I am his now as when you first saw me, dear William' " (chap. 59). However, when, moved by Dobbin's earnest feelings, Amelia finds herself disposed to marry again, we can't help but feel the grip of the story dissipate. Wouldn't it be more proper to say there is nothing whatsoever to reproach in a woman becoming a bride again ten years after the death of her husband? Indeed, most women begin the search for marriage prospects again six months or a year after a husband's death. We witness this kind of thing on a daily basis, and if we feel a sense of anticlimax when the matter is finally settled, that is because the object F of the vow of chastity has long since disappeared, and all that is left is the deeply persisting small f.

(b) It is also often the case that, while the object F itself continues to exist, it no longer rates the emotions heretofore attached. Yet small f continues to adhere as before. Consider, for example, the case of the retainer under the old Domain system who continues to bow and scrape before his lord, unable to reform the feudal attitudes of the past. Or consider the question of the supernatural we referred to repeatedly in the previous section. If one investigates such phenomena from the point of view of the intellect, strictly speaking nothing remains to provoke emotion. Nevertheless, the moment these are incorporated as literary material, one finds the old affects stubbornly attach. These all belong to the phenomenon of persistence.

Conversely, one must also recognize a principle that is the opposite of persistence, where as a large F ages or grows distant in time, the small f that attached in the past attenuates as well. A general survey will yield more than a few examples. Within literary classics as well there are those that aroused the amusement of people of ancient times but have difficulty speaking to people today (just as there are large F that give rise to small f in Westerners but are unable to bring about any f for us). Popular songs, too, possess an extremely intense small f for a period of time, but because this f is completely lost once their moment has passed, no one even sings them anymore. However, since objects losing f in this way is less quantitatively significant than f persisting after the object, it is possible to say that (F + f) retains as before its tendency to absolute increase.

So, it should be clear from the preceding argument that because emotion (what attaches to F) is liable to increase in quantitative terms, while at the same time the number of F itself is also increasing, the (F + f) that constitutes the literary material is essentially prone to increase. We can represent this in the form of the following table:

Time 1	a				
Time 2	a	a'b			
Time 3	a	a'b	ab'c		
Time 4	a	a'b	ab'c	abc'd	
Time 5	a	a'b	ab'c	abc'd	....e
Time 6	a	a'b	ab'c	abc'd	....e	....f

FIGURE 2. Proliferation of Literary Material Over Time

The columns in this table represent persistence. That is to say, if affect a persists from Time 1 to Time 6, literary material (F + a) is available throughout. If this affect a in Time 2 transforms by the principle of displacement to (F + a'), this simultaneously gives rise by the principle of expansion to the element (F" + b). In this way the totality of available literary material gradually becomes represented by the contents of the compartments in the infinitely expandable bottom row of the above diagram. (For reference, the Introduction to Waldstein's *Lecture on the Extension of Art* is worth a look.)

Translated by Joseph A. Murphy

BOOK 3

The Particular Character of Literary Substance

Book 3 points up most sharply the boundaries between literature and science. Count
Okuma Shigenobu's Fifty Years of New Japan (1909)—a series of essays by leaders in
their respective fields on the state of the art in various administrative, military, commercial, and academic disciplines that make up the modern state—contains an essay
on "The Introduction of Western Philosophy" to Japan by Miyake Yūjirō (1860–1945;
better known by his pen name, Miyake Setsurei). Miyake describes lectures by Har-
vard's Ernest Fenollosa in the 1880s, introducing German Romanticism in an amus-
ing way, as "lacking in subtlety and exactness," and producing an impression "akin to
that produced by scratching one's feet outside one's shoes."[1] Miyake vividly captures the
skeptical Japanese students at Tokyo Imperial University—schooled in the subtleties of
Chinese and Indian thought prior to the establishment of the modern educational
system—watching the young American stumble over the introduction of Kant and Hegel. He concludes that while Western philosophy in some ways excels in minuteness of
analysis, most of the strategies are familiar, while the Eastern corpus excels in several
points of organization. "It is most probable that by scrutinizing the bulky literature of
Hindoo [sic] philosophy the greater part of the so-called pure German philosophy may
be obtained" (238). For Miyake, writing in 1909, the element that essentially distinguishes the two is the amount of scientific experiment. Sōseki's contrasting of scientific
and literary truth can be seen to participate in this new terrain, where the classical
legacy of Indian and Chinese thought confronts a Western legacy that, though familiar
in many ways, introduces a new feature. Philosophical questions common to both
traditions—the relation of language and thought; the composition of the mind and the
relation of organism to environment; whether the underlying substance of the world is
characterized by stability and perfection or by ceaseless change—are posed here across
this broad division. The latter, fundamental question appears here and will appear

again in the famous lecture "The Civilization of Modern-Day Japan "(1912). In this sec-
tion Sōseki comes down rather decisively on the side of change.

The question, however, is organized in an interesting way over the division of science
and literature via the question of time. Here one of the central difficulties in interpreting
Sōseki's text is brought into focus. Sōseki moves through a standard set of considerations
in claiming that the truth that obtains in literature is different from the truth that obtains
in science. Though he does not really specify what that literary truth is, by following his
argument it is clear it must lie in true affective experience f; hence it is a matter of indif-
ference if F is scientifically true or not. The difficulty is that, while Sōseki is claiming that
literary practice should be exempt from the criteria and impulse of scientific thought, he
does not say whether they should obtain in literary criticism and theory. This significance
for practice becomes clear in the section where Sōseki argues against the tendency of sci-
ence to analyze in a way that kills literary truth. One can feel the tension of Sōseki in the
classroom in 1904–5 vis-à-vis his students, who are accustomed to the impressionistic
humanism of Lafcadio Hearn and resist Sōseki's effort to "kill" the object,[2] and who is
himself resisting slipping into either position. Hence, whether or not one judges Sōseki's
effort to secure for literature a realm outside science as successful, it says nothing about
how to evaluate his theoretical work. This is a point maintained with clarity by Sōseki but
often elided today in discussions of "literature and science."

N.B.: We have translated the main body of each of the book's two chapters, omitting
the closing section in each case.

Chapter 1: A Comparative Survey of Literary F and Scientific F

That the goal of science is an account of facts and not explanation is clear from the report of scientists themselves. To rephrase the matter, science seeks to answer questions of "How" and does not address the question of "Why"—indeed, it is self-aware that this exceeds its domain. Once an account has been given of the circumstances that gave rise to a particular phenomenon, scientific competence will tend to pause there. However, in order to answer this question of "How," one can't help retracing this question of "what gave rise." Hence, in scientific research there is no shaking oneself free from the concept of "time."

Literature as well is not without this element of "How." However, in contrast to science, in the case of literature there is nothing that requires it to pose this question of "How" in every possible direction. As I just mentioned, one cannot separate the word "How" from the problem of time. And literature certainly cannot wholly be separated from this question of time. Insofar as this question of time leads literature to the question of "How," it is in no way different from science. All novels, romance, epic poetry, drama, and so forth, incorporate time in this respect. As one event gives rise to the next event, one complication gives rise to yet another, and just as the vicissitudes of fate through innumerable circumstances lead to the development of the protagonist's character, these all come back to the question of "How." However, in the case of literature ✓ there is no need, as there is in science, to keep this "How" ceaselessly in mind. The aspect presented to the mind of objects in the material world is constantly in motion and never at rest. Anyone who sets out for the suburbs with his or her box of paints well knows that the same tree, the same field, the same sky exhibit constantly changing aspects, depending on the operation of the light. To observe something that is ceaselessly ✓ changing and fluctuating with an eye strictly to "How" is, like winding an infinite thread, an operation that has no end. The literary author has ✓ the right to take this endless chain of events and cut it at will, and exhibit it as if it is eternal. He has the special privilege of taking some part of hu- ✓ man affairs and the natural world ruled by this ceaseless, endless development, cleave it at a point of his choosing, and exhibit a cross-section divorced from time. Problems as grasped by a painter or sculptor are from the start characterized by such a cross-section separate from "time," and clearly cannot venture outside such a restriction. Because of the fact that literature incorporates "time," its sphere is wider than painting or sculpture; on the other hand, in its aspects of momentary description, spontaneous invocation of lyric poetry, and so forth, it belongs to the same category as painting or sculpture. As such, the F of the literary artist ✓ is not always bound up, like the scientist's F, in this constant curiosity about "How." Consider, for example, the following from Burns:

> Tho' cruel Fate should bid us part,
>   As far's the Pole and Line;
> Her dear idea round my heart
>   Should tenderly entwine.
> Tho' mountains frown and deserts howl,
>   And oceans roar between;
> Yet, dearer than my deathless soul,
>   I still would love my Jean.
> (*Tho' Cruel Fate*)

Because this discloses a momentary emotion, it renders visible a slice of an event that is in time and has a beginning and an end. Consider again Herrick:

> Dew sate on *Julia*'s haire,
>   and spangled too,
> Like Leaves that laden are
>   With trembling Dew:
> Or glitter'd to my sight,
>   As when the Beames
> Have their reflected light,
>   Daunc't by the Streames.
> (*Upon Julia's Haire Fill'd with Dew*)

This is a really simple and honest poem. It simply sings of the dew in Julia's hair and has nothing whatsoever to say about where this dew came from, where Julia is, or the relation of these to the self. That is to say, whereas Burns's poem presented a subjective cross-section, this poem provides an objective slice.

One might well say that while there are categories of literature that do not incorporate time, among those works that reach the level of the highest masterpiece, there are none that fail to touch on this question of "How"? Look at epic poetry, drama, or the novel. Isn't the large part of the interest in the work constructed precisely around this question of "How"? There is something important here. However, it is quite clear that the value of a literary work has never been determined by the quantity of the time incorporated; hence we must ask what does elicit the attitude of appreciation. If one finds in literature the feeling of pleasure at grasping a momentary, transitory phenomenon, this brings it very close to what one finds in painting or sculpture. The major part of our own traditions of waka, haiku, as well as Chinese poetry, consists in this literature of the fragment. Hence to call into question the literary value of a work because of its simplicity and limited substance is a bit premature at best.

The next difference we come to in the writer and the scientist is in their attitude. The attitude of the scientist to his object is that of dissection. Originally we all hold the mundane view that the various objects under the sun exist in their perfect and complete form. That is, we are under the impression that a person is a person and a horse is a horse. However, a scientist is never able to look at the form of a person or a horse and remain satisfied but will, without fail, analyze it into its component parts and cannot stop until he has discerned in each its respective properties. That is to say, the attitude of the scientist is destructive and, vis-à-vis something that exists in complete form from the natural world, will not stop until it has separated it into its smallest component parts. Not satisfied with the analysis afforded by the naked eye, it will utilize a mirror of a hundredfold or a thousandfold magnification to reach its goal. Not content with a complex body, this will be further reduced to chemical elements and these separated into atoms. And one has to allow for the fact that the result of this analysis is often a tendency to slight the complete form established from those constituents, or even to neglect the need to reassemble at all. For example, when they analyze water into H_2O, the gist of the matter is that an object is obtained composed of H and O, not the water itself established by the combination H_2O. What form of dissection, then, is utilized by the literary artist? The novelist dissects character, and when describing material things lists their particular features. If the literary artist did not have this attitude, at the crucial stage of selection and rejection of objects, they would not be able to bring forward for inspection the parts essential for literature and withdraw to the background the inessential parts. In other words, the literary artist would not be able to represent and vivify these things. However, where the dissection of the literary artist and the scientist differ is that the former is always in the domain of the naked eye and never in the microscopic realm, nor does it submit its results to empirical verification. Take a look, for example, at the current debate among physicists on the "conceptual discontinuity of bodies." The argument goes like this: All objects exhibit some elasticity. Hence it should be possible in principle to put them in a cylinder, like air, and compress them. One can take this as evidence for the hypothesis that all material substance, strictly speaking, must be discontinuous.[3] Literature has no part in this debate. A certain skill is represented in Zeising's "Golden Cut," which sought to discover value in experimental terms through a kind of law of aesthetic amputation,[4] but as this is the scientist's domain, a literary artist will rarely give it a second look. This is not to say that the straight line that organizes or the circle that encloses are excluded from the domain of literature. However, to inquire back further to determine whether that line found in the natural world is effective in terms of geometry is simply not an issue. Because they distinguish truth and falsehood only in terms of affective impression, to further distinguish in terms of scientific truth becomes rather a falsehood. For this sensibility the sun rises in the east and sets in the west. The earth does not revolve in an orbit around the sun. Coral is a beautiful branching object made from a red, brittle substance and not a vermin's nest made from polyps. The poet Rossetti got it exactly right when he said, "Whether the sun revolves around the earth, or the earth revolves around the sun is not of the least concern to me." Again, Keats:

> Do not all charms fly
> at the mere touch of cold philosophy?
> There was an awful rainbow once in heaven:
> We knew her woof, her texture; she is given
> In the dull catalogue of common things.
> Philosophy will clip an Angel's wings,
> Conquer all mysteries by rule and line,
> Empty the haunted air, and gnomed mine—
> Unweave a rainbow, as it erewhile made
> The tender-person'd Lamia melt into a shade.
> (*Lamia*, pt. 2. ll. 229–38)

Tennyson also writes partway through *Maud*:

> See what a lovely shell,
> Small and pure as a pearl,
> Lying close to my foot,
> Frail, but a work divine,
> Made so fairily well
> With delicate spire and whorl,
> How exquisitely minute,
> A miracle of design!
>
> What is it? a learned man
> Could give it a clumsy name.
> Let him name it who can,
> The beauty would be the same.
> (pt. 2, sec. 2)

In this way the dissection that goes on in the literary work always has as its ✓ goal capturing the activities of the whole. Singing of the parts in themselves is permissible only insofar as it has an effect in furthering that goal. [We have omitted sections in which Sōseki further explores these issues in terms of George Meredith, Shakespeare, Lessing and others.—Eds.] Hence the method of dissection exists as a resource for the literary artist, with ✓ the goal of synthesis.

Chapter 2: Truth in Literature and Truth in Science   Lit. Truth

It seems reasonable to suppose that what will be valued by the literary ✓ scholar is not scientific truth but rather literary truth. Hence there is no reason to be surprised that, if the situation demands it, the literary scholar ✓ will turn his or her back on scientific truth without regret. However, be- ✓ cause literary truth consists in the truth of the feeling attached to the represented object, this is merely to say that the arousal is immediate. The painter Millet has a drawing that features a farmer mowing hay. It is said that a certain farmer who saw this offered the opinion that it was hopeless to try to cut grass in a stance like that. And so it is, as a matter of fact, undoubtedly an ineffective posture. However, whether or not this is committing to canvas an ineffective posture,[5] as long as the feeling is produced of cutting grass without a trace of unnaturalness, one has to grant that the skill of the painter has produced an artistic truth. As long as one has attained an artistic truth, the person viewing the piece has no need to be troubled by whether or not it demonstrates a scientific truth. Artists of late have taken to studying the composition of the human body from the point of view of anatomy, and no doubt we must celebrate the spirit of these artists in bringing their works even a little bit closer to scientific truth. However, to the extent that people gallop off in that direction without studying artistic truth, in the end they cannot escape failure. Of course, there obtains between the two a subtle relation, but the artistic producer has to retain as his first priority literary truth, and, depending on the situation, it is not altogether inadvisable to sacrifice scientific truth to obtain it. There ✓ is more than one way in which literature turns its back on scientific truth to obtain literary truth. We'll take up a few examples as follows:

(1) Principle of Hyperbole. Book 5 of the *Iliad* states: "Next Diomedes of ✓ the loud war-cry attacked with spear of bronze; and Pallas Athene drave it

home against Ares' nethermost belly, where his taslets were girt about him. There smote he him and wounded him, rending through his fair skin, and plucked forth the spear again. Then brazen Ares bellowed loud as nine thousand warriors or ten thousand cry in battle as they join in strife and fray. Thereat trembling gat hold of Achaeans and Trojans for fear, so mightily bellowed Ares insatiate of battle" (trans. A. Lang, W. Leaf, and E. Myers, p. 108).

This is actually a battle between the gods. And insofar as these are gods, the cry of nine thousand men and the roar of ten thousand are simply devices that make it possible to imagine. Whether Homer is successful in this or not is beside the point; in order to obtain truth in this imaginative scene, facts are exaggerated. If it is because of this exaggeration the representation takes on life, excessive fidelity to scientific truth is to vainly hitch the literary arts to scientific knowledge and interfere with the vivacity of the operation.

(2.) Principle of Abbreviation, Selection. As the preceding discussion has hinted, the contents of our consciousness are not something that admits, strictly speaking, of complete expression in words or characters. Given this restraint, it is frequently the case that the author will select a part or an aspect of the object and through this seek perfectly to convey the gist of the matter. This is the second point on which the person of literature is bound to disregard the truth of science. The argument follows the same lines as the preceding section, so I won't go into it deeply here. Examples all follow the same pattern, so we'll move to the next section.

(3.) Principle of Combination. This refers to the creative work of the poet or the artist, that is to say, the technique by which they gather together and synthesize material actually existing in the world and draw out something that does not exist in this world. Consider Milton's Satan, Swift's Yahoos, Oberon and Titania from Shakespeare's *Midsummer Night's Dream*, Caliban of *The Tempest*, and so on. One would seek in vain for these characters in the real world; hence it would, of course, be irrational to try to observe them from the standpoint of science. However, insofar as the emotion and sensibility we imbibe from these has life and does not ring false in any way, we can be sure that it perfectly concretizes a literary truth. Because it is from the first through feelings that literary elements receive their highest expression, whenever there is success in transmitting this feeling to the reader, we should not hesitate to grant the status of literary truth. Consider some of the later works of Turner. The brilliance of the sea in these works is as if he overturned the paint box on the canvas. The image of a train speeding through a rainstorm is rendered so dark and vast, it is as if the train were running on the surface of the water itself. Given that this type of ocean and this type of land are not to be found in the natural world yet possess sufficient literary truth, and respond to demands above the demands of nature—that is to say, that we recognize here a firm and indomitable life force—we would have to say that in his paintings is to be found not scientific truth but a pure literary truth.[6]

One thing to keep in mind, though, is that what we are terming literary ✓ truth is something that undergoes change with time. We have all witnessed cases where a work of literature is appraised as embodying truth one day and then suddenly loses this status and comes under criticism the next. This is all to be understood as based on the minute-by-minute and hour-by-hour change in the standards by which "truth" is judged.

Translated by Joseph A. Murphy

INTERRELATIONS BETWEEN LITERARY SUBSTANCES

After defining what Sōseki refers to as "the truth of literature" (bungeijō no shin) in book 3, he sets out to discuss the methods by which to convey this truth of literature in book 4. Book 4 is perhaps the most underrated portion of Theory of Literature by Sōseki critics. In it Sōseki spends a considerable amount of space discussing the different modes of representation, which are organized in accordance with the three main principles of associationist psychology, namely, similarity, contiguity, and contrast. Of the first six, five of

	Corresponding figures of speech
A. Similarities	
1. Projection	Personification or prosopopeia
2. Introjection	Metaphor, simile
3. Dissociation	Metaphor, simile, allusion
4. Comic association	Pun, wit
5. Harmonization technique	None
B. Contrast	
6. Counterposition	
a) methods of emphasis	Litotes
b) methods of attenuation	Antithesis
[pseudo-opposition]	Antithesis and climax
c) method of nonopposition	Burlesque
7. Technique of realism (*shajitsuhō*)	None
C. Contiguity	
8. Distance	Temporal (vision)
	Spatial (expansion of vision)

them have rough equivalents in conventional rhetoric. The chart above lists the methods in the order of discussion and may help to clarify his scheme in this book.[1]

In addition to principles of associationist psychology and figures of speech, the four categories of literary substance Sōseki introduced in book 1—sensation F, personification F, metaphysical F, and intellectual F—occupy an important place in his discussion. Since the intensity of emotive f varies (the strongest being sensation F and the weakest intellectual F), the modes of representation discussed in book 4—especially the first six methods—enhance and/or balance the emotive intensity attached to respective F's. Accordingly, discussions of respective methods revolve around the four categories.

With sections 7 and 8 Sōseki takes up technique of realism (shajitsuhō;) and inter-space (kankakuron). In section 8 we see descriptions of what we now refer to as narratology, in which he discusses the distance between the writer/narrator and character. The central focus of section 8 is the issue of perspective and the effect it has on literary substance. That leaves section 7, on realistic depiction, from which we have selected several passages.

Realistic depiction not only deviates from the three principles of associationist psychology but also lacks a corresponding equivalent in rhetoric. As such, some critics have stated that the section seems out of place. It is perhaps worthwhile to note that Sōseki revised his lecture notes in their entirety, beginning with section 7, prior to the publication of Theory of Literature.

"Technique of Realism" is important historically given the fact that the publication of Theory of Literature *coincided with the height of the Naturalist domination of the literary circle in Japan, the champion of realistic portrayal. Here Sōseki compares Romanticism and Realism not in historical terms, as they are often debated, but rather as two formalistic styles.[2] His awareness that realism is a mode of representation and hence a rhetorical style—one that is reinforced by the parallel he creates with the other figures of speech—is clearly evident. Just as romanticism constitutes artifice (gikō), so does realism. Sōseki takes up two elements that comprise this artifice, namely, the choice of materials (shuzaihō) and methods of composition (hyōgenhō).*

I believe the arguments of the preceding section have made clear the sorts of resolution required in the realm of literature. To put it simply, while the scientist is involved in the appeal to reason over disputations of a black and white nature, the literary man seeks to gain control over the emotions—the source of life—to capture and hold it in his hand. It is as if the scientist conducts a trial in a court of law and coolly hands down a sentence. The ministrations of the man of literature, on the other hand, like the care of a loving mother, transcend rational judgment and move our soul unawares. His methods are not on the surface and available for inspection; his decisions are drawn from hidden information and the interior life.

These secrets of the interior are revealed through a variety of special techniques, and when these techniques are skillfully employed, there arises a kind of fascination within us, and we say in this case that the goal of literary truth has been reached.

I have already spent time spelling out the nature of literary truth, so it follows that I must now turn to an explanation of the techniques for transmitting this truth. These techniques were originally systematized in the discipline called rhetoric. However, as typically practiced, rhetoric expends its strength vainly in idiosyncratic classification schemes. If this is not accompanied by inquiry into its fundamental principles, the effect is attenuated. In terms of my theory, the majority of the techniques by which literary truth is effected are little more than a permutation of ways in which concepts can be associated. The explanation offered in chapters 1–6 that follow is essentially the product of elaborating this assertion.

[Chapters 1–6 of book 4 elaborate the various associational techniques: chapter 1, *tōshutsu gohō* (projection); chapter 2, *tōnyū gohō* (introjection); chapter 3, *jiko to kakuri seru rensō* (dissociation); chapter 4, *kokkeiteki rensō* (comic association); chapter 5, *chōwahō* (harmonizing techniques); and chapter 6, *taichihō* (counterposition).—Eds.]

Chapter 7: Technique of Realism

In the preceding sections I distinguished six types of literary technique commonly employed and gave a description of the way they work. I first elaborated four types of associational technique and then touched on the methods of harmony and counterposition. I would now like to discuss the method of realism or transcription (*shajitsu*).

Let's suppose that all things that have the potential to become material for literature can be expressed by the formula $(F+f)$, as I outlined at the beginning of this study. However, for the six techniques we have thus far investigated, the material does not simply take the form $(F+f)$. Rather, it arises through synthesis with the addition of new material $(F'+f')$.[3] Hence the preceding work simply constitutes a survey by means of relatively systematic methods of the types of transformation that thereby arise. What these six have in common is that in order to express one material they employ other materials. It follows that without two or more instances of material these techniques cannot be put into play. In further differentiating these six techniques and treating of their tendencies, there are four points ✓ you need to keep in mind. First, it is necessary to recall that most cases involve two linked materials operating in the same space, exciting our emotions with regard to F to a higher degree than normal. Among the four associational techniques, the first three belong to this type, plus the stress technique in the method of counterposition. Second, you must also keep in mind that there are cases where the two linked materials conflict with each other and produce in us an emotion with regard to F that is less than normal. The principle of mitigation in the method of counterposition belongs to this type. Third, there are also two cases where the two connected materials together incline neither toward F nor toward F' and excite in us a (well-defined) emotion that really belongs to neither. These would be the harmonizing techniques and the method of counterposition. Finally, among the associational techniques point four pertains to number 4 (comic association) and to the subcategory of non-opposition among the techniques of counterposition, in which, despite the two materials being juxtaposed, no particular emotion at all arises from their mingling.

In summary, when we seek to transform the emotion associated with a ✓ particular F by adding F', we find six types that tend toward the direction of intensity and richness, one type that moves in the direction of reduction and deletion, and two types that produce an entirely new emotion unrelated to the emotions typically associated with F and F'. Clearly, of the liter- ✓ ary techniques discussed thus far, the majority have as their goal the intensification or enrichment of F by the addition of an F'. The technique of ✓ realism I am about to discuss arises precisely in response to the predominance of this type of method. Hence what I am calling the technique of realism is likely to have a significance quite different from what you might commonly expect. In the literary techniques I've elaborated in the previous ✓ sections, the problem can be reduced to the following: given a particular bit of material, what sort of expression will yield the highest poetic effect, or else the most beautiful (alternatively the most humorous). As to the question of the selection of material itself, because the techniques elaborated in the previous sections do not incorporate the question, it was placed outside the sphere of the argument. Because realism is a literary technique of the same order as what has been delineated earlier, I intend to limit discussion at this point to the same context. The question to be raised in this chapter, ✓ then, is how particular expressions of a given material constitute the technique of realism and what particular effects are produced. As to whether

the material itself is realistic in some sense or not, we will leave that for expanded consideration of the problem in later sections.

The brazen throat of war had ceased to roar.
(Milton, *Paradise Lost*, bk. 11,1. 713)

This is a bold poetic passage. If you don't like the vagueness of the term
"poetic," perhaps I can use one of my own technical terms, specifying that
among the associational techniques this is an example of projection. Having set this out in detail earlier, it won't be necessary to belabor the details
of how this works as a trope of projection. Setting this aside for a moment,
one fact is indisputably clear. You may wish it were otherwise, but ultimately it's hard to deny that—whether we're talking about Japan, Europe,
England, or even the English living in the time of Milton—people just do
not use language like this in everyday conversation. It goes without saying
it is going to be hard to conjure up an image of everyday people using
tropes based on language not found in everyday conversation. When a
poet faces the empty page, gathers his thoughts, and contemplates what
type of adjective to use in expressing something like battle, he is well
aware of this. This kind of understanding is a specialty of the poet and lies
beyond the capacity of the average person. Because the ability to concentrate the chaos of a thousand men and horses into one line can only be
deployed by a poet, success or failure at this kind of conception is important enough to constitute the definition of a poet. However, poetic diction
is ultimately poetic diction. Because it is produced only after passing
through a sort of speculative labor, we can't call it natural language (leaving aside the fact that we often find surprisingly poetic diction among
uncivilized peoples). Hence poetic language, which, on the one hand,
pushes language to a semblance of battle, separates it from the methods of
everyday expression and is liable to fall into a kind of unnatural mannerism, on the other. When we employ this type of diction to express a given
material, the material may be released from its mundaneness like a firefly,
but at the same time it separates from real expression as the level of refinement rises. If one seeks, on the other hand, to deploy the mode of expression contemporary to society, it goes without saying that we must sacrifice
the advantages of this type of diction and employ a method of expression
(albeit common) that flows naturally to our ears. This is what I call the
method of realism.

From the foregoing it is clear that the goal of the majority of literary
techniques described in the preceding chapters and that of the technique
of realism are different in kind. For example, let's say you are describing a
beautiful woman (i.e., the beautiful woman is the given material). In the
techniques described in the preceding sections, in order to bring out her
otherworldly beauty, the point of inquiry would be how to arrange this
woman's clothing, the quality of this woman's hair, how to arrange items
in the background, and what sort of unattractive woman to place beside
her. The beauty that only emerges as a result of this artifice may well far
exceed in grace and charm a beautiful woman you might meet on the
street. However, the more this expression exceeds everyday life, the more
it departs from our standards and, in a sense, the more we lose our ability
to identify. A beautiful woman you might meet in the street is not necessarily going to step out with the clothing, hairstyle, accessories in the particular arrangement that the poet proposed. While we can't help but be
attracted to the beauty of a woman endowed with these prerequisites of
the poetic realm or the art gallery, since we can't feel keenly a sense of
shared experience, all the more do we seek a beauty endowed with our
own flesh and blood. Suppose we have an ethereal beauty with blue eyes
and golden hair of an otherworldly quality. When we compare her to a
young woman of fine quality from among our relatives, we find ourselves
sympathizing with the latter, the woman we know, despite the fact that she
cannot compete in terms of the depth and significance of association. Because we feel more intimate with the latter as a fellow human, we are more
immediately concerned with her joys and sorrows (leaving aside the question of beauty and lack thereof). One example should suffice. It should be
clear at this point.

We play in the Elysian fields constructed by the poet, enter the Shangri-la
imagined by the painter, and can't resist the gloriously drunken illusion
we imagine thereby. But, at the same time, when aspects of the everyday
life we intimately lead drift before our eyes, and bear us back to a kind of
realistic illusion, this, too, has its own kind of pleasure.

We can get a fairly precise sense of this with reference to the mono-
logue by Shunkan[4] quoted earlier. Shunkan's language displays a type of
artifice employed throughout the Noh libretto (*yōkyoku*) corpus (again
leaving aside the question of whether it is done well or poorly). While
the employment of this artifice means that the emotional charge of the
F contained in his words is heightened, by the same token we are carried

further and further from the sense that we might view him on our level as a confrere. There is likely no one among your friends and associates who would use these means to express this type of thought. Hence, while the words of Shunkan take one step forward in producing a poetic illusion, they simultaneously take one step backward in producing a realistic illusion. This is not just true of Shunkan. To a person, the characters employed in Shakespeare's plays do not hesitate to resort to this type of language. From the point of view of the method of realism, Shakespeare's characters use the most unnatural diction. (The question of the naturalness of the psychology, and of the emotions expressed, needs to be separated from the problem at this point.) By the eighteenth century this type of diction had lapsed into mannerism and left no further room for development. When one reaches the point where one tries to express the F of "moon" by "Cynthia's horn," you see the impasse at which they'd arrived.

At this point, with the world of poetry drunk on this kind of artifice, a reformer named Wordsworth appeared. The preface to the second edition of the famous *Lyrical Ballads* begins thus: "The principal object, then, proposed in these Poems was to choose incidents and situations from common life, and to relate or describe them, throughout, as far as possible, in a selection of language really used by men. . . ."

The purport of the notion of "incidents" and "situations" is beyond the scope of the present argument. But when a point is reached where it becomes necessary for effect to construct poetry out of the speech actually used by real people, the technique of realism I seek to elucidate in this chapter is a point of general applicability. (That this is not necessarily Wordsworth's assertion can be gathered by perusing the preface.) This bit of evidence from Wordsworth not only secures all the more firmly the existence of this law of realism I recognize—by virtue of its basic orientation being different from, nay, flying in the face of the several methods described earlier—it is also evidence that when resistance arises as the world lapses into mannerism, it will unfailingly move off in another direction in an effort to rescue the situation. (Hence anyone who reads Wordsworth's poetry will discover the conditions for realism I've described here.)

Because the technique of realism follows faithfully the methods of expression of the real world, the implication is that this is a means for transferring fragments of the real world in miniature onto paper. What's referred to here as a fragment of the real world, however, is not to say a fragment composed of materials predisposed to description by the technique of realism. To take the passage from Milton quoted earlier, if one were to replace his poetic diction with a common, everyday means of expression not rooted in the technique of realism, "battle" as the substance of the expression will not be burned in our retina with the vividness of a battle in the real world. If it is a question of impression, it is unlikely anyone will soon discover a mode of expression more powerful than Milton's. It is just that the density of poetic inspiration in this passage—which, we recall, is a result of being forged at length through scrupulous attention to technique and dropped ringing onto the paper—clearly puts this on a different plane from the sort of banalities we trade every day, relegated to a place distant from interaction with the world of everyday people. It goes without saying that this thinness of negotiation with the everyday world is a matter of the person producing the expression and not a matter of the content of "battle" being separate from the sphere of ordinary people. In arguing the case for this technique of realism, a good deal will proceed from comparison on this point. Hence the question of skill or clumsiness of expression in other literary techniques remains beyond the scope of this argument.

However, if we take up this problem of relative skill or clumsiness that ✓ we'd set aside and compare these other techniques with the technique of realism, the case for realism goes beyond its merit in activating real characters from society, and the argument can be made *mutatis mutandis* for the expressive value of the given material itself. Because in every case the literary methods discussed in previous chapters energetically employ technique, when they are really successful it is like the charms of heaven are bursting from each passage. However, lose sight of the target for a second and they begin swinging wildly, celestial skills plummet to the human level, human skills end up as bungling, the poet belabors his concentration, and this is often where real unsightliness appears. Sensing this, the poet polishes here and takes in there, losing all sense of dignity, and soon he is covering the page with affectation and pretentiousness without a second thought. In resorting to artifice, it is not merely a matter of expos- ✓ ing maladroitness for all to see, it's even worse. If, on the other hand, we ✓ look at the technique of realism, because realism uses natural language—it does not pass through a process of refinement—because its speech is transient and disposable, it is the least exalted as a skill. It is so close to technique-free that it resists assessment. If one indicates a horse, it says "horse"; if one points out a cow, it says "cow." It is as if it eliminates curiosities. It is pure, artless expression. As artless expression shorn of curiosities, it may not strike people in its capacity to dazzle, but it also avoids losing control over the thickness or thinness of the makeup, which is far superior to making the viewer shudder at the gaudiness of the decoration. The law of realism is guileless expression. It is an expression that does not cover its clumsiness. Hence it is coarse and plain, direct and honest. The expression is simple and unartificial. As a method of expression, the value of transcription of facts is not to be denied. Take "vanished into thin air."[5] It is a relatively complicated expression. Instead try "He left." That's a realistic expression. As such, a person who dislikes the literary flourish of the former will necessarily prefer the straightforwardness of the latter. Let's describe the moon as "Cynthia's horn." This is an associative method of expression. But some might abhor this phrase's distance from the actual moon. Let's try, "moon like a sickle." This is also an associative method. But this is several steps advanced in terms of keenness. Next try "crescent moon." There is no more simple and direct method of expression to be found. Depending on the person and the circumstances, the latter may well be preferable.

The effect of the method of realism in relation to the problem of managing the given material is as explained above. If we want to advance this another step and discuss the preferences of the method of realism in relation to the selection of material itself, there are no small number of points to address. That being said, the strengths of realism as an expressive method do not differ in kind from the strengths of realism as a method of selecting material. In both cases the standard is drawn in terms of everyday life in the living world, and this is made to dance in front of our eyes, such that our sympathy and interest is aroused as with a close companion. There are no gods or heroes in your immediate surroundings. The person described by a realist will therefore not be a hero. When a person who is not a hero wins our sympathy, it is not because of some quality of greatness but because they are average, like us. (They are average, so they are close to us; they are close to us; hence they win our sympathy. To deny this kind of identification [dōjō] would be the same as not feeling emotion at the photograph of a close friend we see every day.) Your immediate vicinity is not full of wonders and mysteries. Hence the sorts of things the advocate of realism will describe are basically comfortably average. At times it will devolve into the trivial. To have your interest aroused by the comfortable trivia of life is the same as sympathizing with an average person. It is rather unusual for the incidents we encounter in daily life to develop and arrange themselves as in a novel. Hence the structure attained by a realist (on the assumption that structure does not occur naturally in the material) will barely deserve the term. (Structure has value in itself to the degree that it exceeds the normal. The further outside the normal, the less likely things exist in the regular course of the natural world. Hence the appreciation of structure for its own sake takes place precisely where its degree of cohesion exceeds the natural and is to this degree unnatural. Even if the technique is close to perfect, the realistic illusion can't help but be damaged because of this.) Likewise, the scenery of a realist is what stretches out before our eyes and has no need to appeal to novelty; so as long as it provides a sense of intimacy and familiarity, that is sufficient. The reasons are the same as those outlined in the case of expression and don't need to be repeated here.

The realist is a poet of the commonplace. He scorns the pursuit of the novel and the extraordinary. Hence, confronted by that common quality and disinclination to novelty, we show a simple interest. If we examine the plays of Shakespeare, we find they are continually involved with the apprehension of extraordinary people and the description of extraordinary events, and this defines the character of his drama. The father is murdered by Hamlet's uncle; then the mother takes up with the same uncle. And not only that: the ghost of the father arrives for repeated meetings. I haven't yet encountered anyone like these characters from *Hamlet*. And a woman like the beautiful Portia—who not only dons a barrister's robes to pass herself off as a man but, without memorizing a single letter of the law, demolishes an obstinate Jewish man's case in court—I have not seen even in dreams. The cruel and unfilial daughters of Lear, the treacherous and perverse Iago—these all lie outside the realm of common sense and are never to be discovered in the people we know. Whether the psychological response of these extraordinary characters in the face of extraordinary circumstances is natural or not, or whether the twists and turns that arise as a result are *technically* interesting or not, is not my concern here. It is just that, insofar as people and situations this unusual might appear around us possibly once in a hundred years, to the extent that one would be excused from wondering if they don't come from another planet, it is difficult to avoid the charge that this is unnatural. Once this charge of unnaturalness becomes inescapable, an opportunity is created for the realist. In this sense the realist school finds itself opposed to romanticism—in the same way it finds itself opposed to the idealist, and to the classicist. That's not to say that there is a value judgment implied. It is just that each has its strengths and weaknesses, and as a devotee of literature you simply need to adjust your perspective, depending on the work. (Because the topic of this chapter is realism, I am going into this in some detail and do not have sufficient space to go deeply into the others. That must wait for another day.)

I began by elucidating the question of realism of expression, moved on to thematic realism, and now I find I've ended up straying beyond the territory of the present chapter. Let's cite a few examples here to tie things up. The eighteenth-century poet Crabbe[6] would have to be classed as a disciple of Pope in terms of formal expression, but in terms of the meanness and commonness of his themes he is a brilliant realist.

[Farm Servants at Meal]

To Farmer Moss, in Langar Vale, came down
His only daughter, from her school in town;
A tender, timid maid! who knew not how
To pass a pig-sty, or to face a cow;
Smiling she came, with petty talents graced,
A fair complexion, and a slender waist.
Used to spare meals, disposed in manner pure,
Her father's kitchen she could ill endure;
Where by the steaming beef he hungry sat,
And laid at once a pound upon his plate;
Hot from the field, her eager brother seized
An equal part, and hunger's rage appeased;
The air, surcharged with moisture, flagg'd around,
And the offended damsel sigh'd and frown'd;
The swelling fat in lumps conglomerate laid,
And fancy's sickness seized the loathing maid.
But, when the men beside their station took,
The maidens with them, and with these the cook;
When one huge wooden bowl before them stood,

Fill'd with huge balls of farinaceous food;
With bacon, mass saline, where never lean
Beneath the brown and bristly rind was seen;
When from a single horn the party drew
Their copious drafts of heavy ale and new;
When the coarse cloth she saw with many a stain,
Soil'd by rude hinds who cut and came again—
She could not breathe; but, with a heavy sigh,
Rein'd in the fair neck, and shut th' offended eye;
She minced the sanguine flesh in frustums fine,
And wonder'd much to see the creatures dine.
(*The Widows Tale*, 2. 1–30)

Though a person familiar with the poetry of Pope will see many similarities in the rhyme and meter employed, in terms of substance they are as
different as heaven and earth. Although the point of description is a farm-
ing household, this is not the farmhouse life of your imagination, draped in
classic, pastoral images, but a kitchen covered in sweat and filth. If one
reads this and charges that it fails to evoke poetic sentiment, the fault lies
with the reader. One need only observe the simple, rough, uncultivated
nature of the lifestyle laid before one's eyes, which is sufficient. What
Crabbe provides us is not a fictive poem but a real rural scene. When one
knits one's brows and summons up sympathy for these rustics, the goal has
been reached. To contrast this description of the dinner table with the passage in Keats's *Eve of St. Agnes*, or the volume *The Light of the Haram* in
Moore's *Lalla Rookh*, is to begin to understand that the inspirations that
move poets to put pen to paper are multiple and diverse.[7] What Crabbe is
seeking here is the realistic illusion. What the other two aim at is a poetic
illusion. (I won't belabor this with a point-by-point comparison, but please
see for yourself.) In addition, works like the riverbank scene in "Peter
Grimes," the part in "Strolling Players" where the actor learns his craft, and
the conversation of the drunken louts in "The Smoking Club" pass beyond
the border of poetry and remorselessly record fragments of real life.[8]

Jane Austen is the leading authority in the world of realism. Her ability √
to score points while putting the most commonplace situations to paper
far outstrips that of her male rivals. Take this on my authority. Anyone
who is unable to appreciate Austen will be unable to understand the beauty
of realism. Let's support this with an example:

"My dear Mr. Bennet," said his lady to him one day, "have you heard that Netherfield Park is let at last?"

Mr. Bennet replied that he had not.

"But it is," returned she; "for Mrs. Long has just been here, and she told me all about it."

Mr. Bennet made no answer.

"Do not you want to know who has taken it?" cried his wife, impatiently.

"*You* want to tell me, and I have no objection to hearing it."

This was invitation enough.

"Why, my dear, you must know, Mrs. Long says that Netherfield is taken by a young man of large fortune from the north of England; that he came down on Monday in a chaise and four to see the place, and was so much delighted with it that he agreed with Mr. Morris immediately; that he is to take possession before Michaelmas, and some of his servants are to be in the house by the end of next week."

"What is his name?"

"Bingley."

"Is he married or single?"

"Oh, single, my dear, to be sure! A single man of large fortune, four or five thousand a year. What a fine thing for our girls!"

"How so? how can it affect them?"

"My dear Mr. Bennet," replied his wife, "how can you be so tiresome? You must know that I am thinking of his marrying one of them?"

"Is that his design in settling here?"

"Design? nonsense, how you talk so! But it is very likely that he *may* fall in love with one of them, and therefore you must visit him as soon as he comes."

"I see no occasion for that. You and the girls may go, or you may send them by themselves, which perhaps will be still better, for, as you are as handsome as any of them, Mr. Bingley might like you the best of the party."

"My dear, you flatter me. I certainly *have* had my share of beauty, but I do not pretend to be anything extraordinary now. When a woman has five grown-up daughters, she ought to give over thinking of her own beauty."

"In such cases, a woman has not often much beauty to think of."

"But, my dear, you must indeed go and see Mr. Bingley when he comes into the neighbourhood."

"It is more than I engage for, I assure you."

"But consider your daughters. Only think what an establishment it would be for one of them. Sir William and Lady Lucas are determined to go, merely on that account; for in general, you know, they visit no newcomers. Indeed you must go, for it will be impossible for *us* to visit him, if you do not."

"You are over scrupulous, surely. I daresay Mr. Bingley will be very glad to see you; and I will send a few lines by you to assure him of my hearty consent to his marrying whichever he chooses of the girls; though I must throw in a good word for my little Lizzy."

"I desire you will do no such thing. Lizzy is not a bit better than the others; and I am sure she is not half so handsome as Jane, nor so good-humoured as Lydia. But you are always giving *her* the preference."

"They have none of them much to recommend them," replied he; "they are all silly and ignorant like other girls; but Lizzy has something more of quickness than her sisters."

"Mr. Bennet, how can you abuse your own children in such a way? You take delight in vexing me. You have no compassion on my poor nerves."

"You mistake me, my dear. I have a high respect for your nerves. They are my old friends. I have heard you mention them with consideration these twenty years at least."

"Ah, you do not know what I suffer."

"But I hope you will get over it, and live to see many young men of four thousand a year come into the neighbourhood."

"It will be no use to us, if twenty such should come, since you will not visit them."

"Depend upon it, my dear, that when there are twenty, I will visit them all."

(*Pride and Prejudice*, chap. 1)

The subject is casual to begin with. The expression is decidedly nonchalant, without a hint of embellishment. This really is the domain of our daily life, its customs and manners. By spreading this unaffected domestic scene out before our eyes, Austen permits us to take pleasure in the minute detail that lies behind objective appearances. Anyone unable to take pleasure in this has become accustomed to the cheap attractions of the market and forgotten the deep satisfactions of the everyday. These days poets and writers seem to want to move the spirit and delight the soul by reaching for the most extreme situations, thinking that if they do not hurl these curiosities onto the paper with an equally extreme turn of phrase they are not really writing. However, these extreme efforts to move the spirit of the reader first find the seed of plot development in placing an average, ordinary person in one-in-a-million circumstances. Thus, all the gravity, pathos, and passion such writers proclaim, and all their melodramas, which seem to refuse all negotiations with the mundane business of daily life—these, too, are nothing more than the embodiment of the actions of average, ordinary people. If one were to argue that the hero is not an average, ordinary person, then there would not even exist a thread of sympathy between this depicted person and we ordinary individuals; and what gravity, poignancy, and passion are produced would drift, without exception, off into the stratosphere, unconnected to the emotion of the real world. When enough of this is strung together, it ultimately only invites the reader's scorn. Hence, however extraordinary and fantastic a melodrama one wishes to produce, the parts need to be played by ordinary members of the real world. At the very least one needs to suppose that this member of the real world would enact this particular gesture in this particular situation. One need not even suppose this. As long as a basic background is put into place such that the reader can imagine that if one were to drag some familiar, local character into this particular situation, he or she would also behave in the same way as the characters in the book, the reader will ultimately receive in his or her heart that sense of comfort. What I mean here by "comfort" is a recognition of a conditional reality[9] whereby, despite the wide gulf between the events described in the work and the facts of our daily existence, we are driven to imagine that if placed in these extraordinary situations we, too, would have to act in the same way. Consequently, the boundary between these extraordinary actions and the ordinary actions of everyday life is rendered fluid, and we may regard them as dissolving smoothly into each other. Because of this continuity between the extraordinary activities of the characters in the book and our own ordinary activities, we are made to forget the clear gulf separating the two realms.

When we return to the question of realism with this result in mind, we are in a position to make a fresh observation. Austen does not simply portray the innocuous conversation between an ordinary married couple. Her task is not complete simply by placing before our eyes an indifferent fragment of living society. Anyone who can read will see that it is a matter of the character of the husband and wife in this passage, which is so vivid that it flies off the page—the easygoing nature of the husband and the timidity of the wife; the husband's indifference and the wife's sensitivity; the husband's unruffled amicability, to the point of slipping in a little gentle teasing, and the wife's absorption in her strategies about their daughters' futures—as if their very lives are contained in the tip of her [Austen's] brush.[10] While it is difficult to know whether the couple will be blessed in its hopes—no one can know what twists of fate lie in store—it is easy to see the general drift of their lives from this one passage. In other words, the deepest meaning of this passage lies in the distillation of an entire life in a single page. The deep meaning, though, is not merely in the distillation. The point is that once we have grasped their character in its normal state of affairs through this distillation, we can foresee its potential transformations as well. Life in this world is characterized by perpetual change, and when the intensity of this buffeting by fate exceeds a certain limit, it may well be that these characters enter another particular boundary condition and enact a particular drama. But hasn't the way this will play out already been prepared by the exposition of their character under a normal state of affairs in this single passage? The twists and turns they will employ in the face of fate signify a path of development out of this normal state more than independence from it. If their actions become completely independent of this exposition, we lose our sense of context and begin seeing two or three people where there was one. The characters would appear like aliens from another planet. Hence, for these two to continue to hold our sympathies and impart to our hearts that ultimate sense of recognition, this normal state of affairs has to include within it all the possibilities for change that might arise in response to extreme circumstances. "Include" may not be the appropriate word. Let's say that deep within there has to be the capacity to activate these possibilities at any time. Hence the description in this passage has depth not simply because it so skillfully distills their characters in a normal state but rather because it simultaneously encloses within it the capacity for change in unusual circumstances. If we accept the implications of this, it seems mistaken to argue that one cannot achieve depth—and a subtle insight into life—without deploying striking events and situating ordinary people in extreme circumstances. They say there needs to be blood on the floor to grab people's interest, that one needs to call down thunder and lightning to create the drama, that it requires one to grind the bones and gouge out the eyeballs to make people cry. That's fine to say, but to mistake this for depth is to miss the point. There is no great trick to impressing the majority of people by placing a marvel before their eyes. But because the attraction is on the surface and lacks implicit meaning, one has to say this is shallow. Infinite sadness can be hidden behind a single smile. For those who can't recognize sadness without tears, this smile has no significance. Rather, I would say it is precisely such instances that possess real depth of feeling. People who know something of the world understand Austen's profundity. People who know Austen's profundity understand something of the depth latent in the quiescent methods of realism.

We have now outlined the realist's expressive technique and methods of thematization. If we go further and take a look at the techniques of construction involved in delimiting the domain of topics, the goal of thematization will become even clearer. In this passage Marianne has taken sick and Elinor is the one who is nursing her. Austen describes it as follows:

> The repose of the latter became more and more disturbed; and her sister, who watched, with unremitting attention, her continual change of posture, and heard the frequent but inarticulate sounds of complaint which passed her lips, was almost wishing to rouse her from so painful a slumber, when Marianne, suddenly awakened by some accidental noise in the house, started hastily up, and, with feverish wildness, cried out—
>
> "Is mamma coming?"
>
> "Not yet!" replied the other, concealing her terror, and assisting Marianne to lie down again; "but she will be here, I hope, before it is long. It is a great way, you know, from hence to Barton."
>
> "But she must not go round by London," cried Marianne, in the same hurried manner. "I shall never see her, if she goes by London."
> (*Sense and Sensibility*, chap. 43)

This passage simply records the half unconscious ramblings of a sick woman who has become feverish. However, the highly agitated state of the patient's nerves in this state allow of two interpretations. In either case she has taken leave of her normal self. This departure from the normal, subjective state either places her in a state of heightened sensibility or plunges her into a state of debility. From the point of view of common sense, an attack of fever leaves one wandering in a state of semiconsciousness and, as with Marianne's senseless words about her mother, foreground the debilitated state with respect to the normal. However, from the visionary point of view of the poet, one can't avoid a quite different interpretation of this phenomenon. In the state of having taken leave of one's everyday self, the life force in the spirit can be dispatched a thousand miles into the distance and can know the past and future of things that cannot be sensed with the eyes and ears. Here the blurting out of occult prophesies unexplainable in normal terms is not a rash interpretation at all. The point where you decide which of these two to follow is the point where you decide between realism and romanticism. Austen is a realist. Observing the way she handles the case of this girl's delirium provides an opportunity to illustrate the contrasting attitude of a romantic author in similar circumstances.

In *Jane Eyre* the heroine lives apart from her lover. Overcome with yearning one moonlit night while sitting in her room, she hears her name called from afar. Pricking up her ears, she finds the voice does not come from inside the room, nor the garden, nor the heavens, nor does it issue from anywhere on earth. However, it is a human voice and undoubtedly that of her lover. A lover in pain, suffering, near madness, the voice calls her name. The author Brontë borrows the voice of her heroine and describes the scene as follows:

> "I am coming!" I cried. "Wait for me! Oh, I will come!" I flew to the door, and looked into the passage: it was dark. I ran out into the garden: it was void.
>
> "Where are you?" I exclaimed.
>
> The hills beyond Marsh Glen sent the answer faintly back, "Where are you?" I listened. The wind sighed low in the firs: all was moorland loneliness and midnight hush.
>
> (*Jane Eyre*, chap. 35)

Jane, hearing her own voice from somewhere in space, is somewhat like Marianne going on about her distant mother. While the descriptive style in the two passages already shows the distinct commitments of the two authors, in the matter of allowing ambivalent interpretation they do not differ. However, despite the capacity for ambivalence, Brontë's preference for the occult becomes clear in the passage that follows. In chapter 37 we find:

As I exclaimed "Jane! Jane!" a voice—I cannot tell whence the voice came, but I know whose voice it was—replied, "I am coming! wait for me!" and a moment after, went whispering on the wind, the words—"Where are you?" ... "Where are you?" seemed spoken amongst mountains; for I heard a hill sent echo repeat the words."

as her lover Rochester's words find their way back to her. We discover in this passage that what the woman hears on the wind is not an auditory hallucination and what the man receives is not a reply in a dream. Rather, across a distance of a hundred miles their lovers' feelings call out and resonate across the spirit world in a manner that escapes explanation by the five bodily senses. When we perceive these mysterious cause-and-effect relations from the point of view of the everyday world, where 2 times 2 still equals 4, we are surprised at first and proceed with some caution. However, once one has set aside the perspective of daily experience and abandoned oneself to the sweet pleasures of a poetic logic, one discovers the entirety of the universe in a single atom and can take the measure of heaven. This is where romanticism finds its identity. (C. Reade, in his work *The Cloister and the Hearth* [1861], would appear to be trying to use this romantic method to addict the reader to an other-than-natural level of emotion.[11] See chaps. 70, 79, and 80 for sections touching on supernatural circumstances. That said, however, these unusual circumstances have the effect of attenuating the dramatic intensity by their very extraordinariness, and when the employment of these situations becomes excessive, the reader loses trust in the writer. Things essentially outside the domain of experience can't escape that occult sense no matter how often they are repeated. It is only the effect itself that is routinized. It doesn't matter how much time you spend rationalizing. The occult and the mysterious is still occult and mysterious. It is only that the ability to inspire fear in people attenuates as it becomes an object of regular discourse. As such, even in a romantic work twice is once too many for a phenomenon like supernatural communication, and Reade's work has to be judged a failure from this perspective.)

Having discerned a central strategy of romanticism in the point of arrangement of subject matter, we may return to the territory of the realists with this new bit of information and take the measure of their difference. We have to wait to see how Marianne's delirious speech is reflected in later passages to take the real measure of Austen's realism. The girl's words were spoken in reference to her mother. The issue is decided when we find out what the mother's circumstances actually were when the young girl spoke those words. Colonel Brandon is a man who set off for Barton to see the mother and inform her of the girl's sickness.

> The shock of Colonel Brandon's errand at Barton had been much soft-
> ened to Mrs. Dashwood by her own previous alarm; for so great was her
> uneasiness about Marianne, that she had already determined to set out
> for Cleveland on that very day, without waiting for any further intelli-
> gence, and had so far settled her journey before his arrival, that the
> Careys were then expected every moment to fetch Margaret away, as her
> mother was unwilling to take her where there might be infection.
> (*Sense and Sensibility*, chap. 45)

From the evidence of this passage it is quite clear that the girl's soul and the mother's spirit have not communicated on a supernatural plane. That is to say, the author has not taken the girl's fevered state as an opportunity to excite the reader's poetic sensibility by depicting a netherworld of meta-physical operations. As a consequence, M. cannot escape being a normal girl and the mother a normal mother. Yet it is precisely because of this everyday quality that we understand that they dress as we dress, eat as we eat, and act as we act, and we do not hesitate to identify emotionally in a way that does not differ from the way we would toward an actual person in our orbit.

M. is a normal, everyday person. The mother is a normal, everyday per-son. Even M.'s sickness is a normal, everyday sickness. (In *Pride and Preju-dice* the young girl takes ill while entrusted to another family.) It is quite unusual when a person takes ill in a novel for it to be just a normal, every-day sickness. In the cause of that—or in its effects—we will discover some crucial significance. As a result of falling ill, [the hero] is nursed to health by a beautiful woman and they fall in love. Or else he abandons wealth and fortune and falls into poverty. Or else one minute they are lying in bed and then they've passed away. In other words, these sicknesses are bound up in their fate. If we think back on our own experience, we get sick all the time, but there is typically no huge influence on our living condi-tions. We catch a cold and get fed thin soup.[12] We get beriberi and eat some red beans. We get an eye infection and stop reading books for a while. But no one has ever tossed into our window the money for the medicine. We don't discover that the woman nursing us is our neighbor's baby girl from long ago. We don't find that our life is saved by the very doctor being driven into penury by our usurer father. In other words, we are sick because we are sick, and the sickness is not made to bear any further significance. Consequently, a normal, everyday sickness is useless in a novel and constitutes the exception. The type of sickness Austen inserts in her novels is precisely this kind of exceptionally useless sickness. This kind of unnecessary element is not sufficient to affect the general drift of the entire work. Do we not have to regard it as a real sickness for exactly that reason? This deception of the reader through the garb of the everyday is a technique that runs consistently through the realist's work, and Austen is its most prototypical practitioner.

This, then, is the distinction between the romantic and the idealist schools, on the one hand, and the realist school, on the other, on the question of thematics (which we can gloss as arrangement of topics). However, the terms "romantic" and "idealist" just came up during the discussion of realist thematics. The earlier discussion of realist expression proceeded with reference to the six literary techniques, and we really haven't brought up the question of romantic or idealist expression. Just as we were able to obtain an opposition between romantic/idealist and realist form in the realm of thematics, I'd now like to return to the various expressive techniques and see if we can't produce a similar opposition between the form of romantic/idealist expression and the form of realist expression. This should allow us to attain a solid overview of the six basic expressive techniques. In order to discern this, the best strategy might be to produce a table where we can compare at a glance the particular characteristics of the six types of expression.

On the left side of table 1 are the six techniques of literary expression, while on the right side is a formal expression of their principal effects. As we know, small f represents the emotion that accompanies the given material F, while f' represents the emotion attaching to the new material F' that issues from the author's head in relation to the given material F. × represents an instance where the relation of f and f' is formally undefined.

As you can see by examining the right column, with the exception of the two points where the relation of f and f' is undefined (×), and (b) in Type 6, where it is (f−f'), all share the formula (f+f'). In short, the majority of the literary techniques enumerated under the six types constitute shades of meaning in this respect.

TABLE 1. Formal Relations of Principal Expressive Techniques

Literary Technique	Literary Effect
Associative type 1 (projection)	$f + f'$
Associative type 2 (introjection)	$f + f'$
Associative type 3 (dissociation)	$f + f'$
Associative type 4 (comic association)	×
Type 5 (harmonizing)	$f + f'$
Type 6 (counterposition)	(a) method of emphasis. . . . . $f + f'$
	(b) method of attenuation. . . . . $f - f'$
	pseudo-opposition. . . . . $f + f'$
	(c) method of non-opposition. x
Type 7 (realism)	f

When we translate the rough trend represented by the formula $(f + f')$[13] into plain language and examine its basic significance, our problem should be solved of itself. Let's suppose that f has both a given quality and a given quantity. Because we do not rest satisfied with the given in quality and quantity, an f' is provided for. If we suppose that f represents emotion accompanying a given experience that is common and everyday in terms of quality and quantity, the author employs technique to provide a new emotion f' that intensifies and ferments the ordinary f until it is something extraordinary. To put it another way, he or she takes the riches of the given world and contrives to double or even triple their value. Or else he or she takes a given quantity of cold water and by adding the heat of f' raises the intensity of feeling to 70 or 80 degrees.[14] In this sense, the techniques of literary expression represented here quantitatively by $(f + f')$ work to reinforce the tendencies of the romantic and idealist schools (elucidated, in relation to thematics, by contrast with realism). That is to say, in place of techniques brought to bear on the given f, the romantic and idealist schools employ from the start material that possesses a high intensity f. Because they avoid cold water from the start and select material that already incorporates a temperature of 80 or 90 degrees, from the point of view of its effect (or at least its tendency) there is a resonance between the two. When the romantic and idealist schools—which gain their identity from this intensification of thematics—find resonance in the expressive techniques

delineated by the formula (f + f'), we come to see that the terms "romantic" and "idealist" do not strictly refer to an effect of thematics but also
apply to the various techniques of expression. Just as we opposed realism
to romanticism, and so forth, in thematics, we can also oppose romantic
and idealist techniques to realistic technique in expressive methods; and
we can include in the terms "romantic" and "idealist" the characteristics
of the methods of literary expression that can be represented by the formula (f + f'). If we agree on this, it appears that what we call realism and
what we call romanticism or idealism incorporate two senses. As such,
from the combination of these two a variety of hybrid forms will arise.
There is realistic expression and romantic thematics. There is realistic
thematics and romantic expression. Both can be realist and both can be
romantic. This relation is expressed in table 2.

Thematics begins at the level of the realists, and after passing through a
number of steps, reaches the intensity of the romantics (or, if you will,
idealists). Likewise, expression begins at the same level, climbs up the
same kinds of steps, and ends up at the same kind of height. All writing—as
it passes in length from a line, to a passage, to a chapter—constitutes an
intertwining of thematics and expression. Hence, as the quantity of each
increases, the possibilities for combination also increase. As such, while
the methods of romanticism and realism receive their identities from the
two polar end points, it is rather a question of degree and more likely that
hybrid forms would arise that would be too numerous to list, pressing
closer now to one, now to the other. Because these hybrid forms individually fall out at points over the axes of thematics and expression but only
come into being as sentences through their recombination, our concrete
evaluation of their literary and poetic merit will undoubtedly be governed
by a taste that has not gone through this relatively intricate dissection.

The numbers within the columns represent the comparative quantity
of emotion that arises in the readers of various schools as they play out
across the techniques of thematics and expression. Occupying the lowest
row, realism takes as its theme the objects of daily life. The objects of daily
life do not often give rise to an extraordinary f. Let's provisionally assign a
quantity of 50 to this f.[15] Because they refuse from the start any gloss or
ornamentation, the expressive methods of the realists will also occupy an
f in the bottom ranks, and we've reflected this by assigning a value of 50.
As one moves up the scale in intensity of theme, one increases 10, then 20
degrees, finally reaching 120. The numbers 120 and 50 are arbitrary and

TABLE 2. Intensity of Expression and Latent Intensity

	Thematics	Expression
Romanticism	120	120
	110	110
	100	100
	90	90
	80	80
	70	70
	60	60
Realism	50	50

simply designate relative level of intensity. The same is true for methods of expression. As one leaves the realm of realism, one increases by 10, then 20 degrees, finally reaching 120.

The particular quality of realism is such that, while occupying the low-est realm in literary expression—in its closeness to nature, in its unwilling-ness to falsify the facts, in its naiveté, in its refusal of artifice, in its ultimate ability to suggest an unexpected profoundness in the fleeting ordinariness of the everyday—it finds itself quite the equal of the romantics. However, the flaw of realism is in the tendency to wallow in mediocrity, to rest satis-fied with a dull tastelessness, to teeter toward its ending undistinguished and without character. The particular quality of romanticism (which we can gloss as idealism) is in the intensity of its stimulus, its freshness, the vastness of its rhythms, its visceral tension, its ability to leave the reader in wide-eyed suspense. If we were to speak of the defects of romanticism, they, too, are numerous. It can be unnatural, gaudy, mannered, childish, comic in its ambitions, freakish in its extravagance. As to which of these two ori-entations to expression and thematics will captivate you, it is a matter of the times, your age, your gender, and ultimately your innate preference. Elizabethan literature represents the supreme expression of romanticism. Later commentators, while stunned at the richness of their imagination, could not help ridiculing their implausible leaps. A man on in years can no longer endure the strain of imaginary stimulus. When he sees young men running around drunk, waving daggers, and breaking down into tears and singing songs drunkenly on sake, does he not stand in awe of their vigor at the same time that he pities their immaturity? Women tend toward extremes, and even a matron with a well-established family shows not a hint of embarrassment at reading the most absurd and nonsensical novels. Austen, on the other hand, was only a couple years past twenty when she wrote *Pride and Prejudice*, and her authority in realism will reign for a hundred generations. These few examples show how our tastes wander and oscillate between these two poles, governed by the era, our experience, gender, and our innate inclinations. For this reason one cannot mechanically dictate what sort of balance and combination would produce the perfect text, one that would last a hundred generations. Though we may determine the categories of our criticism in this way, we cannot likewise determine standards for the whole. If we are forced to play our cards, such judgments can only apply within particular categories. Assuming that standards established and placed on the table for a particular category have jurisdiction in another category invites the most egregious errors. This is the irreducible ambiguity the critic faces.

Translation by Joseph A. Murphy

BOOK 5

GROUP F

In this concluding volume Sōseki moves beyond the level of individual consciousness—the primary focus of the first four books—to the "group F" or "aggregate F" that those individual consciousnesses are said to form in combination. In other words, we move from the realm of psychology to that of sociology, as Sōseki transposes the rise and fall of focal points in individual consciousness to changes in the shared zeitgeist that characterizes a society and its shared "literary F" in a given historical period. In particular, Sōseki takes pains here to analyze the mechanisms driving change in shared literary taste. He differentiates between various types of consciousness and the role each plays in transforming group F. He also explores the mechanisms by which such transformations take place, using as his device the concept of "suggestion" (from associationist psychology), as well as the various rhetorical techniques he explored in book 4. Sōseki's argument here is marked by both an acceptance of and a moving away from tenets of the Social Darwinism that was widely accepted in 1907.

N.B.: We have translated in their entirety chapters 1–3 of book 5, leaving out chapters 4–6, which explore further applications of the book's basic principles to additional authors and literary movements, and chapter 7, which explores the principle of suggestion as a force of transformation in a variety of historical settings.

Thus far we have identified the qualities of those elements in our consciousness that are capable of serving as literary material and offered several concrete examples thereof. We then compared and considered the differences among them and divided them into four categories. Having thus established these categories and noted the various interrelations that exist between and among them, we considered them as modes of expression to show how A would coalesce with B. Finally we traced our steps backward from the mode of expression to enter the realm of the material itself. In the process we spoke of the literary man, in whose consciousness the literary F appears in abundance, and compared his F to that of the scientist. In this chapter we will be concerned with the state of this thing that I am calling "F."

Here we will be discussing the different forms of F. These will include temporal and spatial differences as well as differences that arise between individual persons, between members of different nations, between the ancient and the modern, and perhaps even the difference between our own age and the future as we might imagine it. The difference, noted earlier, between the scholar of literature and the scientist concerns only a small part of this project, but it was of sufficient importance that we felt it necessary to treat it in the preceding section.

In this volume I wish to discuss the different forms of F. However, because these differences are extraordinarily complex and multifarious, many of their aspects are bound to slip through our fingers and we will not be able to theorize them with much precision. Clearly, our net will not be so fine as to capture all the fish that are to be had. But our subject is literature. And in touching upon it we will content ourselves with a rough analysis of the waxing and waning of progress in literature, the distinctions in trends and schools, and the rise and fall of tides of thought. For a complete account we will have to await the work of other gentlemen scholars.

In this volume I wish to discuss the differences that arise in F. I think it best to go back to the beginning of the volume and review what has been said of F thus far before proceeding further with these investigations. In this I am simply acting as one who is careful enough to repair his shutters before there is any sign of rain, and the reader is requested to overlook a certain amount of redundancy. The contents of consciousness over a given unit of time rise and fall in the form of a wave. The highest point of the wave is where the consciousness is most clear. We followed the theories of psychologists and called this the focus of consciousness. We used the letter F to refer to this focal point. We then considered the limits of F and postulated that it was characterized by a purely cognitive nature. For this reason when F arises not on its own but in combination with an emotion, we designate the latter with an "f" and thus arrive at the formula $F + f$. Under the condition that all literary materials that manifest themselves in consciousness must be linked with some kind of emotion, the literary "F" can always be expressed with the formula F + f. However, (F + f) can be considered a kind of F, so that we should be able to consider it a literary F as long as it is not explicitly stated that it is not accompanied by an "f." We have argued for the usefulness of expanding the F of a given unit of time to encompass the great vacillations of our consciousness over the course of a single day, a night, half a year, or half a century, and thereby to express the tendencies present in all or part of an individual's life with the single letter F. We also argued for the appropriateness of capturing and expressing with the single letter F the most prominent focal points of the combined thoughts and ideas shared by individuals across a given age. Our discussion here will primarily concern the categories, transformations, and transitions of this group F. Because our main focus will be with literature, we will assume that the F under discussion is a literary F unless otherwise specified. While our examples may be drawn from areas other than literature, since the literary group F is also governed by the selfsame principles, we will not have cause to fear contradiction or to worry over the difficulty of inserting a round peg into a square hole. Moreover, because this group F is nothing more than an extension of the F of an individual in a given moment in time, the principles that govern the latter can, with certain exceptions, be applied to the former. In some instances we will take the liberty of drawing examples from the latter [individual F] in order to explain the workings of the former [group F]. But it would be far too onerous to explain what we are up to in every instance.

Chapter 1: The Three Types of Group F in a Given Generation

There are three main types of group consciousness. These include the consciousness of imitation, of talent, and of genius. By consciousness we, of course, mean to say the focus of consciousness (F). These distinctions arise with regard to the formal relations between these three forms of consciousness and do not constitute a catalog of the material content of consciousness itself. Because the material of consciousness changes with the passage of time, we can only speak of it within the context of a specific historical moment.

1. We call "imitative" that consciousness easily dominated by outside forces. By "dominated" we mean to say that as it moves from A to B, it

naturally falls into step with others and takes a similar course of action. In other words, it is the type of consciousness that arises from the imitation of the taste, the "isms," and the experience of others. Imitation is a necessary social glue. A society without imitation would be like a heavenly body ungoverned by the laws of gravity. It would splinter into pieces and before long it would collapse altogether. It is for this reason that scholars claim that society rests upon imitation. And it is our great love of imitation that makes them say so. In his *Physiognomy and Expression* Mantegazza writes (on p. 84):

> Call out in the middle of a crowd, "A conflagration! A conflagration!" or begin to cry "Fire! Fire!" while at the same time you run off gesticulating. In the first case many may stop and inquire. In the second there will be a general and irresistible stampede. Gesture is more automatic than speech, and automatically induces imitation. Of this we may convince ourselves by suddenly opening an umbrella in the middle of the street when the weather is uncertain, yet without actual rain, or by putting the hand into the pocket in an omnibus as though to pay the fare. Many umbrellas will be opened and many persons will draw out their pence by the simple force of automatic imitation.

Of course, what Mantegazza says about gesture can also be applied to more complex ideas. The great principle of the struggle for survival has equipped us all with this quality, and those who are lacking in it will be unable to adapt to society and are fated to fail in the most basic aspects of everyday life. The infant is dependent on its mother for many things, but [even with the most attentive mother] an infant without the capacity to imitate others will perish before its bangs grow out. Eating three meals a day is a matter of imitation. To crave sleep for half the night is also imitative. Propriety in behavior and measure in one's manners are learned through imitation, just as one avoids rickshaws in the road and horses in the market to keep from doing injury to one's flesh and bones. Imitation is thus a very necessary thing. The ability to live in a society of adults without inviting constant mishaps indicates that one's thought, one's actions, and one's words are adapted to that society. Thus, when a child imitates an adult it is in order to earn a certificate of viability in the society in which he lives. We are born into this world under nature's command to imitate others. The very existence of society is more than ample proof of how effectively imitation operates among individuals.

Imitation is thus primary and fundamental to the formation and maintenance of society. In addition to this primary imitation necessary for survival, we are prone to exercise the same tendency in other directions as well. This secondary imitation is not a necessary one but results from excessive fascination or affection toward others. An example would be the way children imitate their fathers or maids imitate the lady of the house. In some cases the imitation of pathological tastes can cause a whole society to take leave of its senses. Such was the case with the craze for misanthropic literature in the early nineteenth century. As Georg Brandes wrote, "The melancholy of the early nineteenth century partakes of the nature of a disease; and it is not a disease which attacks a single individual or a single nation only, it is an epidemic which spreads from people to people, in the manner of those religious manias which so often spread over Europe in the Middle Ages. René's is merely the first and most marked case of the disease in the form in which it attacked the most gifted intellects."[1]

To those who would say that this is not a case of imitation, I would argue that while normal imitation is done with subjective intention, the imitation in this case is commanded by nature. It is an imitation that is forced upon us by something stronger than the individual will. Imitation tends to banish irregularities from society and bring each of its members into an orderly and equal array. It gives the appearance of regularity to society's rough surface, bringing this and that into accord, and does not stop until it has done away with the difference between A and B. For this reason people who have this kind of consciousness in abundance have no individual ambition. They rarely take risks that would threaten their survival and inhabit a relatively secure world. The status quo is easily maintained in a society with many such people. This is because such a society is an extremely ordered one in which customs of the past will be followed, the patrimony will be protected, tastes handed down from past generations will be relished again and again, and people will come and go and love and hate together with their old hometown friends. In most cases the majority of society is made up of people with this kind of consciousness. As the majority, they have power in numbers. They are powerful not only in numbers but in terms of actual power as well. But if one evaluates this form of consciousness in terms of originality, its force is extremely meager.

The people who exhibit it strongly tend to be mediocre and ordinary. This is because they care about nothing but conforming and imitating others. In the literary world these are the unremarkable poets and novelists. They poeticize what others poeticize, see beauty where others see it, and make poetry and novels out of things that other people say are poetic and novelistic. This is what I mean by the Imitative Group F.

2. But "imitation" is a word that only makes sense in the context of a comparison between the imitator and the imitated. In section 1 I explained the basic meaning of the "F" of the imitator. In order for the imitator to want to imitate something, he must be provided with an object "F" that is worthy of imitation. This kind of F is not necessarily gleaned from one's contemporaries, nor does it shine for all to see on the summit of consciousness. It can be obtained through custom or from reading. And yet it does sometimes happen that people bring their heads together and are shown the way by some among them who breathe the same air. I do not know how best to designate this proactive form of F, but for now I will call it the F of talent.

As I said at the beginning of this section, it is very difficult to describe the substance of this F. This is because, like the momentary F in our consciousness, it is always changing and never stays in the same place. If one wants to know its nature, one must first demarcate one period of what is given and only then can one come up with a concrete explanation. But although it is concrete, it is limited to one period of the given and therefore difficult to apply to anything else, meaning that as a general theory not tied to a specific time and space it is not in its nature to offer anything more than an abstract explanation.

Our consciousness is characterized by the way—whether it be over the course of a minute, an hour, or a year—it begins indistinctly, rises into clarity at the summit, and then fades back again into obscurity. When one wave cycle is completed, it repeats the process and describes another wave. These wave cycles continue so long as life persists and society exists. For this reason F always signifies movement and change. (To imagine an F without movement we would have to abandon the idea of memory. Because this would mean staying with the same F and not looking left or right or being able to connect what comes before with what comes after, we would ourselves merge with F and be one. And we would not even be aware of this merger.) When confronted with an F that is about to change, we have no choice but to imagine a series of at least three states of F: a, b,

and c. If the group (imitative) consciousness of a certain era is at b, the a
that preceded it exists as a faint flicker on the edge of consciousness. At the
same time, we can hypothesize that the c which will come next is readying
itself in the darkness to gradually emerge from the subconscious and take
its place at the top. In other words, while b currently occupies the focus of
consciousness, like the proud Heike it will sooner or later yield its domin-
ion to c.[2] Thus, the tendency of b is gradually to transform itself into c and
proceed to shape the contents of consciousness accordingly. Because the F
of the common masses usually moves in the same direction, those who are
one step ahead will reach the destination of c that much faster. And those
who are two steps ahead will reach it even faster. People with the F of talent are ten or twenty steps ahead of the masses. And when they reach that
next focal point, they turn around to beckon them on ahead. Unabashed
at being so far behind, the masses cannot turn their heels midcourse and
change direction. This is because no matter how fast or how slow, b must
move on to c. If the point is to go to Shinagawa, it makes no difference
whether you go by train or on foot. To say that you will not go to Shinagawa because you cannot beat the train would be to miss the point altogether. For this reason the waves of consciousness belonging to the talented people are always one wave ahead of the masses. The unevenness of
these wave movements is sometimes the result of conscious effort and
planning, but in most cases it is simply caused by physical and mental
constraints. For example, when a lecture is being given in a hall there are
many things that might induce a feeling of boredom in the students, including the subject of the lecture, the relative skill with which it is delivered, the weather outside the hall, and the air quality inside. In this instance, while boredom is the inevitable destination of all the listeners,
there is no way to know in advance at which point one of them might, in
fact, become bored. The talented ones who first feel the urge to yawn have
no reason to prove it by rushing ahead of the others and precipitating the
wave of boredom by placing the yawn clearly in the forefront of their consciousness. By the same token, those whose turn to yawn comes around
last need not feel inferior. Even though it is mortifying to be the last to
yawn and to face the scorn of one's fellows, the fact is that their time for
yawning is not yet nigh and all they can do is muddle along until the urge
strikes them.

The F of talent arrives where the imitative F ends up, only it gets there
faster. While it is less numerous than the F of imitation, it has superior

force because it is able to incorporate within itself all that the latter contains. People call those with the F of talent gentlemen who are quick to spot an opportunity, or talents with an eye for social trends. But public opinion does not distinguish between people who anticipate things by chance and those who do so intentionally. People are even less likely to realize that the former are relatively more numerous than the latter. There were people who made tens of millions of yen with stock investments, having predicted the industrial boom that followed the Russo-Japanese War. These are clearly people who posses this type of F. But in the case of business ventures it is not only necessary to do a great deal of planning, one also takes considerable risks, and this makes for a situation that is very different from that of a poet writing verses or a literary man writing prose. Creative gentlemen live in the world of taste, and taste has nothing to do with thought. When the creative among us commune with the trends and fashions of the times, it sometimes happens that a precious wine ferments in their breasts and emits a heady bouquet. But much of this happens unawares. If there is nothing inside them to ferment, they are bound to fail in their efforts to anticipate the waves of fashion regardless of how thoroughly they might yield their intellect, how carefully they might calculate, or how exhaustively they might lay their plans. It is not easy to make one's brush follow the commands of the intellect or to compose verses in accordance with a preset plan. There are countless instances from time immemorial of people who have succeeded in the literary world thanks to the F of talent. Byron woke up one day to discover that he was famous. And Kipling's fame for his novels of India can also be attributed to this type of consciousness. (A case like the literary reputation of Marie Corelli is a very different matter. Her success was a result of the fact that her work accorded so well with the general group consciousness, in other words, the F of imitation. This is why she has so many readers and also why it is so mediocre.)

3. The third form of consciousness we will call the F of Genius. One would be hard put to distinguish the F of Genius from the F of Talent in terms of content [*jisshitsu*]. But I will define the F of Genius according to the following characteristics. (The reader will be advised not to fixate too obsessively on the terms "Talent" and "Genius.")

While those who are endowed with the F of Talent are welcomed by society and showered with all the laurels of success, the F of Genius not only fails to attract fame and honor but can in some instances bring those who possess it into conflict with the trends of the age. This is what is meant when we say that the voice of greatness is not heard by the masses, that pearls are cast before swine, that the eastern wind blows in vain in a cow's ear. All of these expressions refer to the vast gap that separates the F of Genius from that of the common folk. Here we must return to the theory of the wave form of consciousness in order to investigate the extent to which this form of consciousness deviates from the rest.

In the last section we saw how while the imitative consciousness remains behind at F, blind to what comes next, in the brain of the talented man F'—the next manifestation of F—is already visible. Someone whose consciousness is already focused on F' while it is still being anticipated by the man of talent could be said to be one step ahead of the latter in his perception of the trend of the times. But what if he not only was conscious of F' but also not only foresaw but was conscious of F" and from then went on to F'''. What if he did not settle for F''' but went on to F'''' and all the way to F^n. Such a person would have run through a whole succession of waves while the majority of people were still fixated on F and the minority of men of talent were just starting to anticipate F'. Sooner or later F will end up at F^n, but for the majority who are now in possession of F alone the gap is so great that they are unable to perceive it anywhere around them. As a result they not only fail to see its value but they reject it. People of the same ilk are smug in numbers. It is in the nature of such groups to exclude and expunge those who have the least claim to belonging. The failure and oppression of the Genius F can be understood according to the theory of focal consciousness. The difference between the common man and the genius is as follows: it is the speed with which they become conscious of F that distinguishes the genius from the common man. The distance between the common man and the genius is the same as the distance between F and F^n. Because F tends naturally to flow towards F^n, there can be no difference in quality between the two. For this reason the difference between the common man and the genius is not the content of his consciousness but its timing [sengo]. And yet since timing is not unrelated to content, a more precise way of putting it would be to say that it is a difference in the content of consciousness that arises from the influence of the time that gives rise to the waves (and not from any other cause). An example would be the difference between the same man in his childhood and in his prime. Since we are dealing with a single person, the child and the man can be said to be the same, but because the child will not become the man until a certain amount of time has passed, the two are different insofar as they are controlled by time. But if you were to show a photograph to the boy of how he will look in twenty years' time, the distance would be so great that he would not only fail to recognize himself but would, in fact, despise the image. Such is the attitude of the common man toward the genius (according to this interpretation).

I do not believe that this interpretation is incorrect. And yet I cannot claim that it is the only possible interpretation. The difference between the common man and the genius from the perspective of focal consciousness admits of two additional interpretations. According to the interpretation given in the last section, the waves of consciousness of the genius differ from those of everyone else only in terms of stage, while the process and order of their transformations do not contradict each other in the slightest—indeed, they are in perfect accord with one another. But while we can allow for this interpretation, we are also free to imagine the following.

(a) In the focus of consciousness of the genius there is something that one might call a core, which, though not visible to others, is its most vital part. It is not our concern here to ask how this core emerged or how it reached its present state. We simply want to confirm the existence of this core. Having posited the existence such a core, we can then reiterate. The F of the genius, like that of the ordinary man, is constantly changing and describes an uninterrupted wave form. But when we cut away one cycle of that wave, we encounter a peculiar phenomenon. We find that in every focal point this core has held its position. Thus, while the movement from F to F' and from F' on to F" is the same as that experienced by the ordinary person, the presence of this core in every successive focal point in the genius's consciousness makes it strikingly different. This core is what in mathematics is called a constant. It has a consistent influence in terms of quantity and quality on the focal points [of the genius]. This means that the F of the genius is not only different from that of other people but is different in a consistent fashion, thus lending a kind of unity to the irregular and unruly variations of F.

Whereas in the last section we suggested that the genius is different from others because he sees a thousand leagues farther and hears from a thousand leagues away, according to this new interpretation the genius is one who never hesitates to see and hear on the basis of his own unique internal core. Because this core behaves like a constant number and is never absent from the genius's consciousness for even a single instant, when it opposes the normal view of things and contravenes common sense it will transform the common F in its own fashion before it even has time to consider [the consequences of] this opposition. And it is often the case that the genius believes this F [of their own concoction] to be normal. This is perhaps why geniuses often invoke the anger or the ridicule of the common folk. And it is why they are often mistaken for neurotics. From ancient times [to this day] the great systems have been formed by gathering together the smallest things. The consciousness of ordinary people comes and goes according to the dizzying multiplicity of phenomena; they are as easily fooled as those monkeys in the Chinese legend who were kept happy with four acorns in the morning and three at night.[3] They are easily manipulated by appearances; they sink or swim and run themselves ragged at the prospect of whatever treasure is before them at the moment. The things they encounter every day are myriad and multiple, but they are simply carried away by them into a glimmering confusion. It is a continuous stream, like a procession of carriages, horses, and people endlessly reflected in a mirror. But those who are able to screw themselves tightly to that single core and remain forever unmoved will, according to the form and quality of this core, be able to gather together the limitless floating dust and discover for themselves one or two perspectives to live by. They may find a god in all things. They may discover the law of the preservation of matter. They may become optimists. They may become pessimists. Once they have established this perspective as they make their way through heaven and earth, the phenomena that reach their eyes and ears may be the same as those of ordinary people, but their consciousness will be radically different. There are some people who are obsessed with corners. For them not only do a measuring box and an inkstone have corners, but they cannot stop until they find a corner in a round tray, in the moon, and in the sun. This is because their interpretation of the world is entirely dominated by the corner that is their core. It is because they always begin with the corner. For them a circle is a modification of a corner. They see a triangle as a square that has lost a corner. And they think of a diamond shape as just so many crooked corners. For these people there is nothing in the universe that does not derive in one way or another from a corner. There are also people for whom the number three is their core. According to them, heaven and earth come together with man to form the three bodies. The present combines with the past and the future to form the three ages. Or, like Dong Yu from the *Romance of the Three Kingdoms*, they go about lecturing people to study during the "three down times," as they put it—the winter of the year, the night of the day, and when the weather is rainy. And not only that. These people think that one is a number two less than three and four is a three onto which one has been added. Thus, for them everything in the world has to do with the number three. When the filial child sees a piece of candy, his first thought is of his parents. This is because his core is filial piety. The beggar sees a piece of candy and hopes to exchange it for some money. This is because his core centers around money. Falstaff went through life focused on all that was comical. And Don Quixote lived his whole life along the axis of chivalry. Darwin saw the animal world, his wife and children, and even God through the lens of evolution. Buson had haiku at his core and it was from this perspective that he regarded the sun and the moon, the stars and their constellations, the lowly and the mighty.[4] Their consciousness was always dominated by this one core. It rose and fell in waves and did not differ from that of ordinary folk in terms of content, but it was always marked with something particular as a result of the influence of this core. This particular quality meant that where most people would experience grandeur, they would laugh out loud; where others would pay respect, they would feel contempt; and where the average person would be struck with wonder, they would remain unimpressed. We can therefore posit that it is the existence of this core that makes it impossible for the genius to mix with the common lot of human beings.

(b) We will now return to the discussion of focal consciousness with the following explanation of the third type of consciousness [genius]. Because ordinary people are dominated by ordinary consciousness, they move from F to F' and then from F' to F" without ever coming to a halt. The consciousness of the genius is not under the sway of the factors that control the ordinary person, so they move from F to A and from A to B without ever stopping. Thus, it would appear that while the genius and the ordinary person both experience F at the summit of consciousness, from that point they proceed in different directions. It is this divergence that we will now investigate.

While the consciousness of the ordinary person moves on from F to F' after lingering at the former for a certain interval, some individuals decline to move along with the ordinary folk and think nothing of remaining at F for a longer than normal period of time. It is not our purpose here to consider the reasons for this temporal discrepancy. Most likely, the decision not to move along with all the rest (a decision that is not intentional but rather the result of the urgings of nature) is evidence of the comparatively greater force exercised by the current F on the person in question. When one is conscious of a powerful F, the force of which monopolizes one's attention, one does not, as is the usual case, simply wait until the wave of that F subsides and then follow along, late though one might be, in the dust of the others who have gone ahead toward F'. The stronger the F, the more pronounced is the tendency to see within it what others fail to notice, to hear what others do not hear, and to feel or think what others have missed. For this reason, when this individual has the opportunity to move away from F, he tends not toward F', where others have already arrived, but approaches a very different place, which we might call "A." Because this A has appeared in the next wave movement as a result of the powerful force of F on the consciousness, except for some exceptional cases, we can be sure that it has arisen not from without the F but from somewhere within it. If it has indeed emerged from inside the F, this would suggest that it is not unrelated to F but a part of F of which we were not clearly conscious in the earlier stage of the wave movement. We can call it a part of F or an attribute of F, or perhaps a relation between two attributes of F.

With this we have explained that the consciousness of ordinary people moves from F to F', while that of certain individuals moves from F to A. And we have also explained the nature of this A. If we now recognize, in the sense of what we have just explained, that the consciousness at A moves on to B, and the consciousness at B moves on to C, we will see that the continuity of focal consciousness of this individual and the ordinary person have only F in common and that they diverge increasingly from each other with each successive wave movement. Thus, while the consciousness of the ordinary person moves away from F in two dimensions, the consciousness of this individual departs from F in three dimensions. I say two-dimensional to describe the movement of the ordinary consciousness because it does not remain fixated on F. It does not resist the diffusion that arises from the stimuli of the outside world, and its waves continue to expand outward. The three-dimensional [or spatial] form of consciousness does remain attached to F, and as a result it discovers new foci within it, and newer ones within those. It plumbs the depths of F and sends its waves forth to its innermost layers.

Having established these two forms of extension, we can see that the former is common among the majority of amateurs and the latter is characteristic of experts, such as artists and academic specialists. But when the extension proceeds beyond the realms of the expert or, to advance one step further, when the waves of consciousness spread only on the inside of F and the individual in question has no interest in focal points in the outside world at all—when they find narrow and profound, intricate and thoroughgoing knowledge and emotion all within the bounds of the single topic in which they specialize, remaining completely unmoved by all other human and natural affairs—we are clearly in the presence of a kind of oddball and a genius. Being both a genius and an oddball, he will not comprehend the customs of society, nor will he conform to the niceties of the world. In some cases he will lack even the most basic moral sensibility. For this reason he will inspire fear and loathing in most members of society.

Among the higher orders of academic specialists, there are some who are unable to respect the strictures of decorum. There are also famous artists who care nothing for what is just and right. Such people are born into this world with the glory of their genius and the curse of their deformity. But they have already made the sacrifice involved in being misfits in order to expand the F inside them to acquire a brilliance and penetration that is a hundred or a thousand times greater than that of the average man. For example, they say that Titian could distinguish a hundred colors where the average man saw only one. This is the fruit of specialized training. It is one of the most glorious examples. But there are also geniuses who have nothing to offer the world and who can only flaunt the disgrace of the genius and the ugliness of the freak. There are businessmen whose only genius lies in making a profit. There are genius thieves and genius con men. There are geniuses at abusing financial power, who seek only to use their power to harass the poor and the weak. These are the noxious and irredeemable geniuses. Not only do they lack the virtues and good deeds that might compensate for their odiousness, but their goal is to spread poison in society. And because, like the other more respectable geniuses, they are also freaks, it is the responsibility of society as a whole to club them senseless and throw them into the bowels of the earth like so many rabid dogs.

Basing myself on the theory of focal consciousness, I have offered three explanations of this F of genius that appears so strange at first glance. I cannot say which of the three is the correct one or even if all three might hold some water, but my interpretation goes no further than this, so I will end my discussion of genius here.

The imitative consciousness, the consciousness of talent, and the consciousness of the genius are the three great divisions operative in every social class [kaikyū] in any given age. But because I have only proposed them for heuristic reasons, when we apply them to the real world we will, of course, discover that human beings do not live their lives like machines cooped up within these clear-cut categories without ever venturing past the threshold. Between the imitators and the men of talent we can identify a family of hybrids, just as we can find a race of half-breeds between the men of talent and genius. In this way you can always split the three [kinds of consciousness] into five, divide those five into a further nine, and divide the nine again into seventeen even finer distinctions. At each level, as one makes finer and finer distinctions these three types of consciousness do not comprise clear stages but fade into each other like a splotch of ink smeared across a white sheet of paper. There is no need to make precise distinctions of same and different, but only to recognize how x flows into y and y melts into z. Because writers of literature constitute one class of society, they are also endowed with these types of consciousness and will occupy a place somewhere along the scale. (For those of you who are interested in the process by which F is nurtured and developed, I recommend Baldwin's *Social and Ethical Interpretations in Mental Development*. For actual examples of the manner of geniuses see Lombroso's *Man of Genius*. Gustave Le Bon's *Psychology of Socialism* is for the general reader and not very profound, but it is worth reading for its account of group behavior.)[5]

In summation, I offer the following analysis of the three forms of consciousness:

1. The imitative consciousness is found in the greatest numbers. For this reason it is the safest bet in terms of profit and loss. But it is void of creative, original value. It grows without distinction, only to wither like the grass and the trees.

2. The consciousness of talent is found in smaller numbers than (1). But its nature is to anticipate the destination of (1), to reach it one wave cycle earlier, and, more often as not, to become a favored child of society. In terms of profit and loss, it is also a safe bet. But its quality is less that of originality than of quickness. And because quickness is only a matter of timing, its influence on society is normally limited to a temporal one. In popular language this kind of person is referred to as a "man of talent" [saishi]. The man of talent is mistaken for a genius by the common folk,

but this is only because they are blinded by his immediate successes and unable to discern his true nature.

3. The consciousness of genius is found in far fewer numbers than (1) or (2). At the same time, his wild and unpredictable nature makes him the most dangerous of the three. In many cases he is trampled underfoot by the vulgar crowds before he even reaches maturity. (And these are the same masses who claim to extol the virtues of genius. It is they who praise the geniuses of old and ask why none has appeared in their own age. And they do so at the very moment they remorselessly crush those geniuses underfoot. This is what qualifies them as vulgar.) But because the consciousness of the genius is extremely powerful, he will clash with the masses and not stop until he either realizes his own ideas or dies an early death in the attempt. In this sense the genius is an obstinate and stupid fellow. If he manages to realize his ambition and have the value of his own creation recognized by society, what once looked like obstinacy and stupidity will be transformed into greatness and his thick skull will shine with the light of glory. He is not concerned with greatness or obstinacy or stupidity. He is moved to accomplish what he does only by the awesome power of his consciousness. For this reason, if you have something to fear from the genius's self-realization, do not try to warn him, do not oppose him, and do not ridicule him. Do not waste your effort needlessly. You must simply take him by surprise and club him to death. If you fear Nichiren you must kill Nichiren.[6] If you fear Jesus it is best to crucify him. When Confucius was trapped in the wilderness between the Kingdoms of Chen and Cai, he did not abandon his principles. And expulsion from school was not enough to make Shelley renounce his atheism. If they had lived their lives in accordance with what the masses thought proper, in what would their genius have consisted?

Chapter 2: The Principles According to Which Consciousness Changes

In Chapter 1 we explained the distinct characteristics of the three types of consciousness that traverse any given age. The purpose of the current chapter is to examine the directions in which changes occur in the group consciousness of an age and the laws that govern this change.

1. The distribution of group consciousness in every age is governed by the laws of suggestion. Suggestion is not a matter of feelings, ideas, or intentionality but rather a way in which a complex sensibility is transmitted from A to B, bringing the latter under the sway of the former. The most extreme example of suggestion is that of a person under hypnosis. If you give such a person a glass of ice water and tell them it is hot, they will suffer the same as if it were full of boiling water. If you place a feather in their palm and suggest to them that it is heavy, they will react as if you had unloaded on them the tripod kettle cast by the Great King Yu of the Xia Dynasty.[7] This sort of thing is widely known and so much has been written of it already that there is no need for further elaboration here. But it is also the case that people who are in a normal state can be affected by suggestion in this way. One physician tells the story of a woman on whom he was about to operate who lost consciousness just as he was placing the mask on her face and before he had even administered the anesthesia. This was a case of extraordinary susceptibility to suggestion. Among the general population it can be said, with certain exceptions, that children are the most susceptible to suggestion, followed by women. Normal men would appear to be much less susceptible, but they are certainly not immune. As Pascal wrote, we often call others idiots, and we need only say so often enough to make them think that they are, in fact, idiots. We need only make them say to themselves that they are idiots and this will suffice to make them believe it. Human beings are made that way.

The preceding examples may be exceptional instances of the workings of suggestion in the world of the imagination, but if we permit ourselves to expand the definition of suggestion a bit, we will find that even ordinary people are constantly subject to suggestion in their everyday lives and that this suggestion brings about changes in their consciousness.

In order to explain this, we will have to return to the wave movement of the focus of consciousness and think again about the manner in which F moves to F'. As a nonspecialist in these matters I am running the risk of getting in above my head, but I will nonetheless venture an opinion since this is so relevant to the theme of this chapter. When our consciousness is focused on F, we can posit that our brain, as it responds to this, is in a state called "C." When F moves on to F', we can further assume that C will follow on to C'. This is so because, while not all of the finest distinctions of consciousness will register in the material conditions of the brain, we nonetheless assume that even the most subtle changes in the one do have some impact on the other, and that each can help to explain the other. Thus, if C is itself a condition for the emergence of C' and C' is the state of the brain corresponding to the [conscious state of] F', it follows that C would also be a condition for the emergence of F'. Because C will not move on to C' in the absence of some kind of stimulus (be it internal or external), the minimum conditions for the emergence of F' can be reduced to C and S (stimulus). (If "stimulus" is not the right word, there is nothing preventing us from using some other term). The nature of this S is yet to be determined, but it seems reasonable to assume that it could come in many forms. When this S, which is variable in force and in quality, impacts C, there is no reason to assume that C would react in a uniform manner. It might react quickly and vigorously to one S and slowly and sluggishly to another. From this we can conclude that C has its own clearly defined tendencies. When such a C is presented with a free choice between two S's, it will accept the one best suited to its own tendencies and combine with it to constitute C', and on that basis it will become conscious of F'. As long as we live in this phenomenal world and sustain the workings of our bodies and our organs, these S's are constantly attacking our C from within and without. Thus, the shift from C to C' entails the rejection of a certain number of S's. While many of them are rejected, the happy S that best suits C will combine with it to give rise to C'. If we were to translate this process into the language of consciousness, we could say that the move from F to F' normally takes place through a competition among various S's. Moreover, because we can also consider even this S as having a conscious content of its own, we could reformulate the above proposition to state that the move from F to F' normally takes place through a competition among various Ⓕ's. Ⓕ indicates not the meaning that exists within the focal point but that which remains on the edges or beneath the level of consciousness. In this way, when F moves to F' it receives a number of "requests from Ⓕ's and selects" the one that is most powerful and best suited to the tendency of F. Thus, the successive foci of our consciousness are governed by the principle of suggestion. It is not that F' suddenly appears out of nowhere to vanquish F from its seat at the focus of consciousness but rather that it has already been subtly suggested to us before we become clearly aware of it.

2. We have postulated that C has its own tendencies and that S can be strong or weak. We also posited that S can have different qualities. If C has its own tendencies, then F must have tendencies as well. And if S can have

different qualities and strengths, the same must be true for F. Departing from these assumptions, we can make two or three deductions that will have bearing not only on the facts of our everyday experience but also in the realm of literature, where their application will lead us to some extremely interesting conclusions.

a. In the absence of a powerful S, F will proceed to F' in accordance with its own natural tendencies. The natural tendency is established by experience, such that F will move on to the F' in the order determined by the most oft repeated experience. In other words, our consciousness moves from one content to another through habit of association, and it moves in an order and sequence that are also determined by habit. This process is itself repeated over and over. For example, when the image of a rickshaw emerges in our consciousness, we are bound by habit to call the image of the rickshaw puller into the focus of our consciousness. Since, under normal circumstances, most people's consciousness is not subject to any special S, the sequence of their associations usually proceeds in this natural fashion. In this sense their consciousness emerges in an imitative fashion and proceeds according to convention. Because the imitative consciousness tends to coincide with conventional consciousness in terms of content and order, there is nothing stopping us from substituting one for the other. There are innumerable examples of this in literature. For some people the phrase "the birds are singing" inevitably calls to mind the line "in the Eastern sky." In the same way the words "this day" are always accompanied by "the weather is fine." I will have more to say about this problem in a later section.

b. If (a) was the instance in which F moves most easily according to its own tendencies on to F', in other cases we find that F will select and move toward the F' that offers the least resistance. That is to say, when there are multiple suggestions at hand, it will choose to focus on the F' that is least damaging to its own tendencies. That which does not damage its own tendency is, of course, something in close proximity to itself, so we can safely assume that the F' toward which F moves will bear some similarity to it. (The reader will have noted that the relation between [a] and [b] is similar to that between the imitative consciousness and the consciousness of talent.) Once we have understood how the similarity between F and F' facilitates the transformation from one to the other, it will be self-evident why the literary techniques discussed earlier are necessary, how they occur to the writer, and why they afford pleasure to the reader. Among the literary techniques discussed, I listed four types of association. Our examination of the qualities of each of these types of association simply involved taking an F' in order to explain a given F. Whatever part of F might have been the subject of our explanation, the fact that we were able to explain it using F' would no doubt indicate that the latter had some points in common with F. Having something in common means that the resistance of F' to the tendency of F is minimal and that the transition from one to the other is an easy one. It is perhaps for this reason that we resort to these techniques not only to add F' to F—and thereby to magnify the effect—but also because they help make the transitions smoother. (The fourth type of association is based purely on phonetics, which, as I have already discussed, makes it very different from the other three. But there is no reason to consider it an exception in terms of the effect it has [in a certain sense] in promoting transitions.)

What can be said about the four types of association can also be said, with a few minor changes, about the techniques of harmony and contrast, so I will say nothing more of them here. From all of this we can draw one conclusion. The transformation of F should not be sudden or abrupt, working better in a gradual fashion. What this conclusion has to tell us about the nature of historical change will be discussed in a later section.

c. When F has a certain tendency but is unable to develop in accordance with this tendency in the manner of (a) and also unable to develop in a way that satisfies some but not all of its inherent tendencies in the manner of (b), it may transform into an F' that is either unrelated to or in opposition to its own nature. Given that this new F' has completely ignored the tendency of F, it must be very forceful indeed. If it is not so powerful, it must wait until the development of F gradually loses momentum of its own accord. We can easily find examples of (1) by examining any section of the continuous waves of consciousness of our daily lives, whether we are laughing and enjoying ourselves, be it during the day or during the night. Whether associations in the manner of (a) or of (b) are more or less numerous will depend on the particular disposition of the individual, but it seems that people whose physical and mental activity is vigorous are comparatively more prone to (c) than those who are old and infirm. The F and the F' that form the initial and final phases of this type of transformation are contrasted, in a certain sense, with the F and F' that one finds in the case of the general populace. If all other points are the same in the transformation from F to F', F'', F''' and on to F^n, it is the contrast between

F and F' that will provide the greatest stimulus to change. In the case of (b) F' comes to consciousness because it is similar to F and provides little resistance. But in the present case things are very different since F' contrasts highly with F and exercises a powerful stimulus: it attacks F by surprise and occupies its place to become F'. I will for the moment leave aside the question of how this works on the level of history and set it as my task to provide a couple of familiar examples from literature. In my explanation of (b) above, I mentioned as examples the four types of literary association and harmony. I hope it will be helpful to the reader to understand the relation between the two if I follow the same method here and draw examples of literary techniques to explain what is going on in the case of (c). "Counter-position" [taichihō] was the sixth literary technique I listed above, which I further divided into emphasis, softening, contrast, and incongruity. Because contrast [katsuihō] properly belongs to (b) in our current discussion, I will not consider it here. But emphasis and incongruity [futsui-hō] (particularly emphasis) are based in precisely this kind of association. The main point of emphasis is to place an F' after F and to magnify the value of the former through contrast. However, because it is the strength of the stimulus that must thus magnify the value, the force of the stimulus must be the cause of F' overwhelming F. In other words, the force of the stimulus facilitates the transition from F to F'. The same can be said, with a few minor differences, about incongruity, and so I will spare the reader any further analysis here. In precise terms there would seem to be no problem with (2) either. This is so because we have hypothesized that when an unrelated or opposite F' takes the place of F, it must await the gradual development and eventual depletion of the momentum of F. The fact that F develops so gradually means that F is, in fact, A and B—that there is a series of A, B . . . in the interval between F and F' so that the transition cannot be said to be immediate. If we change our perspective slightly and regard the problem from another direction, we will see that this case is, in fact, worth thinking about. If we assume that F naturally exhausts itself, it will appear that F is transforming itself. But if F does not change its focus while F' slowly moves from the subconscious to the edges of consciousness and then gradually toward the focal point of consciousness, we can say that in the end the two are *effectively the same*. There is such a thing in Zen as sudden enlightenment, whereby one approaches enlightenment without knowing it over many years of training, only to wake up one morning and find the whole universe transformed. This kind of experience is not limited to Zen. It happens in daily life as well. (I do not see any reason why Zen alone should have a special right to such experience.) We call the transformation instantaneous only because we are not aware of the new consciousness as it emerges. On the surface it appears sudden, but in reality it is gradual. It is a slow and steady transformation. In history we call this transformation a reaction [*handō*]. A reaction according to this interpretation is thus not something that happens suddenly but rather a gradual phenomenon. At this point there is no need for a detailed consideration of the transformation of F in historical terms. But we can find an example, as we did earlier, in a corner of the literary world. The technique of softening [*kanwahō*] that I mentioned as one of the techniques of opposition is an excellent example of this sort of transformation. In softening one adds an F' to F that will dampen the impact of the latter. Dampening the impact demonstrates that F is too heavy (when F is immobile) or that it is extreme (when it is mobile). When F is too heavy the contrasting F' will eventually crowd into focus with great speed, and when F is extreme the contrasting F' will gradually take over. In both cases it is the same in that F has exhausted itself. In this sense the technique of softening has not only the effect of softening but is also one of the most useful methods for the transformation of F.

I have tried to investigate the transformation of group consciousness by first going back to the principle of wave motion that forms its basis and clarifying the rules of its transformation, following which I have used my so-called literary techniques as examples. In this way we have discovered that all of the methods of expression I have cited are applicable. However, the last method—that of realism/sketching—does not work by using an F' to explain an F (it does not work by combining two elements) and for this reason it could not be used as an example. This is because transformation cannot be theorized without at least two separate states of F and F'.

The laws of transformation that we have discussed in this chapter can be summarized as follows.

1. The transformation of our consciousness is governed by the law of suggestion.
2. The transformation of our consciousness normally takes place through a competition among "a large number of Ⓕ's." In some instances there can also be competition between F and F'.

3. This competition is natural. It is necessary. And when this competition among different suggestions is absent, then

4. We merely repeat the content and sequence of consciousness determined by habit and convention.

5. Transformation is gradual and not sudden or dramatic. (Reaction may appear sudden on the surface but it is, in fact, orderly and gradual.)

6. When the transformation is sudden, this means that there is a contrast between the two successive states. (In cases where it is not about contrast, there must be an equal or greater stimulus.)

The wave movement of the focus of consciousness applies to any temporal span, be it a minute, an hour, a day, a year, a decade, or the duration of an individual's life. What one can say about the transformations that take place over the course of an individual's life one can also say about the transformations of group consciousness among individuals who live in the same time. As I argued at the beginning of this section, mutual consciousness accumulates to form a vast river of time that transforms and develops across spans of centuries in chains of cause and effect for all eternity. If this proves untrue in the real world, my entire theory will crumble at its foundations and I will have no other piece to play. All I can do is look closely into my heart at each instant, look back over the years of my experience and that of others, look forward to the spirit of the age, and open my eyes wide to read the book of history and examine the vicissitude of the ages. Having established that my theories are not far from the facts, I will not hesitate to apply the principles arrived at in the preceding sections to my own life, to that of others, and to the whole current age until I can envision the vast and wondrous unfolding of history itself and apply it to the billions of people acting separately and together, moving and transforming themselves as a group in the awesome and irresistible vortex of history to which we have given the name of providence.

Chapter 3: Application of the Principles (Part 1)

The purpose of this chapter is to take two or three of the principles we established in the previous chapter and apply them to actual cases as a way of illustrating the transformation of group consciousness. We will take our examples from the lives of individuals and also from historical eras. In most cases our discussion will remain within the confines of literature, but we will also find that the import of our argument extends to all kinds of manifestations of human dynamism. I do this not out of a gratuitous desire to complicate matters but because the range of applicability is itself so expansive that things naturally relate to one another.

Suggestion is natural and necessary. When we read the general history of an era, we can recognize that its dynamic manifestation has a peculiar quality all its own. This is true not only of history in general. We can find the same striking phenomenon in literary history as well. (One gains the same impression when viewing the career of an individual writer of literature.) One era (or author) will be comparatively rich in sensuous materials, and the life of literature will be devoted to extolling the beauty of nature. Another age might be more concerned with human affairs, such that every book written must tell stories of loyalty and filial piety to the exclusion of all else. Or people might be so preoccupied with tales of the supernatural that a work in which nothing of the bizarre or mysterious appears is not considered literary. It may be that no work is considered worthy that does not apply some philosophical principle to each and every interaction—that does not, for example, discover the transience of the tumbleweed in even the smallest detail.

But these are all very crude explanations. When the characteristics of an age are complex and difficult to discern, many-faceted and hard to grasp, the reader or critic may well be aware of them but unable to articulate them. They may manage to articulate them, albeit not thoroughly. Or their explanation may be thorough but not clear. They may end up utterly confused and spouting a lot of blather. But this is the fault of the critic and the reader and not because the age does not have its peculiar quality. This is because, despite its lack of clarity, they will be aware of it at the back of their minds. It will appear obscurely in their mind's eye, like villages glimpsed on a map that is submerged in water. No one could fail to note the difference of tone when comparing a Chinese and a Western poem. But they might falter if asked to come up with a precise characterization of the difference. It is hard to imagine anyone who could fail to make the distinction, but if such a person were to exist, they could not be considered a critic or a reader of poetry at all. The disability of such a person would go beyond the likes of color blindness to approximate full-out blindness. The characteristic of an age may not be a simple matter of light or dark, complexity or simplicity, difficulty or ease; but it will most certainly exist. (It is the first responsibility of the critic to have a clear sense of this characteristic. Having sensed what it is, he or she can then compare it to periods that came before and after and for the first time understand its positioning, its value in a certain sense, and also begin to grasp some of the practical logic [*jissoku*] of its transformation. This is the second duty of the critic.)

Just as it is clear that this characteristic will exist, it is also undeniable that it will change. The cause of change is as easily discerned in discrete parts of the individual consciousness as it is in the totality of an individual consciousness and in the consciousness of the entire group. To put it simply and subjectively, we might offer the obvious explanation that consciousness changes because people grow tired of one thing and move on to others [*ken'en*]. In his *Pain, Pleasure, and Aesthetics* Marshall argues that the difference between pleasure and pain has to do with time.[8] He argues that there is no qualitative difference between the two, but that one will change to the other with the passage of a certain amount of time. On this view, pleasure and pain are not objectively different. Rather, it is in the nature of our constitution [*soshiki*] that the duration of a pleasurable feeling past a certain point will transform it into pain. Not being a psychologist myself, I do not have the expertise to evaluate Marshall's claim in detail. But it would seem to be born out by our own daily experience as well as on the larger scale of the successive trends of the world of letters. Of course, we can also discover instances that contradict this principle. But it is clear that upon closer examination it is easy to find that this psychology does, in fact, hold true within a given sphere. When I was living in a boarding house in London, there was an old man of more than eighty years living in the same establishment. I say an old man, but he was really more like a machine. His life was so regular that not only did he rise, sleep, and take his meals at the same hour every day, but he also took his walk at the same time and place and read his newspaper at the same time and in the same chair. I have no idea from what age he began to live his life in this manner, but it was natural for him to persist for years in behavior that other people would have to change after a week or two. When I first observed this man, I wondered how he could bear such monotony. I thought his behavior quite mysterious and difficult to understand. But once I entered into his circle and had a chance to observe him more closely, I easily discovered that what had so astounded me at first was not such a different world after all. This old man inhabited a monotonous sphere and never took one step outside it. When seen from the outside, his world appeared unimaginably tedious. But if one took a step inside that sphere, one could see that it was changing all the time, or, rather, that he was pursuing change. Take his newspaper, for example. It would indeed be monotonous to read the same newspaper at the same time and in the same place every day, but in fact the content of the paper was different 365 days a year. While this old man was admittedly an eccentric the likes of which one rarely comes across, there are actually countless people who resemble him in one way or another. A specialist with his specialty and an artist with his art are both like this. Fujii Chikugai was a poet who for his entire life wrote nothing but Chinese poetry consisting of four lines.[9] Sosen was a painter who painted nothing but monkeys.[10] And there are others who paint only tigers or orchids and bamboo. There are people who read *Faust* in their youth and go on to read it dozens of times over. The most interesting cases are those aficionados of *jōruri*, *rakugo*, or Noh, who draw a tight little circle around themselves and never tire of playing around inside it. But if you look closely, you will see that they are all like that old man in London, who sought out variety and change within a monotonous world. It is for this reason that I say that characteristics must change. And the reason for this change can be summed up in the notion of boredom [*ken'en*] referred to earlier. Boredom is a common enough phenomenon, but it is boredom that governs the behavior of human beings and there is nothing to be done about it. Taste in literature never tarries long in the same place. It must always develop and change. But since this transformation is governed by boredom, it does not mean that it necessarily progresses from the vulgar to the lofty. (That the transformation of taste does not always entail development is an inevitable conclusion of the application of Marshall's theory to this question.) All we can say is that change must happen. Transformation is a factual truth.

Having recognized that change will never cease and that this is a truth born out by the facts, we arrive at two propositions. The first is that suggestion is necessary. Without suggestion there can be no transformation. The inability to change results in pain. The second proposition is that suggestion is natural. It is suggestion that makes change possible. And change is a fact. If there had been no changes to Malthus's theory of population, we would be condemned to repeat its propositions in the same form as they have come down to us. But then along came Darwin, who spent ten years going over the same ground as Malthus until, finally, he was inspired with the new F of the theory of evolution and the world lurched in a new direction. Darwin was transformed as an individual and so were the minds of his whole generation. Without transformations of this sort our reason will stagnate in a single place and pain and suffering will result. Carlyle's writing was incisive and original, and he commanded richer powers of expression than any other man of his era.[11] But Carlyle's day would not last forever, and soon he would yield his place to Meredith, whose style was even more expertly forged.[12] Thus, as C., one of the great masters, was rising to the very summit of the wave of contemporary novel writing, he was not only offering his writing to the consciousness of the world but was also planting suggestions for M. C. did not perish, but neither did those who followed in his wake content themselves with extolling the virtues of C. alone. Some obvious examples would be the way Shakespeare drew from Holinshed or Tennyson elaborated on the legend of Arthur. Those who are the first to make something out of a suggestion are called pioneers. When the consciousness realized by a pioneer gathers momentum and infects the imitative consciousness of a generation, the waves of the group consciousness are stimulated into action and we move into a new realm. Literary history offers an excellent example of this in the way the Classicism of the eighteenth century gradually faded from the focus of consciousness to be replaced by Romanticism. When the great tempest of the French Revolution hit the group consciousness and hoisted the standard of liberty, equality, and fraternity uppermost in the minds of the general populace, the consciousness of the literary world responded by entering the stormy fray of politics itself. Dowden's *French Revolution and English Literature* provides a detailed account of the relations between the two.[13] This kind of transformation is a cross-section of the tempest that is stirred up when the political group consciousness is transmitted to the literary group consciousness. If the literary world rejects the transformation of taste that results, poetry and prose will lose their vitality and become like so much grain rotting away in the stores of a too peaceful nation. No matter how hard they might push or pull, a thousand men of talent and a hundred geniuses will not suffice to produce even a single revolution of the sluggish wheels of conventional consciousness. Thus, we are governed by the characteristics of the age we live in, and to have talent or genius is only one condition for success. Those who are born in an age of comparatively dramatic transformation can rise to greatness overnight. But in an age when consciousness changes slowly and sluggishly, the heroes and the brilliant minds are apt to live out their lives in vain, caught in traffic with the mediocre.

I stated earlier that transformation is natural and necessary. I also pointed out that it is nothing more than boredom that governs this transformation. For this reason it is natural to assume that when we compare the F of one period to the F' of the next, the latter does not necessarily represent an advance or improvement over the former. This is all the more true in literature, where taste is of such vital importance. In science F' often uses the F of the preceding period and supplements it with something new. Because this new element is added according to the demands of reason, in one sense it can be said that F' is more advanced than F. But in the case of the transformation of taste, the tendency is not to supplement what came before but to erect something entirely new and thus to move away from the earlier stage. Of course, because one is not free to abandon the earlier stage altogether, certain similarities will persist. Thus, F' is not necessarily an advancement over F. (It would be extremely useful to examine the transformations of taste to determine whether they represent development [*hattatsu*] or mere change [*henka*]. My shallow learning affords me neither the materials nor the knowledge necessary to consider this in a very thorough fashion. But if I were to apply what meager brain power I do have to the question, I might venture to say the following. When the transformation of F takes place within a single sphere, one can identify some elements of progress. But if the transformations possible within that sphere are exhausted or abandoned and, under certain conditions, transformation moves into another sphere, the relation between F and F' will no longer display any signs of it being a matter of progress or development.) I am emphasizing this point because the vulgar crowds tend to look at the trends of the time and fail to realize that they are the result of mere likes and dislikes, which leads to the misunderstanding that every change in taste necessarily represents a development for the better. In other words, they think of their own tastes at the moment as the most perfect and mistakenly take them to be the only standard. Of course, it is perfectly natural to render judgment using one's own current tastes as the standard, and far be it from me to criticize anyone for so doing. I simply want to point out the danger of failing to understand that while one's standards may apply in one sphere, they must not be extended to other contexts. People who do not understand this have the unfortunate tendency to evaluate all kinds of things that lie outside their ken based on their own standards. The standards and tastes that one has at any given moment mostly fall within a single sphere. But when one traces back the waves of development that led to the acquisition of tastes within this sphere (to the point where they become one's standards), one will find not only the tastes from this sphere but also those of many other spheres from which the current ones have flowed. All of this is to say that we have acquired our current tastes only by passing through the spheres of numerous others. But it would be a terrible mistake simply to look to the past of one's consciousness and assume that because it lies in the past it is necessarily less evolved than it is at present. It does not require an expert to know whether the tastes that lie in one's past have changed by degree or are different in nature. To conclude that the tastes of the past are childish in comparison with those of today, particularly when the tastes in question are of a different quality entirely, is never acceptable even if such a judgment is made only with regard to one's own consciousness.

Sir W. M. Conway wrote:

The history of art relates to the succession of styles, not the stages of a long development. Civilization may steadily increase, the political organization of peoples may grow continuously more complex and efficient, education may spread downward, the standard of Life may rise, but Art takes a course of its own. No possible growth of civilization will give us another Sophocles, Shakespeare, or Raphael. Artists equally great may arise, but they will never surpass these men in their own kind, nor anyway rival them. The great artists that are to come will be great in some new fashion. The great schools of the future will not express the old ideals in a better way, but new ideals in a new way.

Individual styles develop and decay, but styles merely succeed and do not surpass one another. The ideal of any period expresses the joy of the people of that period, and there is no evolution of joy. The emotion is forever the same, but called forth by ever-varying stimulus.... (139–40)

But from the beginning up till now men have changed their ideal from age to age, by modifying it from moment to moment. The faith of one generation has differed from the faith of another. Enthusiastic preaching founds what infidelity in turn destroys....[14] Permanence in repose, triumph in victory, perfection of form, grandeur of ideal character, superhuman majesty, boundless pity and love; these and a thousand more have been the Ideals, which men have worshipped and loved, lived and died for, painted and sculpted and sung, each in its turn, since man became the creature that we partly know. (141–42)[15]

There is more than enough in Conway's theory to support my own. But because his purpose is to show how ideals succeed one another, he has not gone into much depth as to how transformation takes place within a single sphere (or a single ideal). I want to focus here on his proposition that once we have developed to a certain extent within a specific sphere and made the decision to consider that this level of development will be our standard, that standard will only be applicable to the successive periods within this sphere. People may start out with this position and critique everything that lies within one sphere, but they then overstep their boundaries and end up invading other spheres. In literature this kind of invasion happens all the time. The invaders do not see the crime in what they are doing and the invaded are inclined to accept their pronouncements and aspersions without resistance. The chaos that presents itself might appear worrisome, but on closer inspection we will see that there is nothing forced or unnatural about this confusion of spheres. Things are very different when it is a matter of taste. Whether the object of our aesthetic critique is a painting or a poem, there is no need for us to accept the command that we remain within a single sphere when exercising our critique. Length is the sphere in which the long and the short are measured, and quantity is the sphere in which we consider weight. It is not possible to sit in the sphere of length and consider weight, and it is a waste of time to sit in the sphere of weight and measure long and short. For this reason those who are interested in length and weight must remain in the same sphere. However, with painting and poetry, no matter what school or style, we have the freedom to weigh in from whatever sphere we choose. To say we have that freedom is to say that we can make our own critique no matter what sphere we are in. The most powerful aesthetic is the one that sits snugly at the focus of our present consciousness. And this aesthetic is one of many existing within a single sphere. For example, there is currently a school of novelists which holds that the ideal of the novel is to present *a kind of truth* about life. The focus of consciousness of these people (who can be found in Europe and in Japan) is dominated, in terms of taste, by this one standard, and they tend to judge every piece of writing from this angle. The strange thing is that every work they write about can indeed be sufficiently critiqued from this perspective. This is because the differences between individual artistic works are not as clear as the differences between liquids and solids, which can be understood only according to certain uniform standards. But *the truth of life* is only one of many aesthetic standards. The trend of the time has caused us to linger a while over this particular aesthetic ideal, but it does not represent progress. We cannot help but hold *the truth of life* as our standard because many of us have accepted it, according to a certain relation of cause-and-effect, as the taste of the current age. Our ability to evoke this truth and to critique it has certainly progressed somewhat owing to the fact that our taste and consciousness have been able to achieve a certain amount of developmental change within the same sphere. For this reason all works can be critiqued, and we can come up with at least something to say about any work according to this standard. But this depiction of *the truth of life* is a matter of contemporary taste (in other words, it is a trend). For this reason anyone who claims that it is *appropriate* to critique all works with this one standard because today's tastes are more developed than those of the past is sadly mistaken. These are people who do not understand the principle of the transformation of consciousness with regard to taste and who assume that because their own tastes have developed their entire lives, from childhood to adulthood, within the confines of a single sphere, the same must be true for the taste of humanity itself over the ages. In the previous book I classified literary materials into four types. I do not know whether these four categories were the right ones or not, but if there are, in fact, four distinct types of material, it would be easy to arrive at ideals with regard to each of them. These four types of ideals would then be ideals for literature as well. But *the truth of life* only relates to one of these ideals—that of intellectual materials (of which it is only one component). It is possible to critique anything that expresses this ideal on the basis of this ideal. But to judge something whose goal is to express some other ideal in terms of this one is to go where one does not belong. It is not an intentional invasion but rather a result of the confusion and chaos that comes of an inability to recognize the existence of boundaries. It is certainly possible to judge me as a teacher according to the ideal of the teacher. But to anyone who would use that same ideal to judge me as a friend, as a parent or child, or as a citizen, I would say, "If you want to critique the different me's by the same standard, you won't fail in doing so, but your critiques will clearly not be able to differentiate their objects."

I have already stated that suggestion is necessary. I have also argued that it is natural. I pointed out that change takes places as a result of boredom. For this reason change does not always mean that progress and current tastes are more developed than those of the past. When there is development, it is possible only within the same sphere. I argued that it was a mistake to judge something in one sphere while standing in another. Thus, we inevitably face the problem of how aesthetic judgment can be possible. The purpose of this chapter was not necessarily to consider such a method, but my pen has naturally brought me here and I will close the chapter with a short summary.

The taste of the present is the standard for everyone. This is not because it deserves to be the standard. It has simply become the standard naturally for lack of any other. When the taste of the present is such that it can be limited to a single sphere, it will not be able to escape from that sphere to serve as a standard for anything else. If the tastes of the present are diverse, it is possible to place one's focus in a number of spheres simultaneously and make judgments based on the standard of the best that can be achieved in each sphere. Those who are able freely to move their focus through a number of spheres are known as writers, artists, and critics with a broad range. The works of those with a narrow range can be exhausted with a few words, just as the arguments of narrow critics can be summed up in a pair of phrases. Being a writer, artist, or critic of broad range requires a freedom and range of movement and transformation. The freedom of transformation is a matter of innate talent, a natural gift. And the range of transformation is determined by how much one reads, thinks, listens, and observes.

Translated by Keith Vincent

PART TWO

OTHER WRITINGS ON LITERARY THEORY, 1907–14

1907–14

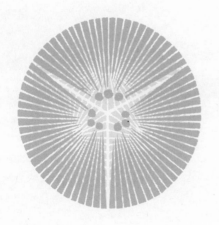

Statement on Joining the *Asahi*

In April 1907, Sōseki resigned from Tokyo Imperial University and the First Higher School and joined the Asahi *newspaper. The contract stipulated a remuneration of two hundred yen per month and a twice-yearly bonus, with all fictional works to appear in that paper. It also left him free to publish nonfiction works such as* Theory of Literature. *Sōseki's resignation from the elite university to take up a position in what was still considered a vulgar profession shocked many. He explained his decision in the following short article, which was originally published in the pages of the* Asahi *newspaper. It has become one of his most famous pieces of nonfiction.*

Since I resigned from the university and joined the *Asahi* newspaper, everyone I meet has a surprised look on their faces. Among them are some who ask me my reasons. There are some who praise my momentous decision. Personally I had not thought that quitting the university and becoming a newspaper man was such a particularly wondrous occurrence.[1] The question of whether or not I would succeed as a newsman was doubtful from the start. It is natural if people expect me to fail, saying, in surprise, that it's reckless to alter the course of ten or more years in a single morning.[2] I admit that I surprised even myself on that point. Nevertheless, if you are professing surprise because I relinquished such a great honor as

---

Nyūsha no ji (Tokyo *Asahi* newspaper, 1907)

that of a university position, then I would ask you to desist. A university may well be the breeding ground of scholars of distinction. It may be the hiding place of such worthies as professors and holders of doctoral degrees. It may be a place where one can become an imperial appointee if one perseveres for twenty or thirty years.[3] It may be a place with various other advantages. If you think about it like this, it's a fine place indeed. As for the applicants who slip in through the Red Gate[4] and try to enter a course of study—not given to calculation, I am ignorant of their exact number—there are so many of them that you could easily waste a great deal of time by walking about and questioning each one. One can understand what a fine place the university is even from this fact. I also am quite in agreement. But by "agreement" I mean only that I agree with the fact that the university is a fine place. You should not jump to the conclusion that I have expressed any notion that journalism is not a fine occupation.

If being a newspaperman is a profession, then being a university man is also a profession. If it were not a profession, then there would surely be no need for the desire to become a professor or a holder of the doctoral degree. There would surely be no need to receive a raise in one's monthly salary. There would surely be no need to be made an imperial appointee. The university is a profession just as the newspaper is a profession. If the newspaper is a vulgar profession, then the university is also a vulgar profession. The only difference is that one means doing business as an individual and the other means doing business as part of the government.

I lectured at the university for four years. The circumstances were such that as of this April I had fulfilled my obligatory period of service, that is, twice the two years I spent in the West by government order. Even though my obligatory period of service had passed, if I had otherwise been unable to support myself, it would have been my intention to cling fast and hold firm, not letting go even to the point of death. While in this grim frame of mind, I was suddenly consulted by the *Asahi* newspaper as to whether I would join their company. When I asked what my responsibilities would be, they said it would be fine if I just supplied compositions related to the literary arts, in suitable quantities at suitable times. For me, whose life and soul consist in writing about literature, there could be no greater blessing than this, no conditions so agreeable, no occupation so honorable. It would bear no relation to the question of whether I might succeed or not. It would bear no relation to striving and sweating, troubling one's mind over things like professorships, doctoral degrees, and imperial appointments.

When I was lecturing at the university, I was beset by incessantly howling dogs, which was most unpleasant. Half the reason why my lectures were so awful was because of these dogs. On no account can I imagine it was due to something like my lack of scholarship. It is most regrettable for the students, but as it was all the fault of the dogs, I would ask you to take your complaints to them.

The most agreeable thing about the university was the time I spent looking at the newly arrived magazines and other materials in the reading room of the library. However, given the press of work it is a great pity that I could not make as much use of this as I would have liked. It is also unfortunate that whenever I entered the reading room, the library staff in the next room would thoughtlessly speak, laugh, and joke about in loud voices. Attempting to halt their elegant amusement was an enormous task. One time I respectfully wrote a letter to the university president, Mr. Tsuboi, humbly asking for his action in the matter.[5] The president took no notice. This is the other half of the reason why my lectures were so awful. It is most regrettable for the students, but since it is the library staff and the university president who are to blame, I would ask that if you have a complaint, take it up with them. To have it thought that I am lacking in scholarship would be exceedingly troublesome.

As far as the newspaper is concerned, they say that there is no need for me to show up at the office. It will be enough if I do my work every day in my own study. Doubtless there are many dogs in my neighborhood as well, and people will undoubtedly appear who will cause an uproar like the library staff. But that has nothing whatever to do with the *Asahi* newspaper. No matter how unpleasant, no matter how disturbing these things may be, I will be able to do my work for the *Asahi* newspaper with enjoyment. Truly, if an employee can do his work for his employer with enjoyment, then this may be called a splendid situation.

As an instructor at the university, I was receiving an annual salary of eight hundred yen. With many children and high rent, I could not possibly live on eight hundred yen. I had no choice but to run about between two or three other schools, barely managing to make ends meet.[6] Even a Sōseki will suffer from nervous exhaustion if worn out by such ceaseless activity.[7] On top of that, I had to write. I will allow that I may be writing to suit my own fancy, but the Sōseki of late cannot feel he is alive unless he is writing something. And that wasn't all. If I didn't read books for my teaching, or for the cultivation of my own mind, I felt shamed before the world. It was for these reasons that I was reduced to a state of nervous exhaustion.

Over at the newspaper, I have been banned from earning money as a teacher. Instead, they will give me enough salary so as not to suffer from want of funds. If I can make enough to get by, I will no longer need to suffer from the excruciating intricacies of English words like "that" and "it." Even if I were told not to quit teaching, I would definitely quit. The very next day after I did quit, a weight was suddenly lifted from my shoulders and an unprecedented amount of air filled my lungs.

On quitting the university, I went to Kyoto for a visit. There I met my old acquaintances—fields, mountains, temples, and shrines—all of them so much more pleasant than the classroom. A nightingale, performing acrobatics on the branch, swelled with its first song of spring. Turning my heart to the sky above, I exhaled the dust of the last four years from the depths of my lungs. All this, too, I owed to becoming a newspaperman.

There is a saying that goes: "Heart is won by heart." For the sake of the *Asahi* newspaper, which placed this eccentric in an environment perfectly suited to eccentrics, it is now my happy duty to work to the best of my eccentric ability.

Translated by Rachael Hutchinson

Philosophical Foundations of the Literary Arts

What follows is the edited transcript of a lecture Sōseki delivered in 1907 at Tokyo Art College. Originally published in the Asahi *newspaper, it provides a more accessible survey of many of the theoretical issues that Sōseki had expounded at greater length in his* Theory of Literature, *which was published shortly before the lecture. There are, however, subtle differences in the positions Sōseki takes here and in the published book. The transcript appears in its entirety.*

(When I was invited to give a lecture at the inaugural gathering of the Tokyo Art College's Literary Society, I accepted on condition that—since I am an employee of this *Asahi* newspaper—my remarks should be published here. Although I knew it was an imposition, I asked the chair to provide a stenographer. The chair kindly agreed, and four or five days after my talk the transcript was forwarded to me, together with a kind message. But when I glanced at it in its raw form, I found it a muddle, unsuitable for publication or for offering up to readers; the overall structure was lacking and in places my turn of phrase was awkward. I had no choice but to rewrite the entire thing. When I set to work on the transcript, every section seemed to require amplification, and the manuscript ended up twice as long.

Bungei no tetsugakuteki kiso (Tokyo *Asahi* newspaper, 1907)

It is in the nature of this sort of argument that if one does not read it all the way through in one sitting, one's train of thought will be interrupted, the lines of reasoning will get tangled, and the natural flow of ideas will be impeded. Nonetheless, the space available on the pages of a newspaper is limited, so, despite the inconvenience, I will divide this up into daily installments of one or two columns in length.

The work that follows, composed under these conditions, maintains the form of a transcript from a public lecture, but it can just as well be considered a new essay drafted by me, the lecturer, for my company. It marks my second appearance before our readers, after my "Statement on Joining the *Asahi*." As an employee of this company, I believe I have an obligation to the greater public to outline my views on the literary arts and to clarify my beliefs and aspirations.)

I am a man who has not often delivered public speeches—in fact, it would be more accurate to say almost never. I am frequently asked to do so, but up to now I have turned down those requests. I simply didn't want to. On top of that, I didn't feel capable of doing it. Classroom lectures are another matter. Until quite recently I delivered them on a daily basis, and I like to think I am fairly proficient at those. Unfortunately, however, the request today was for a public speech, and so our prospects are fairly bleak.

In fact, when Mr. Ōmura called on me the other day to ask me to give this speech, I at first declined. Realizing from the start that it would turn out badly, I knew how sorry I would feel for him if I accepted. But he seemed unwilling to take no for an answer. He kept urging me to do it. "Just do it," he said. "You can talk about anything you like, just do it—please do it!" Still reluctant, I racked my brains—whereupon he announced that it wasn't even necessary for me to give a speech. If I wasn't going to give a speech, I asked, what exactly would I do? He graciously replied that all I had to do was attend. If I merely showed my face, he would be satisfied. If all I had to do was show my face, there was no need to hesitate, and so I cheerfully made up my mind and promised to appear. That is how I come to stand before you today. Unfortunately, my face is not all that much to look at. Merely offering you this face seems inadequate, so I suppose I should say something. I still find it impossible to adopt the formal tones appropriate to a speech—"Ladies and Gentlemen of the audience!"—so my talk will end up sounding more like a classroom lecture than a formal speech. Even for classroom lectures, however, my usual policy is never to speak impromptu but instead to write everything down beforehand and then read it aloud in the classroom from beginning to end. But for today's talk I have had no time to do that, nor any opportunity to pull my thoughts together. As a result, even though my remarks will be something like a classroom lecture—a form in which I pride myself at having some skill—the outlook for today's talk is nonetheless not promising.

I find it quite interesting that you here at the Art College have formed this literary society in an effort to cultivate your knowledge and taste in the field of literature, beyond the confines of your own artistic specialties. Moreover, as President Masaki has just remarked, the relation between literature and art is quite deep. That you, the representatives of the latter, should take an interest in the field of literature and would even consider the sorts of slipshod talks that my kind has to offer—well, in terms of bringing our two fields into contact, it is a great honor for me to be the first to be chosen to set his views before you. That is why I was determined to give this speech today, even though I doubt my ability to carry it out. In pointing out that I made you a pledge I am ill equipped to make good on, I do not mean for you to feel somehow obliged to me. I am fully cognizant of the great honor you do me by inviting me to appear here. Nonetheless, I warn you again that I have no talent for making speeches, and that even as a classroom lecture my remarks will fall short. They will, I think, be painful to listen to. I ask your indulgence in advance.

With that, let me begin. When I say "Let me begin," it may sound like I am launching into a formal presentation, but that is hardly the case. I have before me only three or four pages of rough notes. My remarks here will be nothing more than the contents of these three or four pages. If I were to read them straight through, it would all be over in fifteen minutes. Even for a hastily improvised speech like this, that seems woefully inadequate. Therefore, I plan to proceed by expounding extemporaneously upon the contents of these three or four pages. I have no idea yet how or where I will expand them. At times I may take a detour and find myself stuck, unable either to go forward or return to my starting point. I will be using, that is, a most unpromising method of expansion. On top of that, my starting point will likely make little or no sense to you. So whatever happens here, please don't be surprised. As you listen, please rest assured that in my conclusion I do intend somehow to plunge down into the depths of the relationship between art and literature. Just now, in his speech, President Masaki referred to the "show-offy spirit of the ordinary hacks." The starting point of my talk may seem vaguely lofty, but at my destination I intend to settle down into the show-offy spirit of the ordinary hacks, right alongside President Masaki.

So, to begin with, I am standing here. All of you are sitting there. I am standing down here, while you are sitting up there. That I stand here like this and you sit there is a matter of fact. To state this factual matter differently, I am the self, whereas in relation to me you are something other than the self. To use a more complicated mode of expression, what we have here is an opposition between self and object. In sum, the world is made up of a mutual opposition between the self and objects. All of you surely feel that way, as do I. Everyone understands things in this way. Moreover, with me standing here like this and you sitting there like that, there exists between us a certain distance. It may be a distance of one or two *ken*, or perhaps even twenty *ken*. By the way, how big is this lecture hall? At any rate, it extends over a certain number of *tsubo*, and within that span I am standing and you are sitting.[1] This extension is called space. (You knew that without my telling you.) In sum, there is a dimension called space, and all objects occupy a certain position within it.

Second, today's speech began at one o'clock. I don't know when it will end, but I am fairly certain that at some point it will end. More than likely it will end before the sun goes down. I will make my haphazard remarks and then, after I finish, Mr. Ueda will take my place and give what will no doubt be a very interesting talk. After that we will adjourn. My talk and Mr. Ueda's speech are both events that will pass by, and without the dimension known as time this passing by could never take place. This, too, is something that is already clear and requires no special explanation.

Finally, there is the question of why I have appeared before you, running off at the mouth like this. I would be somewhat bothered if it were thought I had done so out of sheer whim or eccentricity. In fact, there are perfectly good reasons for my appearance here: the aforementioned kind invitation from Mr. Ōmura; my rather rash acceptance of the same; my sense of obligation after having accepted; and so forth. The result of all of these combined causal factors is, as you can see, my appearance before you, dressed in my frock coat. This sort of relationship, whether human or natural, is known as the law of cause and effect.

We may sum up as follows: in this world there exists an "I" and a "you," and we are located in a vast space, within which we each act out our roles in a drama that unfolds across time, an unfolding that is governed by the law of cause and effect—or something along those lines. We have to accept that there is an "I," a "you," something called "space," and something called "time," and that there exists a law of cause and effect that governs us. These are all self-evident to everyone—even to me.

And yet when we think about these things more carefully, they begin to appear doubtful. Quite doubtful, in fact. Ordinarily, of course, everyone accepts the above without question—as do I. But when we stand back from common sense and reflect more carefully, we begin to suspect that something is amiss here. Somehow this doesn't seem quite right. Why? Take the "I," for example: the I who stands before you in his frock coat and high collar, who seems to exist so solemnly, moustache and all, before you. In fact, the true nature of this "I" is quite problematic. You can see the frock coat and high collar with your eyes, you can touch them with your hands—and yet, of course, those are not me. These hands, these feet—the ones I scratch when they itch, that I rub when they hurt—in sum, is this body me? No, that doesn't seem right. There are feelings called "itchiness" and "pain." And there are sensations of scratching and patting. Other than those, we have nothing. What exists here is neither hand nor foot. What exists are phenomena of consciousness that, for convenience's sake, we call "hand" and "foot," just as we have phenomena of consciousness that we call "itchiness" and "pain." In sum, what exists is consciousness— and the activity that we call being conscious. Only this is certain. Anything beyond this we are unable to prove, but this much is clear, beyond dispute, and requires no proof. When you think about it this way, what we usually call "I" is not something that exists objectively out in the world. Rather, as a matter of convenience we give the name "I" to what is, in fact, a continuous stream of consciousness [*ishiki no renzoku*]. But why, then, you may ask, is it a convenience to go to all the trouble of positing this otherwise superfluous "I"? It is because once we posit this "I," then as its flip side we also posit the existence of something other than the self—the existence, that is, of "you." In sum, we establish the distinction between self and object. Despite the difficulty it entails, this is a necessary expediency.

In saying this I am denying not only the existence of the self (or what we commonly call the self) but also your existence. Despite the fact that there are a large number of you here listening today, you only seem to be here. I'm very sorry for you, but you don't actually exist. Perhaps you find this upsetting, but I'm laying down my fundamental arguments here, so please do me the favor of hearing them out as arguments. To put this in its most basic form, which may sound impertinent, apart from me you have no objective existence. I said apart from me. Yet this "me" also does not exist, at least not in the form of an "I"—and so how could you possibly exist? No matter how angry you may get about this, it won't change matters. You sit there. You sit there thinking that you are sitting there. Even I think that you are sitting there. But to say you are there is merely to say that I happen to think you are there. No matter how much I may want to go beyond simply thinking you are there, I am unable to prove anything beyond that. Usually when we want to ascertain the existence of something, we first examine it with our eyes. Having seen it with our eyes, we touch it with our hands. Then, after touching it, we may try smelling or tasting it. We might not need to go through all these steps to ascertain your existence, but, as I said earlier, when I see with my eyes or hear with my ears, in the most fundamental sense what I am actually doing is experiencing the consciousness of sight or hearing, and this consciousness cannot somehow be transformed into an independently existing object or person. If I look at or touch you, the image of students in black school uniforms with gold buttons appears—but only as a phenomenon in my conscious mind. I have no means of ascertaining your existence beyond that. This being the case, we can only conclude that if I don't exist, then neither do you. Consciousness is the only thing that can be said to exist—to really exist. When a gold button appears before my eyes, what we really have is the consciousness of a gold button. The ceiling of this hall is a bit sooty—because I am conscious of sootiness. This is not meant as a complaint, by the way. I'm not saying the ceilings at the Art College are sooty, only that I am conscious of sootiness. Of course, I can't prove the objective existence of that soot, so you shouldn't take offense.

That is the first point I wanted to make. If we set aside our daily common sense, when we look at the world of selves and things, we realize that we cannot claim that objects exist independently of the self, nor that the self exists independently of its objects. To put it another way, without the self there are no objects, and likewise without objects there can be no self. "Objects" and "self" necessarily appear in tandem. We use two different words to express them only to make things easier to understand and as a matter of fundamental principles. Since the two cannot, in fact, be distinguished from one another, we don't really need a separate word to express their mutually indistinguishable status. Accordingly, the only thing that clearly exists is consciousness. And we ordinarily refer to this continuous stream of consciousness by the name "life."

When I refer to a continuous stream here, it includes the sense that consciousness is in flux. To say that it is in flux is also to say that

1. there must be some distinct moments of consciousness
2. these various moments takes turns ebbing and flowing
3. insofar as this ebbing and flowing is apparent, the moments of consciousness must also be clear
4. the flux of consciousness must be governed by certain laws

But this already makes the problem too complicated, and this is not the occasion to bring up such a difficult topic, so I will simply proceed with my talk without discussing these, entrusting them to your own future studies. With regard to the last of the above four points—the principles behind the flux of consciousness—in book 5 of my *Theory of Literature* I have provided my own imperfect views on the subject, so perhaps you can refer to that. In fact, now that I think of it, why don't you all go right out today and order a copy of *Theory of Literature*. At any rate, what exists is consciousness. There might not be any objects or any self, but consciousness exists beyond a doubt. And this consciousness is continuous. We may or may not be able to explain through philosophy or evolutionary theory why it is continuous, but there can be no doubt that it is continuous. Having established this fact, I proceed to my next step.

If we pause here and recall the opening of my talk, we will find that something strange has happened. You'll remember that I prattled on at the start about how there is this thing called "I" and that there is also this thing called "you." I went on to claim that both of us were bumping around in this oddity known as space, and that we were paddling our way across this mystery called time, all the while under the strict control of a fearful thing known as the law of cause and effect. And yet when we stood back from common sense to ponder these matters, we seem to have reached precisely the opposite conclusions. It turns out that all of our benchmarks—objects, the self, and so forth—were missing from the start. We can't distinguish the world from the self; it's all become quite a tangle. I don't know exactly at what point this reversal took place, but we seem to have fallen into a glaring contradiction. (Space, time, and the law of cause and effect are also caught up in this reversal. For the purposes of this talk, however, I will take those up later, and their status will presently become clear.)

Why has this contradiction arisen? When we think about it carefully, nothing really can be said to exist, and yet, according to our common sense, the universe is so packed with the various forms of creation that you couldn't be rid of them all even if you tried. I'm not Mr. Tobari, but I can't help wanting to say, "Look, here is the world, and here is Chikufū.[2] Why has this contradiction arisen?" This is an enormous question. If I went to the trouble of trying to argue this in all its complexity, it would use up a great deal of your time. Out of necessity I can give only a very rough outline of the problem in the limited time I have. If some eminent philosopher were here listening, he would no doubt attack me, pointing out the flaws in what I have said. Nonetheless I somehow have to square away this huge problem in the short time allotted, and so, of course, I cannot possibly offer a full explication. Yes, I admit it: my imperfect rendering is imperfect. But shouldn't you at least admire my pluck? Besides, even if I were asked to give a more profound account and allotted all the time I needed, I don't think I'd be up to the task. I've done about as well as I can, I think.

Now, why has this contradiction arisen? It wouldn't be difficult to give a quick answer to this question. As I said before, what we call life consists of a continuity of consciousness. (To say "we" is misleading since it suggests the independent existence of self and other, but I use it here as a convenient shorthand.) Moreover, we seem unwilling to interrupt this continuity. In other words, we don't want to die. We wish nothing more than for this continuity to continue. I can't explain why we wish for this. Nobody can explain that. All we can do is acknowledge it as a fact. Of course, an advocate of evolutionary theory might say that this desire had gradually developed over a long period of time and might even be able to point out something about the process of its development. To wit, he could argue that all of the beings who did not possess this tendency, who did not conduct themselves in the world in conformity with this tendency, ended up dying out, and that those who remain today are the ones who were filled with a strong desire to live. This may be the reason that the type of people who cling desperately to life, even to the point of ugliness and indecisiveness, seem to thrive in our world. This, too, is only a partial explanation, but to proceed further and try to determine the ultimate cause behind this tendency is futile. It would require us to resort to something like a Zen koan, such as the one that asks: If all things can be returned to a single cause, then what is the cause of that cause? Schopenhauer refers to this tendency as humanity's blind will to live. That is a remarkably apt expression, and I am tempted to borrow it myself. Yet if I were to set this striking notion alongside my previous proposition about the continuity of consciousness, I would be undermining my own assertion that nothing exists except the continuity of consciousness. Regretfully, therefore, I will set this question aside and simply regard this tendency as one aspect of consciousness, that is, as one of its attributes. I will regard the concept of "this tendency" as being something that emerged only after a process of abstraction and considerable development. In the end, we can accept as fact only that "we seek continuity of consciousness." Stated more simply, we can accept as fact that "consciousness tends toward continuousness."

When we speak about consciousness, about continuity, and about a tendency for continuity, we inevitably imply both the unity of consciousness and its internal differentiation. Insofar as it is continuous, our consciousness must be continuous between A and B. That is to say, we must be able to distinguish clearly between two instances of consciousness, A and B. Moreover, to say that we can distinguish between them is also to mean that we can unify consciousness, or unify similar instances of consciousness. For example, take the form of consciousness we call "vision." This word was first coined only after—as a result of analysis that allowed us to distinguish our experiences of the consciousness of vision from our senses of touch or taste—we unified all of those experiences into a single form of consciousness. Once consciousness has been internally differentiated in this way, we tend to link this particular form of consciousness to the mechanism known as the eyeball and to think that the eyeball presides over this form of consciousness. If, for the time being, we conflate our consciousness of vision with the functions of the eyeball, it seems that long ago—before this internal differentiation into distinct functions took place—our power of sight was not centered on the eyeball. Perhaps long ago I saw things with my entire body; perhaps I tasted things with my back. I think the division of labor between eye, ear, nose, and tongue is a very recent development. Once this division does take place, however, we lose our versatility. Now, if you get cancer of the tongue, you can no longer eat food with your heel, and if you should be so unfortunate as to catch a dose of the clap, you can no longer do your business with your belly button!

It's all quite inconvenient. But insofar as we can speak of the *continuity* of consciousness—and insofar as the meaning of this *continuity* is clear—then the contents of this continuous stream of consciousness must be clear. If the contents of consciousness were unclear, then we could never be sure if it was continuous or not. This would go against our fundamental tendency. Nay, it would go against the fundamental tendency of consciousness itself. Moreover, the processes of internal differentiation and unification of consciousness naturally develop as a result of this fundamental tendency. We can hardly imagine how far this differentiation and unification will go in the future. Nor can we know how complex our senses will become in response to this. I believe that things that we cannot see today, things that we cannot feel, perhaps even things that evade our five currently known senses, will gradually emerge onto the stage of consciousness. We simply have to be patient and wait.

To repeat, we are concerned here with the "continuity of consciousness." If we divide this phrase in two, we have "consciousness" and "continuity." The problem we face splits in two: What are the contents of this consciousness and what are its sequences? If we then recombine these, we return to the problem of what contents of consciousness are continuous in what sequences. When we encounter this question—and it is a question we must undoubtedly encounter, since it arises as a necessary consequence as soon as we acknowledge the existence of consciousness and its continuous nature. Moreover, this question also necessarily includes the possibility of choice. This question would never arise if there were not some measure of freedom, some margin for making choices. The very appearance of this question implies that it can be answered in more than one way. The forms by means of which this question is resolved are given the name "ideals" [*risō*]. To sum up, we possess a tendency to want to live (or, more precisely, consciousness tends toward continuousness). From this tendency there arise choices. As a result of these choices, there arise ideals. In this way a tendency that originally aimed only at simple survival undergoes development, and we start to desire a specific kind of life, one that possesses a certain kind of significance. In other words, our ideals gradually evolve as we make choices concerning what sort of sequence we want our continuous consciousness to follow and what sort of contents we want to include in it. The ideals of literary writers, which I will discuss a bit later, also arise in this manner.

Let us think again about the word "continuity." As I said before, when we say, "Yes, consciousness is continuous," then it must be continuous between clearly distinct instances. Moreover, as this consciousness that is clearly distinguishable between distinct instances moves forward in its continuity, it necessarily follows a sequence in which A *recedes* as B *emerges*. Saying that there is a sequence here means that A and B cannot occupy consciousness simultaneously. We are conscious of B after A recedes, so that when we are conscious of B we are no longer conscious of A. Nonetheless, if we can distinguish B from A, this means that beneath our clear consciousness of B some consciousness of A must also persist—even if it is relatively indistinct. We ordinarily call this indistinct form of consciousness "memory." The strongest degree of memory is located in the upper strata of consciousness—the clearest strata—while the weakest degree is located in the lowest strata of consciousness—the least clear strata.

In this way the continuity that is consciousness necessarily includes memory, and the existence of memory necessarily involves time. This means that time can only be said to exist when there is a continuous consciousness of some content, and that time does not exist independently out in the world, outside its relationship to consciousness. In other words, it names a relationship that exists between different instances of consciousness, a relationship that can only exist if we have consciousness to begin with. Therefore, to speak of this relationship independently, without reference to consciousness, is permissible as a convenient abstraction, but we should not regard it as something that exists on its own. To use this water pitcher here as an example, it's as if we were to take from it only its white color and assert that this whiteness existed independently of the material object. On first thought it seems that there is a thing called time that flows on and on, and that incidents and events develop and fluctuate in the midst of that eternal stream. However, what has really happened here is that our powers of differentiation and synthesis have developed to the point where they have, as a matter of convenience, abstracted out this thing called time and granted it existence. The logic of this is like extracting the perfume from a rose and then claiming that the rose exists in that perfume. It seems to me more appropriate to say that perfume exists in the rose. But time and space (to which I will turn presently) are difficult problems—according to philosophers, they are quite tricky—and so when I lay out my crude ideas in slipshod fashion like this, you had best not give them too much credence. Then again, if you give no credence whatsoever, we won't get very far either. It seems best to have you give credence until my speech is finished. When you leave for home later today you can start doubting me.

Next, let's turn to the continuity of consciousness, that is, when A recedes and B emerges. We sometimes encounter the following sort of situation: you are conscious of A, and then you are conscious of B. But you can also reverse the order and be conscious of B first and then move on to A. Furthermore, expanding or contracting the time in which one is conscious of the two does not change the relationship between them. This means that this relationship is relatively independent of time, that it is a fixed relationship. In such a situation, we realize that this relationship cannot be explained in terms of time and so instead we call it a spatial relationship. This, too, is a relationship that exists between two instances of consciousness, meaning that space cannot be said to exist independently of consciousness. Grammar consists of rules that express the mutual relationships of words arranged into sentences, whereas children are apt to think that first there was grammar and then subsequently sentences were produced. But first of all there were sentences and words; grammar merely indicates the relationships that exist among these. In this sense we can say that grammar exists within sentences in the same way that the concept of space exists between the two concrete instances of consciousness. When, for the sake of convenience, we abstract this out and arbitrarily project an increasingly vast space out there, we begin to feel as if things were scattered across a limitless expanse. The theory of space, however, is another tough nut to crack. I'm told that Newton asserted that space exists objectively, and that Kant said it was something known intuitively—meaning that what I've said may not be quite accurate. It may not seem accurate to you, but that's fine—as long as it is what I think. I can spout these things that perhaps only I believe as a necessary result of your request that I give a speech—and if I don't mention these things first, I'll never be able to get around to talking about literature.

So, as a result of a process of abstraction, we bestow objective existence on time and space. In order to render these meaningful, we further fabricate something called numbers so as to have a convenient method for measuring them. Never before has there been anything in this world so queer and bereft of actual substance as numbers. Nor, for that matter, is there anything like them now. Numbers are signs that make it easy to measure the relationships of continuity in consciousness—forward or backward, left or right—irrespective of the content of that consciousness. It must have been quite a task to come up with signs like this, lacking any actual substance.

Within the continuity of consciousness there are cases where two phenomena—and sometimes more than two—always appear in the same order. After A, then B necessarily appears; it always appears, and there is never the slightest change in the order of their appearance. We have bestowed the name "cause and effect" on this sort of relationship. Moreover, we then isolate this sort of relationship and for it we fabricate the notion of a law of cause and effect. "Fabricate" might seem a strange word here, and yet given that we are creating something here where nothing exists, it is clearly a case of fabrication. Any cause and effect that does not adhere to a phenomenon of consciousness is an *empty* cause and effect. The law of cause and effect and its ilk are utterly *empty*; they are nothing more than hypotheses posited for the sake of convenience. To try to get by, without realizing this, simply by muttering something about being under the sway of the great law of the universe is, in effect, to cower in terror before a paper tiger of one's own making. The so-called law of cause and effect is nothing more than an index designed to provide, at a glance, the information that—at least up to now—such and such has always been thus. It is a convenience, but it is the height of folly to assume that in the future no continuity will appear that transcends the current "law." It is for this reason that persons of discernment find nothing strange in things that ordinary people find inexplicable. This is because they are aware that innumerable relations of cause and effect exist beyond those already known. They operate on a different level from those who, hearing the bell sound, assume that it must be lunchtime.

Before proceeding, I would here like to sum up the points I have made thus far. (1) We are under the sway of a desire to live. To put this in terms of consciousness, consciousness tends toward continuousness. (2) This tendency gives rise to choices. (3) These choices give birth to ideal forms. (4) In actualizing these ideal forms, consciousness adopts certain *special* vectors of continuity. (5) As a result, consciousness undergoes internal differentiation, clarification, and unification. (6) The unification of instances of one kind of relationship bestows objective existence onto time. (7) The unification of instances of another kind of relationship bestows objective existence onto space. (8) Through a process of abstraction we have created numbers and use them to render time and space meaningful. (9) We have unified the instances of certain kinds of relationships that occur within time and given them the name of cause and effect. Through a further process of abstraction we have created the law of cause and effect.

That, more or less, is where things stand. When we think about this, it means that space, time, and the law of cause and effect are all mere suppositions made for convenience's sake, that none of them exist in reality. At least that is what I am saying. It's fine if you think otherwise. To each his own. For now, though, I wish you'd accept this supposition. We won't get very far if you don't. If you ask why it doesn't bother us to posit such unnecessary suppositions, it is because in our ordinary, vulgar way of thinking, people only care about surviving. We really are shallow creatures: if it means we can go on living, we're happy to spout any lie or carry out any wrong. If we fear it might hinder us in living not to posit the existence of space, we immediately fabricate space. If we sense it might hinder us not to posit the existence of time, well, then, we say let's produce time—and we do. In this way our various abstractions and suppositions are all lies devised in response to our overwhelming, desperate anxiety. They are, in fact, truths derived from falsehood. The great expediency of these lies is apparent in how we have learned to repeat these lies for any number of years until, in today's degenerate and corrupt world, I believe these lies to be truths, just as you do. We don't suspect or doubt them but instead are only too pleased to grant recognition, openly and without hesitation, to these mere suppositions as if they were actually existing things. They say that poverty dulls the wit and troubles cause us to lose our bearings.[3] When we face difficulties in life, we are only too ready to compromise ourselves. In sum, these are lies that arise when our interests are at stake, and they have about as much truth in them as a prostitute's tears on New Year's Eve. If you wonder why this is so, just think about it. If you didn't believe there was such a thing as time, nor the numbers by which we measure time, well, then, if I promised to give a speech on Saturday, I might show up on Sunday. We would all be inconvenienced. And if you didn't believe there was such a thing as space, nor the numbers by which we measure space, well, you wouldn't be able to dodge streetcars or find your way down from the second floor. You'd walk smack into the wall of a police box and then step on the tail of a dog—that is, you'd meet with all sorts of unhappy results. It's the same situation for our law of cause and effect. If we do not lend to these the right of existence, we expose ourselves to great danger. We'll believe almost anything when we feel endangered. As for the brave souls who refuse to partake in this nonsense, well, they're all dead. Therefore, those of you who remain alive and well today are all dishonest, while the upright ones have all passed away—having been run over by streetcars, fallen into the river, or gotten themselves arrested at the police box.

Once we have space and time, it is a rather simple matter to divide consciousness up between self and object. Simple is hardly the word for it, in fact. It's as if we established the pedestals that are space and time solely so we'd have someplace handy on which to install self and object once we'd distinguished them. As soon as the pedestal is ready, we go into action, as if we had been waiting for it. We latch on to our consciousness and throw it out there, latch on to it and throw it out there—throw it out there just like an *awamochi* maker plucks out individual bits of pounded rice *mochi* and tosses them into a dish of *kinako* soybean flour. If we say the *kinako* flour is time, then we have *mochi* past, *mochi* present, and *mochi* future. Or, if we say the *kinako* flour is space, then we have far *mochi* and near *mochi*, *mochi* here and *mochi* there. Even now, there you all are, 150 of you, sitting there in front of me. Please excuse my impertinence in saying this, but as a matter of convenience, I've just tossed you out there. We are fortunate to live in an age in which space already exists, even if it is just a lie, and it seems a waste not to put it to good use. And so I've thrown you out there because, well, it's all so convenient: there you sit, a hundred or more of you, so prim and proper. If it seems impertinent of me to talk about throwing you out there, just be glad I didn't decide that you were all *mochi* rice cakes.

This capacity for projection combines with our capacity for differentiation, which I mentioned earlier. We are thus not content simply to identify things as merely being other than the self. Rather, we assign various names to them and thereby draw distinctions among them. For example, we classify them as being either sensible or supersensible (by which I mean such impalpable entities as spirits and deities—leaving aside the question of whether these actually exist). The category of the sensible is further subdivided into colors and shapes that are visible to the eye, sounds and reverberations that are audible to the ear, odors that can be smelled by the nose, tastes that can be detected by the tongue, and so forth. In this way the distinctions drawn are further broken down into increasingly narrow spheres. As this function of differentiation proceeds, and as our sense perception grows more and more precise, the distinctions we draw become increasingly minute. Moreover, our capacity for unification is also active at the same time, so that, on the other hand, we combine things into broader categories: plants, trees, animals, people. We don't stop there, however: the category of plants is broken down into violets, dandelions, and primroses; the category of trees is broken down into plum, peach, and pine; the category of animals becomes cows, horses, monkeys, or dogs; and that of humans becomes warrior, farmer, artisan, or merchant[4]—or, again, old or young, male or female, elite or vulgar, mature or immature, wise or foolish, righteous or evil. Today the distinctions a botanist can make among plants and flowers are no doubt a hundredfold more refined than those that you or I can make. Likewise, painters such as yourself can no doubt distinguish dozens more hues of color than the ordinary person. If we ask why this is so, it becomes clear that at bottom these differentiations are prompted by our determination to live well. In order to be able freely to choose one specific continuity of consciousness (in order to provide us with the widest possible range of choices), beforehand we expand the range of our consciousness. When a person like me looks at grass, it all looks the same green. Even if I want to be conscious of various different kinds of green, I am unable to do so because my capacity for differentiation is not sufficiently developed. At least insofar as colors are concerned, I simply am unable to live a life rich in variations and complexity. I am little better than blind. It's really quite unfortunate. According to one critic, where people like me see a single color, the painter Titian recognized fifty. This is not simply a matter of saying he was precious because he was a painter. It means that as a human he could lead a relatively versatile lifestyle. The greater the range of materials available to our consciousness, the greater our freedom to choose and live out a specific continuity of consciousness. In other words, he stood in a better position to actualize his own ideals. This is what made him a versatile person. This is not limited to the realm of colors. For example, persons poor in the ability to engage in intellectual speculation live an inner life so barren as to deserve our pity—just like my own inability to experience colors. No matter how wealthy or high-ranking such persons may be, their particular continuity of consciousness is unfailingly monotonous, undistinguished, and lacking in ideals. Unable to distinguish between high and low, noble and vulgar, right and wrong, crooked and straight, they lead lives as oblivious and dull-witted as that of an amoeba. People of this ilk treat everyone as if they were all the same. They are really quite troublesome: when you point out the stupidity of their shortcomings, they turn on you as if you were the fool. But that is a topic for another day. The feet of my speech seem to have slipped into a ditch at the side of the road. I shall straightaway crawl back out of this ditch and resume my forward progress.

As I have noted, in contrast to the *self*, we project *objects* out into space, which, through the function of differentiation, we break down further into ever finer distinctions. At the same time, we also exercise our capacity for differentiation with regard to the self, so that we distinguish between body and mind. Furthermore, we distinguish between the mental functions of the mind: intellect, emotion, and will. We can also make further distinctions between the various attributes of these functions, breaking down intellect or emotion even more finely. Questions of this sort are the specialty of those known as psychologists, and so they are best addressed to them. In their work, however, psychologists are prone to isolate these functions from one another and to deal with them in an abstract manner. Dividing them up into intellect, emotion, and will may be an appropriate classification schema, but these three functions are, in fact, not independent of one another, nor do they operate without mutually affecting one another. No matter how minutely we may analyze a function of the mind, when it is seen as a whole in most cases it ends up including all three—intellect, emotion, and will.

Accordingly, to distinguish rigidly between these three is merely a useful abstraction. To depict for people the operations (taken as wholes) of the mind in the smallest details of its analytical functions without resorting to this sort of abstraction is primarily the task of literary writers. Therefore, the work of literary writers has likewise undergone a development in its powers of differentiation, rendering to consciousness with increasing clarity that which is amorphous and drawing increasingly finer distinctions between the contents of consciousness. For example, if we look at ancient texts—such as the *Tale of the Bamboo Cutter* or the *Taiheiki*—although we find many different sorts of people in them, in fact they all seem quite similar. It's also the same with Saikaku and his ilk. In other words, those authors saw people as being basically all the same. Today, however, with our more highly developed faculty of differentiation, we can no longer be so indiscriminate in how we view people. If a work today lacks skill in making fine distinctions between the characters' mental functions or in providing detailed depictions of the traits it has distinguished, it is out of synch with the times. When a person lacking this sort of discernment tries to depict people, it ends in failure as surely as when a color-blind person decides to paint a picture. To put this in terms that will be more familiar to you as specialists in painting, it's the same as if one lacked the visual ability to distinguish between the white of a piece of paper and the white of a tablecloth. Given today's highly developed visual sense, such a person is incapable of expressing the ideal forms for color. Likewise, a literary writer who lacks the insight required to draw fine distinctions between men who are otherwise of similar character, disposition, circumstances, and age will never win acceptance under the terms of today's highly developed perception of humanity. A literary writer who wants to depict people cannot simply be a good writer; he must also have highly developed powers of discrimination with regard to people. In our advanced age, a man not equipped with the most advanced powers of perception—not simply as a writer but as a person in general—had best not try his hand at it.

This is not, however, how the world sees it. The world at large thinks of a novelist as someone who keeps himself fed and clothed by working his writing brush no different from a cabinetmaker or a paper hanger. It holds a university professor in much higher regard than a novelist. It holds a regional bureau chief for the Ministry of the Interior in higher regard than that. And a member of the cabinet or a rich man or an aristocrat is held in even higher regard. It's quite strange, really. If a novelist were to teach us some new fact about what people are really like, we would have to say that thanks to this novelist we had been pushed to develop a step further, that he had cleared away a patch of thorns blocking our evolutionary path. (I don't mean to imply that the merits of a novelist are limited to this. I only mean to show that he is in no way inferior to a bureau chief or the holder of a doctorate.) If you gentlemen were to say there is no novelist in Japan today who lives up to this, I would answer as follows: The fault lies not in my definition of the novelist. Rather, the fault lies with the novelists of today's Japan (including myself). Our bureau chiefs are hardly worthy of the title, just as our doctorates are hardly worthy of that title and likewise our novelists are hardly worthy of that title. But I seemed to have again slipped off of my main road and back into the ditch. . . .

In fact, I have not yet reached the point in my talk where I can take up the topic of literature. I was explaining our capacity for differentiation when I somehow went off on a tangent about the powers of discernment of literary writers—particularly novelists. This does not constitute the whole of their task. As I said before, I was just offering up one aspect of his task as it relates to the topic of our capacity for differentiation. In order to reach the point where I can speak about the field of literature in something like its entirety, I will have to advance by way of some rather broad generalizations. I will dip my oars in now and see if I can row us there.

As we have seen, through our faculty of differentiation we distinguish between objects and the self. From among the objects we distinguish between natural things, people (that is, other people viewed as objects), and supersensible divinities (insofar as we acknowledge the objective existence of divine beings). Likewise, within the self we distinguish between intellect, emotion, and will. In terms of possible forms for linking these three functions of the *self* with the *objects* external to the self, there are clearly three options. To wit, there are people who exercise their intellect on objects, people who exercise their emotions on objects, and people who exercise their will on objects. Of course, these three functions are not essentially independent of one another, and so when we say they exercise their intellect, their emotion, or their will, we mean that they *primarily* exercise that function, not that they exercise only that one function to the exclusion of the others. Now, among these those who employ intellect in order to clarify our relationship to objects are commonly called philosophers or scientists. Those who employ emotion in order to savor our relationship to things are commonly known as writers or artists. Finally, those who employ will in order to remake our relation to things are commonly called soldiers, politicians, tofu makers, or carpenters.

This differentiation among the contents of consciousness indicates that there is a wide range of possible streams of continuity these contents can follow, which, in turn, indicates that there is considerable latitude in choosing among the possible ideal forms—that is, among the specific types of continuity of consciousness from which we choose in leading our own lives—that I referred to earlier. One person might prefer to live out a continuity of consciousness that tends to employ the intellect—and thus becomes a scholar. Another might adopt as their ideal a continuity of consciousness that tends to employ emotion—and thus becomes a writer, a painter, or a musician. Still another who desires a continuity of consciousness that primarily employs the will ends up as a farmer or a rickshaw puller—or even, in a few special cases, may fight battles, pursue adventures, or even plot revolutions.

Having divided human ideals into three broad categories, if we ask which ideal characterizes us—that is, I who have the honor of speaking here today and you gentlemen who do me the favor of listening—the answer, of course, is the second. We choose a life of emotion; this is not to say that we never want to employ our intellects, but rather that our ideal requires us always to be connected with our emotions. I don't expect you to be convinced merely by my saying "our ideal is emotion." In order to persuade you of this, I need to explain in more detail exactly what it means when I say "we take emotions as our ideal."

I said that people who live primarily through their emotions savor their relationship to objects. But in order for people to savor their relationships to objects, it is sometimes necessary to clarify those relationships and at other times to alter them. For these reasons, a person of emotion must, of course, sometimes operate as a person of intellect, just as a literary writer must simultaneously be a philosopher and a person of action (a creator). Yet a person whose primary goal is to clarify these relationships may, in order to better clarify them, abstract those relationships to the point where they can no longer be savored. Given three apples, such a person is satisfied if the relationship known as "three" is clarified; he forgets all about the apples and pays heed only to the number three. Literary writers also need to clarify relationships, but they do so in order to savor those relationships more fully than before. It would make no sense for them to clarify those relationships to the point that they can no longer be savored. Accordingly, while it is well and fine for literary writers to understand the relationship named by the number three, they will never forget about the apples sitting there. It's the same when a literary writer exercises the faculty of will. His purpose is not simply to alter the relationship with the object but rather to alter it in order to make possible a fuller emotional response to it. For this reason a literary writer will change the relationship to an object only to the extent that it doesn't go against the workings of his emotions. For example, we might place a stone next to a pine tree, but we would never chop down the pine tree to sell as firewood—unless we were really hard up for money. Once our lovely pine tree goes up in smoke, there is nothing left on which to work our emotions. I hope this helps clarify somewhat what I mean by savoring our relationship with things. In order to savor our relationship with some object, that object has to be something concrete. When, through the workings of intellect or will, we destroy a concrete object, the literary writer loses the ability to savor that relationship. Therefore, we stick with our concrete objects and employ our intellects and wills only to the extent that we do not destroy the concrete character of the object that was capable of arousing our emotions in the first place. That is what I mean.

This means that the literary ideal cannot be realized in the absence of some object of sense perception. (If we were to discuss this in any detail, a number of questions would arise, but I lack the time to go into these. Roughly speaking, though, there is no reason to doubt this proposition.) To put it simply, even in the case of formless and odorless divine beings, when we want to depict them in words or picture we have to borrow sensible properties. This is why the God of the Old Testament and the gods of ancient Greece were all portrayed as possessing voice, shape, or other palpable manifestations. Accordingly, we are justified in defining the ideal of literary writers as being to manifest some kind of emotion by way of some object of sense perception. Two distinct issues arise here. First, what is the object of sense perception? The second concerns our "some kind of emotion." In what way is it manifested via an object of sense perception? What part of the object is involved? When we say "by way of some object of sense perception," we face the question of whether the object of sense perception is a mere tool used to express the emotion or whether the object of sense perception is what arouses the emotion itself in the first place. The various responses to these questions allow us to present a rough sketch of the different forms of literary ideals that exist. I won't provide my answers to these questions strictly in the order given above but instead will number my explanations here to make them easier to follow.

1. At the outset today, I started with the construction of space and time and said that the two worlds of self and objects arise from them. I said the world of *objects* included nature, people, and divine beings (when regarded solely as things)—everything that exists other than the *self*. Since divine beings are not actually objects of sense perception, they are not at issue here. When a god appears in literature, it always appears by way of

something perceptible, so that its appearance belongs to the same category as other objects and hence does not call this definition into question.

We are left, then, with natural objects and with human beings. When we encounter nature or a person, we have an emotional response. In other words, when we encounter the sensible features of a person or something from nature—its coloring, its outlines, its size, its proportions, its softness or hardness, the way light reflects off of it, the sound it makes—we respond according to our taste, that is, according to our likes and dislikes—meaning that ultimately we have some emotional reaction. This is what makes it possible for us to savor our relationship with sensible objects. Moreover, it prompts us to want to experience the consciousness of the highest possible relationship with that object. One possible means for realizing this ideal form is through a poem, while another is through painting. The most pronounced form of this emotional ideal is called our aesthetic sentiment. (In fact, there are many other ideals besides the aesthetic. If, for example, we experience one kind of relationship that we call sublimity and another kind of relationship we call aloofness, there is nothing preventing us from speaking of a sublime sentiment or an aloof sentiment. In fact, the unfolding of our function of differentiation would naturally bring us to this result. The way Westerners trumpet on only about beauty and aesthetics causes us no end of mischief.) Those who try to realize this sort of aesthetic ideal in relation to natural objects become painters of traditional landscapes, or they become poets of the Chinese style or of Japanese haiku, singing the praises of natural scenery. Those who instead try to realize this sort of aesthetic ideal in relation to people become poets who sing the praises of beautiful women—or painters whose oeuvre consists of portraits. The nude portraits that have caused such a stir lately both in the West and in Japan are the result of those who struggle to make this one limited ideal their life's sole purpose. However technically demanding this may be, in terms of the range of ideals available to literary writers, it represents only one possibility. I'm told that if you paint a nude, people declare that you have mastered the art of painting. I can't say much about painting, but isn't this just the result of the eastward march of contemporary French fashions? At any rate, it makes no real difference whether we speak about this in terms of painting, poetry, or prose. A person taken up as an object of sense perception represents only one possible choice among the many available perceptible objects, just as the aesthetic sentiment represents only one kind of emotional reaction we can have when we encounter a person as an object of sense perception. Insofar as that is true, the beauty of the nude body may be something quite lofty, but it is also only one narrow segment of the full possible range.

Whether we speak of the beautiful, the sublime, or the aloof, each represents one way of savoring our relationship with objects, and the choice among them is a matter determined by the particular ideals espoused by the literary writer. As a result of further differentiation, the range of possible ideals available might expand—and we have no way of knowing how far this process might go. However far this division into new types may progress, though, the new ideals produced would still be born of the relationships that occur when we encounter objects of perception as objects of perception. That is, the sentiments that might arise in such cases would still be those that arise when we take up the object itself as our main concern and should not be confused with the sentiments that arise when we use the object as a tool or medium through which to take up indirectly something other than the object itself.

2. In terms of the relationship between self and objects, I hope that I have sufficiently explained the ideals and sentiments we hold toward objects. Next I will turn my attention to the self.

a). As I have already discussed, we can differentiate three functions within the self: intellect, emotion, and will. I also noted that those who clarify our relationship to objects primarily by means of the intellect are philosophers and scientists. It only seems natural that—since this is a matter primarily of clarifying that relationship—it would fall within the domain of philosophy or science, but if, in order to clarify this relationship, we summon up some emotion, then to the extent that this relies on our emotions we must call it a literary function even if it does involve the use of intellect. Moreover, as I have already explained, if we want to satisfy our feelings even as we employ our intellect, we cannot do so in the absence of some sensible object, that is, we cannot achieve this solely through relationship itself, abstracted away from the object. In other words, in order to exercise our intellect in a literary fashion, we need to borrow some sensible, concrete object; only through the mediation of such a concrete object can we render literary the workings of the intellect. If we do this, we have fashioned a new literary ideal—an ideal, that is, in which, using some object as a means, we obtain emotional satisfaction by clarifying our relationship to that object through the workings of our intellect. Let us call this the ideal of truth. This ideal of truth is thus an ideal for philosophers and scientists, as well as for literary writers. The latter, however, differ from the former in that they are bound by an additional condition—that the truth be expressed *through some concrete object.* We can differentiate between various ways of manifesting this truth, that is, between various ways of employing the intellect. Human mental functioning (in this case we cannot, as in [1] above, regard a person as a simple object of perception) generally proceeds according to the known laws of cause and effect, or in response to some new significance that is developed through additional differentiation beyond the previously known laws of cause and effect. For example, imagine a novel that depicts a parent and child engaged in a fierce argument when, suddenly, a fire breaks out and fills the house with smoke. They forget all about the argument and help each other escape from the fire. This feels right not only to the writer but also to the reader. In clarifying the relationship between parent and child in this situation, the novel utilizes the intellect of the author and reader even as it satisfies their emotional sense of truth. Or, again, imagine a novel that depicts a devoted couple who in a time of great famine forget their love for one another. The husband steals the wife's gruel and eats it up. This, too, might provide a similar satisfaction to author and reader in that it clarified the relationship between husband and wife in a certain situation. (From the standpoint of human mental functioning, there are many kinds of truth. Some of these may at times directly contradict others, and yet they all remain truths.) The kind of literary writers who like to write this sort of story take truth as their primary ideal.

b. The second mental function that we possess is feeling. As I said earlier, those who work by taking feelings as their ideal are literary writers. This point, however, can easily give rise to confusion, and so I would like to explain it more fully before proceeding. Simply to say feelings is ambiguous. This is because the feeling that moves us to produce a work of literary art and the feelings that we experience when we are enjoying the work must be distinguished from the feelings that are depicted in it, the feelings that are employed as material in the work itself. When we see an object of perception directly as an object of perception, one kind of feeling arises; this feeling is one of the ideals of a literary writer. When, on the other hand, our intellect is moved through the mediation of some object of perception, another kind of feeling arises. This feeling, too, is one of the ideals of a literary writer. Next, when our feelings are prompted through the mediation of some object of perception, we necessarily have yet another kind of feeling. Even if these two feelings were identical in content, to treat them as the same thing, the same entity, will confuse our discussion. For example, if through a certain object of perception the feeling of anger appears, the feeling that we obtain through a work depicting this might be anger of the same quality (of course, at times a different sort of emotion will arise), yet these two are not the same thing. The first anger is a cause, whereas the subsequent anger is an effect. To put this into clearer terms, the first anger is an anger that adheres to the object of perception (even if the source of the anger that is in me is only projected outside of me and thereby established elsewhere). The subsequent anger is one that arises entirely within the self. Having made this distinction to prevent confusion between the two, I will move on. The logic here, however, is basically the same as I explained in (a), when I discussed how we love the workings of the intellect and bestow onto these one kind of feeling. The happiness, anger, sadness, and joy that are active in our psyche form the larger part of our consciousness. Moreover, when they are manifested objectively, when we recognize them in some so-called object (in most cases another person), this, too, greatly stimulates our feelings. However, this stimulus, based on the conditions I described earlier, is something we only receive when the feeling is manifested by way of some concrete thing or person. If you are interested in feelings but, like a psychologist, you deal with them in the abstract as inanimate things, you will fail to deal with them in a literary fashion. It is true, however, that feelings are more readily dealt with in the abstract, as compared with intellect and will, but I do not have time today to explain this in any detail.

In this kind of ideal one can also differentiate between various kinds. To begin with one possible norm, one can express a relation of love via some thing—well, this is much clearer if we make it a person rather than a thing. To express a relation of love via a person is the ideal of eight or nine out of ten people we call novelists. This relation of love can be further differentiated into various types. For example, there is the love that results in a marriage, or the feverish love one succumbs to like a disease—but these old-fashioned kinds hardly ever appear in novels nowadays. More cynical varieties might include a woman who marries even as she remains infatuated with another man, or a couple who finally realize their dream of being together and who begin fighting the very next day. In sum, one can identify any number of different ideal types with regard to this—though "ideal" hardly seems the right word.

Next we have loyalty, filial piety, chivalry, friendship, plus all the other honorable sentiments, which, together with their assorted differentiated variations, can also serve as norms. In general, we can refer to norms that include such honorable sentiments as belonging to the ideal of goodness. I wish I could speak in more detail about this, but time does not permit.

c. The third mental function is will. For will to be manifested in literary terms, it, too, must follow the previously mentioned condition, that is, it must be rendered concrete via some sensible object. In doing this, the sensible object is a tool, thanks to which the workings of will are rendered distinct. The tool in itself, however, is simply a tool; it takes on importance only when a will is expressed through it. Take the example of a sake serving bottle. I suppose there are some sake serving bottles that are in themselves valuable porcelains, but if their bottoms fall out, they can't pour sake and so will sit there among the plates and cups, unable to serve their owner's will. Or imagine, for example, that I want to convey the image of a cannonball flying through the air. There are two ways of looking at this. One is to stick strictly to the sensible, which would belong to the case I described in (1) above. The other is to try to express an extraordinary, overwhelming force via this sensible object—something we do because it is impossible to depict such a force in and of itself. In this case the cannonball is merely a secondary device and our primary target is the terrific force that it expresses. While this force may be partly natural and partly mechanical, it also represents the functioning of will.

If we see someone climbing Mount Fuji in winter, we call them a fool. They may well be a fool, but if through this fool a certain kind of will is manifested, we may be justified in ignoring the overall foolishness to focus solely on this manifestation of will, solely on this properly literary aspect. In such cases where a fool risks his precious life—swimming across an ocean strait or crossing a desert—everything else is being sacrificed for the sake of living out a certain continuity of consciousness, one characterized primarily by an act of will. If this is manifested in a literary fashion, then we cannot deny that it is literary. Likewise, when it is done for the sake of the nation, or of the Way, or of humankind—when will emerges in tandem with the sort of honorable sentiments I discussed in (b)—it elicits extraordinarily lofty feelings. What we call the courage of the weak is an instance of this.

In English this is called heroism. The feelings that heroism elicits in us are quite powerful. On my way here today, I happened to see black smoke pouring out of the tall smokestacks at the Arsenal, and I was struck by a certain emotion. When you think about it, there is something vulgar about a smokestack. If you want to know what is dirty in this world, well, few things are dirtier than a coal-furnace smokestack. Furthermore, when I think that the black smoke is really the exhalation of a throbbing desire to make money, it all becomes even more repulsive. What's more, the smoke is bad for my lung condition. And yet, and yet—I forget all about that and find myself struck by a certain emotion. This feeling is a perfect example of the kind of emotions that are elicited by a manifestation of will. If this is the case even for the smoke at the Arsenal, a case of genuine heroism must elicit a truly magnificent feeling. Almost none of today's literary writers take this sort of feeling as their ideal. And, of course, it is possible to further differentiate this ideal. Kusunoki Masashige at the battle of Minatogawa—as he committed suicide declaring that he wished for seven lives so that he could devote each to battling the enemies of the emperor—is one example.[5] The priest Daitō Kokushi, who was never able to sit cross-legged style, vowing during his dying moments that "today, of all days, you'll do as you're told" and forcibly bending his stubborn legs, paying no mind to the fresh blood that stained his priestly robes, main-taining his seated meditation as he breathed his last: that is another. We can differentiate this into a variety of types, but the norm shared by all is our sense of the heroic.

With this, my general survey and explanation of the ideal types espoused by literary writers is complete. To sum up, one type is the feelings we have toward some sensible object in and of itself (e.g., the aesthetic ideal). A second consists of those cases where the three functions of intellect, emo-tion, and will operate through the mediation of some sensible object. These can be divided up into cases where (a) the intellect is at work (e.g., the ideal of truth), (b) the feelings are at work (e.g., the ideals of love and morality), and (c) the will is at work (e.g., the ideal of the heroic). Strictly speaking, I should here explain how the feelings that arise through asso-ciation from these four broadly distinguished ideals merge into one an-other, but time constraints do not permit that.

In general, we can divide the ideals of literary writers into these four types. This classification schema is slightly different from the one I used in my *Theory of Literature*, but this is only natural, given that my point of departure today was different. Moreover, this schema seems clearer and more appropriate, so I don't think the difference between the two will cause the reader any harm.

Now, as I said before, though we can distinguish between three kinds of mental functioning—intellect, emotion, and will—these do not manifest themselves in isolation from one another. Moreover, in the literary arts their functioning is always manifested through sensible objects. Therefore the sentiments aroused in response to these four types are always mixed up together, so that in reality they do not appear in works in such clearly distinguished form. Nonetheless, there are four types of ideals—no less than four. When we take up a particular work and investigate it, one of these four ideals strikes us as being the most pronounced in it. Accordingly, to a certain extent we are able to determine the ideal to which a given work adheres. It is also undeniable that these four ideal types are continually subject to waxing and waning of their power under the influence of the age and of specific individuals. In some ages, for example, it may be that works that do not satisfy the craving for beauty will not be regarded as literary. But in the next age, as ideals fluctuate, beauty is not enough: only works that manifest truth will be deemed worthy of being crowned with the name literature. Or, again, a certain person may declare that he wants neither to produce nor to read works that do not satisfy his sense of morality. Another person might declare that he doesn't sense any literary quality in the absence of an expression of will and a sense of the heroic. Each of these eras and each of these persons is entirely correct. If, moreover, there was a person who voiced a lack of preference between the four types, then we should judge him the person with the most catholic of tastes—and therefore the most correct.

Which of the four types comes into fashion in which ages and which is most desired by which sort of persons? These are interesting questions but I must also omit them due to time constraints. I do, however, want to point out one thing. These four types, as their names imply, each possesses the right to stake its own considerable claims. Since each constitutes a literary ideal, we cannot find any grounds for claiming that any of them should be subordinated to any other. No one can possibly rank them according to differences in degree of importance. To claim otherwise is an act of sheer folly, like an irresponsible teacher who grades exams without reading them. All we need to say is this: we are influenced by our age, and so we tend to prefer works that adhere to one or another of these ideals. Likewise, given my individuality, I choose works that can be gathered under the rubric of one or another of these ideals. Because there is no disputing taste, it's simply a matter of stating what one likes or dislikes. To spout fancy arguments with trumped-up rationales for that which cannot be justified simply because you're embarrassed to assert your groundless likes and dislikes is merely to make excuses, like saying you don't like eating octopus because you have a weak digestive system. If you really liked octopus, then no matter how poor your digestive system, you'd find a way to scarf it down—all eight legs.

For this reason, each of these four ideal types possesses rights equal to all of the others, and each marks a standard that should not be infringed upon by any of the others. Accordingly, to insist on beauty as the standard in evaluating the ideal of truth is like trying to play a fork in chess when the pieces aren't in the proper position. It's like criticizing someone's appetite for food based on their sleeping habits. If you were to conclude that someone ate so much because they were a habitual sleepyhead, who would listen? If you asked someone to bring you a measuring cup so you could measure out a yard of fabric, would anyone heed your request? People who would take the reading off an outdoor thermometer and then declare, well, it sure is a tall mountain—we should probably measure their feverish delirium with that same outdoor thermometer instead of a proper medical thermometer.

The misguided criticism I am referring to here is not, however, a matter of pointing out the absence of truth in a work that otherwise manifests beauty. Rather, it refers to criticism that says the work is *no good and unacceptable* because it lacks truth. In fact, it may not contain truth—but it does not need to do so. When something is not there, who would pretend that it was there and ask to receive it? To fail to see the beauty that actually is there is to snuff out the life of a work that someone has taken the trouble to produce. Pointing out that a man is as bald as a teakettle but has white whiskers is fair enough, but if someone then declares, no, a bald head simply won't do—well, then, we lose the poor whiskers too. The Niō temple guardian gods carved by Unkei, are fine expressions of the stirring of will.[6] Yet their bodily physiques are hardly suitable for dissection on the autopsy table. If someone were to critique them on this basis, calling them failures because they lack truth—well, the failure here would lie with the critic who says this. Millet's painting of evening prayers expresses a feeling of profound remoteness.[7] That is all you need to see in order to appreciate it. If you were to point out that the painting lacks any stirring of will, I suppose we could tolerate this. But if you were to call it a failed painting because it lacks any stirring of will, then you are like a frog at the bottom of a well, peeping out through a narrow pipe but believing you see the whole wide world of literature.

There is, however, a difference between cases where one ideal is expressed while the others are merely omitted and cases where the others are instead deliberately attacked. Leaving out the others is a simple case of omission, but when the others are actively attacked, it is a direct transgression against those others. In such cases the ideal that the author takes as his standard must be manifested in the work with such extraordinary skill that consigning the others to oblivion seems plausible. This is exceedingly difficult to pull off—even for a genius. Accordingly, what happens in most cases is that the merits and demerits of the various ideals cancel one another out, and what is left is simply the bare core of the work. After all, even the famous Fujimura store's *yōkan* sweet bean paste loses its charm when placed in a chamber pot. Someone who ignores the chamber pot and gobbles it down is truly a rare aficionado of *yōkan*. Or, again, a person with a scholarly aptitude should make a wonderful teacher, yet if he is a profligate it is nearly impossible for him to pass the qualifying examinations. If it's just a matter of his moral conduct not being up to the highest standards, that's one thing, but if he spends all his time and money drinking in the red-light districts, stuffs a two-yard-long bill from a bar in his pocket, and staggers into class, it will, of course, hurt his reputation on campus. Likewise, no matter how many strong points a literary work may have, if it has weak points that undermine those strong points, and if those strengths aren't so toweringly strong as to make us forget the weaknesses, then, unfortunately, it will be criticized. And this really is unfortunate. It is unfortunate because this is a judgment made only after recognizing both the strong and weak points of the work. I have no desire to fall in with the ragtag rank-and-filers who spend five or six years making the same monotonous complaints.[8]

We are now finally ready to proceed to the topic of the ideals of our contemporary literary arts, and I'd like to talk big for a few minutes. What is the ideal of our contemporary literary arts? Beauty? No, it isn't beauty. Perhaps the same is true in painting and sculpture as well, but I am ignorant of them, and so I will focus your attention on this: as far as literature goes, it is certainly not beauty. The only written works today that draw their vital force from beauty alone belong to the shorter poetic genres. There are certainly no such novels, nor any dramas. To go into detail on this would take too much time, and so I'd like to leave it at this and move on to my next point. If the contemporary ideal is not beauty, is it the good, or perhaps love? These ideals, of course, are woven into the fabric of any number of works, but they are far too frail to serve as the main ideal for our contemporary age. Is it then the heroic? If the heroic were the ideal of our contemporary age, things would be more promising, but the fact is that we need to look in precisely the opposite direction. There has never been an age so lacking in heroism as the present, nor has there ever been a literature so reluctant to exalt heroism as that of our contemporary age.[9] This is clear when we consider the fact that our contemporary age has produced not a single tragedy capable of summoning up a sense of the heroic. Given that the ideal of contemporary literary arts lies not in beauty, nor in the good, nor in the heroic, it becomes clear that the ideal consists of a single word: truth. Were I to cite examples, I could go on forever (proving this would be quite cumbersome). It can't be helped, so I will simply leave it at this one word: truth is the ideal of contemporary literary arts and literature. For the time being, please simply accept this as fact. Incidentally, through internal differentiation this truth can be shown to include various types and degrees. If we assembled and sorted through the various writings of England, France, Germany, and Russia, we could likely point out all of the main variations. I have no intention of registering a complaint about this. As I said previously, truth is one of the four ideals, and being one of these, the fact that truth has gained force and has put the other three into a relatively dim light is a natural and inevitable outcome, something akin to the way the flow of time has caused the old-fashioned *itchōgaeshi* hairstyle to give way to the new modern *sokuhatsu* style. There is, however, one important thing I would like to point out about this.

Namely, as human powers of observation deepen, they become narrow. In our world, as you know, there is nothing so narrow as the narrowness of a specialist. To be narrow is not necessarily a bad thing, so some might dismiss this charge. But at times being narrow causes trouble. For example, a doctor who is excessively passionate about his narrow field of specialization, unable to leave it behind whether asleep or awake, might end up carrying out some horrific scheme, like giving his wife poison so that he can explore the results experimentally. The world is a vast place. In that vast world it would be a sad thing indeed to lay down a single cotton thread and walk carefully along it, looking to neither side, believing that it constituted the whole world. If it were simply a matter of being sad, well, in such cases only the person in question has to endure it, but to insist on following a single line like this often ends up causing trouble for others as well. We can learn this simply by walking in the street. Even if the traffic officer tries to control the flow of traffic, shouting "Keep to the left," "Keep to the left," as if he were trying to earn his monthly salary hour by hour, the people headed in the four directions cannot all walk in a straight line, headed in the same direction at the same rate of speed.

In this wide world people walk at their own pace and in their own chosen direction, and when they happen to meet, if they seem likely to collide, in the absence of some compelling reason they must yield the road to one another. Likewise, each of the four ideals possesses equal rights with all the others as it walks through life. Each walks according to its own desires, but since their rights are all equal, when they are in danger of colliding they must reach some mutual settlement and resolve things peacefully. In order to reach such a peaceful resolution, none can presume the right to choose on its own authority what road to walk. In sum, the world becomes wider only when we recognize that the people coming from in front and from the side are each attending to their own business and that each has their own reasons. If we are like the doctor I mentioned earlier, digging ever deeper into an ever narrower sphere, this becomes impossible. The law of disassociation[10] describes how we see only those aspects about which we are passionate and disassociate the others, setting them off to the side. The others are simply left out; they never even catch the eye. This may be very convenient for the person in question, but for others—that is, for other people who don't want to proceed in that same direction—it can cause much trouble. If the first person is at least aware that he is causing trouble, he may try to improve the situation, but when that person lives in his own narrow world, lacking any awareness that other people live outside of it, then it is hopeless. The bad habit of contemporary literary arts to value only truth seems in danger of falling into this pattern. Nay, in fact, I am afraid that it has already done so.

When one stresses the truth, one feels justified in writing anything at all, so long as it arrives at truth. If, in giving full play to truth, one merely disregards beauty, goodness, and the heroic, that is fine. But if one goes a step further and, for the sake of truth, actively harms beauty, impairs the good, and tramples the heroic, then advocates of truth may celebrate, but one shouldn't expect advocates of beauty, goodness, and the heroic to be cowed into silent acquiescence. To say it can't be helped since each ideal has a different purpose is valid only insofar as any given ideal causes no harm to the others. To remain ignorant of this firm rule of not harming others, and to run about noisily proclaiming this to be a world of truth, a world of truth, is like allowing the streetcars to run wild wherever they please on the road, ringing their bells, because it is supposedly a world of convenient transportation, a world of convenient transportation. People who love streetcars so much that they refuse to go anywhere unless they are riding in one might be pleased, but people who walk, ride in rickshaws, or use bicycles would find this most inconvenient.

In the literary arts, however—whether it is on the side of appreciating or on the side of producing—there is a process of disassociation. (I spelled out my views on this process of disassociation in the *Theory of Literature*, so please refer to it.) When taken to extremes, it results in some odd phenomena. For example, think of those paintings of nudes that hang in broad daylight, fully exposed. According to ordinary social mores, a nude body is something not to be seen; it is something indecent. Say what you will about how Westerners view this matter, it's the same there. I can vouch for that. Nonetheless, in order to manifest the sensuous beauty of the human body, we have no choice but to use a nude, that is, we have no choice but to commit an indecency. This is where a conflict takes place. Moreover, as civilization progresses, this conflict becomes more and more violent, with no hope of a peaceful solution. To resolve it would require us either to change our social mores and habits or to discard the sensuous beauty of the human body. Unwilling to yield on either, we instead impose a settlement by fiat on this intractable conflict in the form of a self-contradictory pledge. To wit: "While we are under the sway of the sensuous beauty of the human body, we will forget all about the social indecency of the naked body." If I use the obscure terminology I introduced earlier, this amounts to promising to view painted nudes while disassociating our sense of indecency. It is thanks to this pledge that painted nudes have enjoyed such a long life and not—as some painters and literary critics seem to think—because public attitudes toward painted nudes have become more tolerant. In the same way, streetcars can be dangerous, but they are also convenient, and so the Tokyo Streetcar and the Electric Streetcars are allowed to exist—under the condition that we disassociate the sense of danger by confining them only to certain streets. If painted nudes—or, for that matter, the Tokyo Streetcar and the Electric Streetcar—get too full of themselves, their right to exist can easily be taken away. But once we establish the pledge to disassociate them, then no one minds. It is the same for truth. Works that primarily employ truth are fine as long as we set the condition that each of the other ideals will be forgotten, that is, disassociated. Saying such works are acceptable doesn't imply that they should swagger about proudly but simply that their existence can be tolerated. They should adopt an apologetic attitude: "I'm quite sorry about this, my fellow ideals, but it really is important to me, so I hope you'll tolerate this." To establish these conditions, however, the emotions elicited by truth must be so powerful and so skillfully employed as to make it possible for us to forget the other ideals. I am doubtful that today's works meet this standard.

I have been arguing in quite abstract terms, so let me try to explain my thinking by way of a few concrete examples. Say we have a man who pretends to be mute. He is suspected of something and so is arrested by the police. He realizes that he will get in trouble if he answers their questions, and so he decides to act like a mute. The police officer has no choice but to keep him in custody. The next morning the "mute" gets very hungry. Remembering that he is supposed to be mute, at first he simply bears it, but in the end, when he can't stand it any longer, he blurts out in a loud voice, "Give me something to eat!" What if we wrote a piece along these lines? The skill required to turn this into an interesting novel would revolve around the question of whether it manifests a kind of truth about a certain kind of man placed in a certain kind of situation. That's where the interest would lie. This being the sole focus, there is, of course, no room for beauty, goodness, or heroism. In other words, it doesn't include even a smidgen of any ideal other than truth. If you ask me whether this is a flaw, I don't believe it is. The simple lack of the other ideals in itself does not damage the work. The sense of interest elicited here by truth provides sufficient reason to read it through to the end, disassociating the other ideals.

Next, let us imagine the following type of story. Suppose there is a beggar. As he wanders from place to place on a certain day and at a certain time, he approaches a certain town and realizes he is quite hungry. Luckily for him, he comes upon a quiet house and, finding it deserted, steals some bread and wine and eats and drinks to his stomach's content. He heads for the outskirts of town, whereupon he becomes sleepy. Just as he is nodding off, a woman from the town happens to pass by. His stomach full of food and his head full of wine, the beggar now has only one desire: as soon as he sees the woman, he immediately follows the dictates of his beastly lust. This, apparently, is the gist of a story by Maupassant, though I haven't read it myself.[11] The person who told me about it expressed repeatedly how interesting it was. It may, in fact, be quite interesting. But the interest lies in its unflinching depiction of how a person in a given set of circumstances might act if he were placed in a certain situation. The interest here, however, unlike my previous example of the story of the mute, lies not just in how it manifests the truth. This story actively attacks the other ideals. Insofar as we do not completely forget the other ideals, we will lose all interest in the story and it will seem pointless. What's more, it will likely be roundly criticized by those who adhere primarily to the other ideals. In this case the convention of dissociation will likely never be implemented. Insofar as this is not implemented, the work will not survive—or, more accurately, it will not be permitted to survive. The more the world at large declines and abandons its sense of morality, the lower this sort of ideal will sink. In other words, because the moral sense of the general population has grown dull, authors and critics likewise pursue ideals in another direction, leaving the place of morality vacant behind them. In the end, we arrive at the feeling that as long as you express the truth, who cares about goodness? If that's the sort of society today's Japan has already become, then perhaps it can't be helped. Otherwise, it seems a bit too hasty to assume that just because Western society has declined and its literary ideals now favor truth above all others, we should immediately follow suit and import this through Kobe and Yokohama, without a thought for the possible consequences.[12] Few nations in history, it seems to me, have been eager to import the bubonic plague from abroad. My language here may seem hyperbolic, but it remains a fact that when we look at the writings of foreigners, we find ourselves unable to effect a proper disassociation and, as a result, we find them unpleasant.

Shakespeare's *Othello* is not a contemporary work, but it provides an example of this. Its plot development and character descriptions achieve a sense of truth; having taught the work two or three times, I am fully cognizant of this. Yet whenever I finish reading it, I'm left with a bad feeling. I get no sense of the tragic or the heroic but instead feel oddly oppressed. If I had more time, I would analyze this feeling and explain it to you, but I haven't yet been able to put my thoughts in order and can say only this: it is a most unpleasant work. I am mystified that, given all the critics who have discussed Shakespeare, to date none of them has discussed this matter. In the final analysis, I think this is likely because they take up the work using as their only standard the ideal of truth. Among contemporary works, those that practice this vice are simply too numerous to mention. The woman Hedda Gabler, for example, lacks for nothing, and yet she deceives people, torments and makes fools of them, behaves outrageously—she is from head to toe a thoroughly unpleasant woman—yet the creator of this unpleasant woman is the acclaimed Henrik Ibsen.

Or suppose there is a petty clerk whose wife is a woman overflowing with vanity. One day, through connections, he manages to obtain an invitation to an evening gala, or some such event, hosted by a minister of state. He thinks that his wife will be overjoyed if he simply offers to accompany her to it, but she unexpectedly takes a hard-line stance, insisting on the unreasonable: her clothes must be this, her hair ornament must be that, and so forth. Since it is such a rare opportunity, her husband bends over backward and somehow manages to satisfy each of his wife's demands. Is that enough to get her to accompany him? No, she sticks to her hard-line position. She declares that she won't go to the party unless she has diamonds, rubies, or similar fine jewelry to wear. This, of course, disconcerts her husband, but he comes up with a plan: by chance a friend's wife happens to own all kinds of jewelry, and he solves the crisis by borrowing a precious diamond necklace just for the evening. On the night of the ball, the wife is overwhelmed with delight: she dances, prances, leaps about, laughs—and as a result she somehow manages to fling away and lose the precious borrowed necklace. The two of them turn pale, and the wife naturally regrets having danced so wildly, but it is too late now: the diamonds won't come back on their own accord. After discussing what they should do, the couple have no choice but to borrow a huge sum of money, after which they scour the streets of Paris until at last they find a necklace that looks exactly like the one they borrowed. They buy it and return it to the owner right on time, saying nothing about what has happened, and thereby manage to get through the immediate pinch. But now they have to struggle to repay the loan. After all, even in Paris it is the custom to pay back what you have borrowed. The previously vain wife turns over a new leaf: she takes over in the kitchen, cooking their meals and doing the washing by herself until her hands grow chapped. They economize on everything, eating only potatoes at mealtimes, until after several years they are finally able to pay off their debt. But the wife ends up looking like an aged servant girl from the lowest classes: her face and hands are misshapen and she possesses only the humblest of clothing . . . .

One day the wife, as always, takes her basket and goes shopping for cheese or some such thing, when she happens to bump into the woman from whom she borrowed the diamond necklace years earlier. That lady is a fine, high-class wife, while our heroine now looks for all the world like a servant girl—or, given her age, a former servant girl. She naturally feels a bit awkward about saying anything but finally makes up her mind to speak and announces, "Well, my, my, how unexpected to see you here!" Naturally the other lady has long since forgotten all about her. She looks surprised to be approached by a servant girl. But our heroine doesn't lose her courage and proceeds to tell the whole story, step by step, explaining how, in order make good on the woman's diamond necklace, she had been forced to make unendurable sacrifices, and that, accursed by those sacrifices, she had ended up in her present state. Whereupon the other lady begins to laugh, explaining that the diamonds were always just paste gems. That is how the story ends.

This, too, is a work by Maupassant.[13] It ends with a great flourish, certainly one of Maupassant's strong points. We may be inclined to applaud him for providing us a rare glimpse into what we take to be the true nature of fickle Parisian society. That is the ideal that this work adopts—as well as the source of its unpleasantness. Faced with a terrible situation, the wife abandons her vanity and lowers herself to the level of a servant girl from the countryside. Only after years of hardship does she manage to pay back in full the overwhelming debt—this is conduct of the highest order, undertaken for the highest of motives. If Maupassant had even a touch of moral sympathy, he would, at the very least, have rendered vividly the wife's fine disposition. In fact, the wife's remarkable sincerity is given no play whatsoever. It can't be called deliberate, but the wife is unintentionally fooled and forced into working absurdly hard when it is entirely unnecessary. Despite her diligent and faithful efforts, she receives no reward—neither spiritual nor material—from either Maupassant or his readers. Even if we want to show sympathy, everything is portrayed in such a ridiculous fashion that we are checked from doing so. This is because of the final line of the story, which the author sets up as a particularly witty and flippant punch line. With this single line Maupassant renders his readers—who are no doubt as rich in moral sense as anyone else—incapable of bestowing sympathy even on a clearly deserving object. This is a work that portrays a good deed and thereby stirs in us a desire to show sympathy, but then it forbids us from actually showing any sympathy. Even though it does bore down into one kind of truth, it does harm to the ideal of good, and I cannot endorse it.

Let me provide one more example. I will turn to Zola. An old man marries a bride much younger than himself. Although they are married, for some reason they cannot have a child. Anxious about this, the old man consults a doctor, who, feeling obligated to make some sort of suggestion, comes up with an odd answer: he says that if they go to the seaside and eat a certain kind of shellfish, they will be able to have children. The old man is delighted to hear this and immediately takes his wife to the French equivalent of the Ōiso beach resort. There the wife soon becomes friendly with another man who is visiting, a man who in age and all other respects is perfectly suited to be her husband. The two of them jump into the water and swim about together every day. The old man stays back on the sandy beach each day, watching them in the distance, in his heart admiring the energy of the young people. One day the three of them go for a walk along the shore. The old man, not being so nimble, avoids the rocky parts of the shore by walking up on the embankment instead. The young people walk briskly along the water's edge, not minding the waves. They walk five or six hundred yards and come upon a cave near the shore, whereupon the two enter it. Then, for better or worse, the tide rolls in, temporarily blocking their way out. The old man sits above the cave opening watching white sails in the distance, waiting for the tide to recede so the two can come back out. Bored, he happens to recall the shellfish the doctor had recommended, takes them out, eats some of them, waits a bit longer, eats some more, and then waits a while longer, so that by the time the tide finally recedes and the two emerge, he has polished off a considerable number of shellfish. So far, so good. When he takes his wife back home, the effect of the shellfish is immediately apparent, for the wife becomes pregnant that month. The grand finale comes when they have a beautiful baby—I'm not sure if it is a girl or a boy—and the old man is completely satisfied. I don't know what Zola was thinking when he published this work, but in my view this is a work that couldn't be written if you didn't go even one step beyond the previous Maupassant example in the direction of abandoning one's ideals. If you go and visit the vaudeville houses and other entertainments favored by our own lower classes, you will sometimes find the strangest things winning applause. You would find it strange because the parts that earn the most applause are the parts that would cause any ordinary person to furrow his brow. If Mr. Zola and his ilk were to come to Japan and appear in our vaudeville houses, I am certain they would pack the house.

While I of course cannot claim that all contemporary literature has fallen prey to this vice, no one can dispute that most of it does follow this tendency. It also seems correct to note that this bias toward overvaluing the truth gives rise to a more or less pathological phenomenon. When you gentleman see a detective, I imagine you don't think of him as your equal. And yet when that detective goes home, he has a wife and children, and he is as popular among his neighbors as anyone. That is to say, it turns out he isn't a beast, lacking in all moral sense. He may even be a man of culture, one who enjoys browsing through the scroll paintings at night markets or contemplating the occasional bonsai plant. When, however, this detective takes up his duties as a detective, he only has eyes for digging up facts. To call this a case of seeking the truth might seem irreverent, but there is nothing wrong with saying that the essence of a detective's job is to seek the truth—in the basest sense of that word. Accordingly, his appearance and manner when he is carrying out his duties are not those of an ordinary human being. He has no sense of morality then, no sense of beauty, much less any notion of the heroic. Even if he were to encounter something of great beauty, something tremendously good, or something lofty and noble, he would remain unmoved. I hope I never become a detective. To be a detective, you have to deprive yourself completely of three of the four ideals humans hold dear, and even for the one out of four that remains, you have to devote yourself blindly to its very lowest form. Such a human being is, of course, no longer really human. If we thought of him not as a human being but rather as a machine, then he would at times be quite useful. It is precisely because they are useful that the police bureau employs so many of them, keeping them on monthly salaries. But because they are doing the work of a machine, they themselves ought to adopt the corresponding attitude and give up their status as human when they are carrying out their duties; to do otherwise would be an insult to the rest of us ordinary humans. It may be quite rude of me to compare contemporary literary writers to detectives, but insofar as they take pride in publishing works that advocate truth alone and disregard all other ideals, then in their status as authors they are deficient human beings—whatever their status as individuals may be. I cannot help but declare them pathological. (As I noted before, the four ideal types each possess the same rights and privileges, and none should infringe on any of the others. It may be difficult to obtain equal satisfaction from each of the four types. A certain degree of mutual infringement may also be inevitable. In such cases, though, the infringing party must possess a remarkably strong and unique characteristic, one that is sufficient to cow the infringed-upon party into silence. On this point, the example of *Othello* that I cited previously seems the easiest to defend. As for Zola and Maupasssant, I derive the same sort of vulgar feeling from them as I do from detectives.)

As I have said repeatedly, in the literary arts there are four ideal types, just as I've already noted that these can be further divided into various subtypes. These four ideals are the ideals of the literati, and yet they are also the ideals of humanity in general. Therefore, a literary writer who possesses all four in their highest forms would be the person possessing mankind's highest and most extensive ideals. Moreover, a person possessing the most extensive and highest ideals would be a person capable of influencing others. This means that the literary arts are not simply a matter of technique alone. The works of an author of poor character are capable of transmitting only the most common of ideals, or perhaps no ideals at all, and therefore have only feeble powers of influence. It is only when techniques are employed in order to give full play to an outstanding character, to have it rain down on the heads of others—it is only then that the achievements of the literary arts will shine brightly until the end of time. When I say "shine" here, I don't mean that the author's name will be spoken or that the world will be filled with his praises. I mean that the excellent character of the author will permeate the hearts of readers, spectators, or listeners—that it will become part of their flesh and blood, handed down to their children and grandchildren. This is the only sense in which those who devote themselves to the literary arts can be worthy of being passed down to future generations. It is not a matter of earning a two- or three-line entry in the biographical dictionary. It is not a matter of having one's own self passed down. The only things that can be passed down are printed words. When the self is in this true sense passed down through one generation and then to future generations, only then do we first realize that devoting oneself to the literary arts is not some idle pastime. Only then do we become conscious of the fact that the self is not merely an individual but rather a part of the whole that is the spirit of society. Only then do we awaken to the immense impact of the literary arts on public morality. Starting from a simple will to live, we have carried forward our increasingly differentiated ideals to the present day. To actualize these ideals through the means at hand is to render the purpose of our existence into something higher and more distinguished. That which realizes most fully the greatest ideals is an accomplishment that contributes to the basic purposefulness of our existence. In this sense, the man of letters is in no sense an idler, a worthless person. Even someone like Bashō, whose haiku seem passive in nature, or Li Po, whose poetry celebrates debauchery—these are not idle persons. Their lives were filled with a significance greater—and their contributions to the ultimate purpose of human life were greater—than those of any government minister or any rich and powerful family.

Ideals are nothing in and of themselves. They are merely possible answers offered in response to the question of how best we should live our lives. In this sense, the paintings of an artist and the writings of a literary author are all answers proffered to that question. Men of letters do nothing more: the world sets the question before them and each, according to his own devices and his own interpretations, presents to the questioner his version of the answer. In order to be effective, this answer must be clear; if it lacks clarity, even a brilliant answer will fail to achieve a meeting of minds. What we call technique is the set of tools that a man of letters uses in order to achieve clarity in his answer. A tool, by its very nature, is not the final end of a problem.

Perhaps you will say that you understand this. Or perhaps you will say that you do not understand it. Those of you who understand will not need this, but for those of you who do not yet understand, let me explain a bit more. I've just said that technique is a tool. At first glance that may seem clear, but when we step back and think about it, it actually becomes more complicated. When we are asked what technique is, we are usually stumped for an answer. Often we say that it is a means for expressing some kind of thought. And yet we are here dealing with a thought that has been manifested only by means of the technique. That is to say, in the absence of the thought we can't really consider the technique on its own, just as in the absence of the means used to express it we cannot observe the thought on its own. If we proceed with this argument, we find that the distinction here between technique and thought is highly ambiguous. To put it in terms of this piece of chalk, it is as if we tried to detach its white color from its shape as chalk when discussing it. If we take away the white color we lose its shape, just as if we take away its shape the white color vanishes. What seems to be two is in fact one, just as what seems to be one is in fact two. To argue this in terms of philosophical principles would get quite complicated, so in order to make this easier to grasp I will explain it by way of a concrete example. In fact, this is an example I used recently in one of my university lectures and I think it will do the trick here.

Here are two sentences. The first is from Shakespeare, the second from Defoe. If we compare them, the distinction between technique and content should become clearer.

Uneasy lies the head that wears a crown.

Kings have frequently lamented the miserable consequences of being born to great things, and wished they had been placed in the middle of the two extremes, between the mean and the great.[14]

In general terms, the meanings here are clear and require no explanation. Shakespeare's words describe how the head that wears a crown can rarely rest at ease, just as Defoe's words lament the misfortune of being born to high estate and tell how kings often wish they lived somewhere between the two poles of high and low. Of course, the former is a line of verse, while the latter is a prose passage taken from a long novel, so that if we placed it in the context of the whole work, its meaning would be open to debate. But if we isolate these two phrases and evaluate them independently, we find a great difference in their technique. I will discuss this again later, but note that in terms of their content it should be clear to anyone that they are basically the same. Accordingly, if we take them up in terms of their idea, we would be perfectly justified in seeing them as identical. And yet, while they may be quite similar in terms of their idea, the feeling we get when we read these two phrases is quite different. Recently I had reason to revisit Defoe's works, and in rereading them I happened to come across this phrase. Recalling the above line from Shakespeare's *Henry IV* [*Part* 2], I was surprised to note that, despite the similarity in the contents, the feelings the two elicited were quite different. Until I tried to dissect the reasons for this difference, I was unable to understand it clearly. What I will describe for you now is my attempt to dissect the feeling I had then.

To start with the Shakespeare, this passage does not attempt to express in words the physical and mental state a king experiences over a period of years (ten or twenty years, or even the whole of his reign). Rather, it expresses this by encapsulating it within a single instant. This is quite skillful. To explain this in greater detail, although the word "uneasy" seems to express a certain vague state of mind, it is, in fact, a highly acute and effective word. For example, when you sit on a chair with a broken leg you feel uneasy, just as you feel uneasy when your trousers start sliding down because you've forgotten your suspenders. All express an unsettled state. Of course, an unsettled state implies the passage of a certain length of time, and yet it is a state that seems to pass before our eyes in an instant, without requiring a long time. Therefore, even when it describes a state that continued over a long period of time, this word "uneasy" reduces it to a single instant, a single minute, so that like a picture it instantly elicits an image of that state in the mind.

Some might object to my explanation here, saying: "Yes, I see. What you describe as the state of being uneasy may well exist. But you have described an uneasy state that exists for the body, not for the mind. It may be possible to cut out a cross-section from the uneasy state felt by the body across a long interval of time and use it to reflect the image of that state in the mirror of mental imagination, but the uneasy state felt by the mind—worry, for example, or anxiety—does not form itself into a palpable impression in this way." In response to this attack, I would reply as follows: That such a state of being uneasy exists is beyond doubt. It undoubtedly exists, and yet there is no need for me to consider it here. Even if a king's uneasiness is a mental state, there is no need to consider it as such. More than that, we are here given no opportunity to consider it as such. Directly after "uneasy" comes "lies." This "lies" is a word that applies to concrete things. Accordingly, when we read the word "uneasy," even before we can begin to wonder which sense of "uneasy" this involves, we find it connected directly to the word "lies," and so it becomes clear which sense of "uneasy" is intended.

Even granting this, some may still criticize me as follows: "But 'lies' has the same double sense. Of course we can use it in the sense that you have suggested, of a tangible thing, but the word is also often applied to intangibles. Therefore, 'uneasy lies' does not necessarily give rise to the clear image that you *claim*." I would answer this criticism as follows: If you want to say that "uneasy lies" does not give rise to a clear impression, then you should just go on to read the third word here, "head." This "head" is clearly a concrete thing. Of course, even "head" can be interpreted in a metaphorical sense, but anyone who reads the entire sequence, "uneasy lies the head," will not interpret this "head" as referring to some abstract mental capacity or power of thought. Everyone will interpret this as a physical head—the kind with hair growing out of it. And insofar as "head" is understood to be a concrete object, then "lies," too, will certainly be understood in the tangible, physical sense. Seen in this light, it also becomes difficult to take "uneasy" in the sense of something invisible and immaterial. Of course, we do not know how long this condition of being "uneasy" will persist, but even if we were to say that it was a state continuing over a long period of time, during the interval in which it continued to exist it would always be a state that was visible to the eye. And since it is a state that is always visible, if we were to cut some instant out of it, that cross-section could represent the whole span of time. To put it differently, even for a state that persists for ten or twenty years, we are able to summon it up in our mind as something reduced to a single instant, as something boiled down or concentrated into a single instant. Shakespeare's poetic language takes this boiled down, concentrated impression and sets it before the reader in a single glance, like a flash of light. This is a question of manipulating time. It is a poetic effect, revealing in a single instant a state that continued over a long period of time.

There is, in fact, another feature particular to the Shakespeare passage. In addition to the temporal aspect I've just discussed, this all has a spatial aspect. We can dissect this as follows. If we were to ask whether the word "king" is a concrete noun or an abstract noun, most likely everyone would reply that it is concrete. And they would be correct: it is, after all, a concrete noun. And yet, if we perceive in it only the concrete, it will be comparatively difficult to produce a clear image. If we are told to draw a picture of a king as if before our eyes, we are initially unable to produce a sketch. In our brains the image of "king" that we hold is quite vague and unfocused. But when we are told "the head that wears a crown," our concept of "king" suddenly becomes quite clear. Up to this point we have understood it only as something concrete, but, in fact, this region of our knowledge is quite ambiguous and incoherent. Like looking at something with eyeglasses having the wrong prescription, we can see clearly only that this thing exists independently, that it is independent of other things, but the contents of the thing remain vague. When, however, we are told "uneasy lies the head that wears a crown," we feel as if the image has suddenly come into clear focus. The word "king" alone requires us to imagine the whole extent of a king as a person, and the effort to imagine that whole extent ends up muddling or dispersing our effort at thought. In order to avoid this, we need to limit our imagination to one relevant point—and yet there are so many possible points that we don't know where to direct our imagination. This is where Shakespeare steps in to tell us that, among all the possible points, this is the best one on which to focus our imagination. What he tells us to focus on is not the foot or the hand. Nor is it the backbone, nor, for that matter, the king's belly. No, it is the head that wears the glittering crown; that is where he points his finger and says, "There, if you focus only on that, you will be able to imagine the king clearly." We, who until this moment were stumbling about aimlessly, our gaze scattered blindly across the whole range of possibilities, once we heed this advice and direct our gaze in the indicated direction, then, lo and behold, we see the king. In fact, what becomes clear is only the limited relevant point, and yet this relevant point stands in for the whole—as the essence of the king. If we imagine it clearly, then it is the same as if we imagine the whole clearly. In other words, Shakespeare tells us where we should look to capture the essence of the object. This essence is not merely effective in conveying the whole. It also makes economical use of the reader's powers of attention by rendering unnecessary any dispersal of focus on things other than the essence, by making it possible to strip away completely the inessential. To understand this essence in terms of spatial distribution, Shakespeare has taken an extensive object, the king, and transformed it by reducing it to nothing more than "the head that wears the crown." He has, that is, boiled a six-foot man down to his head, less than a foot in height.

When we look at it in this way, we see that Shakespeare's phrase has condensed both time and space, boiling them down to produce a vivid image of a long period of time and a vast expanse of space. It's as if we were looking at a distant scene with our naked eye, a scene only vaguely in focus, but when we view it through a pair of binoculars, the dispersed scene is neatly reduced to a sharp image that registers on the eye. Here the degree of magnification of the binocular lenses has been adjusted for us by none other than Shakespeare. This is why we obtain a sense of the poetic when we read Shakespeare's phrase.

Now, when we read Defoe's phrase, the effect is completely different. In this fellow's writing style, he writes at length to depict lengthy things and briefly to depict brief things—that is, he makes not the slightest effort to condense matters. He makes us look at even distant scenes with the naked eye. Not only does he fail to adjust the degree of magnification of the lenses, he doesn't even provide us with a pair of binoculars. It is, on the whole, a rather witless mode. We might even be justified in calling it a writing style that ignores the reader's convenience, a careless and even unkind writing style. No one could complain if we described these as sentences lacking in elasticity and resilience. No matter how far these sentences may need to go, they know only how to plod along on the same two feet they were born with, utterly lacking in the ability to invent a rickshaw—not to mention a steam engine or an electric train. This is why they give us a prosaic impression. Prosaic sentences ride neither horses nor trains; lacking cleverness, they are sentences that know only how to walk. This is not meant as criticism. There are times when it is fine to walk. But to wear down your feet the whole year through, to plod along at the same pace whether you are headed to a fire or a funeral—it's fine, I suppose, if that's how you prefer to do things, but it sounds rather foolish. Defoe was a remarkably productive author who wrote some three hundred volumes in his lifetime. We might think of him as a rickshaw puller of an author.

This ends my critique of the passages by these two writers. What have we gained from this critique? The awareness that, in the literary arts, technique is crucial. In the absence of technique, even a clever thought will fail to have an impact. Shakespeare and Defoe expressed the same thought, and yet the results are—as we have seen—remarkably different. We conclude that, despite the similarity of the original thought, this great difference is due entirely to technique. Apparently some members of the Japanese literati have lately been trumpeting all over the place that technique is useless. I have yet to hear a clear explanation of this and so cannot really say much about it. But if you accept the explanation I have given here, I believe it is impossible for anyone who claims to be a literary writer to disregard technique. Moreover, I do not believe that the explanation I have given here is mistaken, logically or otherwise. If you are of the opinion that so long as the piece being played is the work of a famous composer, it doesn't matter how badly it is performed, then perhaps you will believe that technique is irrelevant in writing as well—but I, for one, do not accept this view. Among those who see technique as useless, apparently there are many who proclaim that what is crucial is to touch upon the essence of human life. That, they say, is the goal, and any technique will suffice so long as you reach it. I have yet to hear a clear explanation of this position, and so I do not really understand what they are saying, and yet whenever I hear such words I am left with a strange feeling. Even if he has the command to touch upon this, an author who has no clue about where to touch upon it will be at a loss. To shout blindly, "It's all about human life, human life," without having a clear explanation of what human life really is, well, it's like sounding a fire alarm when you see a tiny spark. The clique that runs around pushing people out of the way like this seem to be doing well, but I suspect that they will end up causing no small amount of mischief. If, before they started demanding that we touch upon human life, they were to clarify matters—to say this is what human life is, and this is what it means to touch upon it, and that is why technique is meaningless—then we would need to take them seriously. Until that happens, I will hold off. On the other hand, if you want to know what I mean when I talk about touching upon human life, I would be happy to provide you with a clear answer—which, by chance, happens to be the topic I will take up next.

I don't want to keep you waiting, and so I will move on to my next point. Compared to those literati who run around insisting that literature touch upon human life and that technique is irrelevant, painters—well, you painters aren't so full of noisy bluster as we are, and you seem to devote yourselves more soberly to your studies; you don't run about blindly setting off alarm bells for no reason. When I look at your mode of practice, it seems to me that you are not so much concerned with whether or not you touch upon human life as you are devoted to polishing your technique. It goes without saying that I am utterly ignorant in the ways of painting. I don't have any right to stick my nose into the field of painting, but sometimes a complete outsider can be useful. Besides, I don't have many opportunities such as this to appear before you gentlemen, and I am making an argument here that applies to the arts as a whole, and so I will plunge right in.

When you paint a person, you use a model, just as when you paint flowers or trees you do so by sketching from real life, whether out in the field or indoors. I think this is perfectly fine and feel that it is an infinitely more serious form of study than that of we literary writers, who are content to sit in our little four-and-a-half-mat rooms, lining up at whim whatever unlikely characters, settings, and events we happen to dream up. The efficacy of your practice is widely accepted, and you hardly need me to comment on it. To proceed here despite my ignorance, I will at least mention what I believe I do understand about this. By undergoing this kind of training, I think you acquire two distinct things. First, your visual sense becomes clearer with regard to the object's size, shape, color, and so forth, and you become more skillful and quicker at depicting in detail this sharpened perception. Second, as the lines and points that you use to depict the object become relatively independent from the actual form and color of that object, you acquire a kind of skill in manipulating these. This second point is a question of technique, and yet since it also involves the manifestation of certain ideals, we cannot see it purely as a question of technique. In fact, up to now Japanese pictorial arts have tended to define value primarily in terms of technique. Despite this, if we leave the eyes of the beholder free to appreciate the work at will, they often elicit great interest by finding in each work the expression of some ideal—in other words, by finding in it an expression of the painter's personality. For example, a single line (even though that one line does not make up the whole of the picture) may manifest a vigor that reflects an ideal associated with the painter's will, just as a curve may manifest a certain ideal with regard to beauty. A certain clarity and lucidity in the relationship between bold and fine may harbor traces of the intellect or of feelings—a reserved sense of gentleness, for example. (By their very nature it is unavoidable that ideals of intellect or emotion are relatively indistinct.) In this way, lines and points themselves come to harbor ideals. Just as with the inscriptions on old monuments or the samples of master calligraphers found in copybooks, it seems quite plausible that the argument that you can tell someone's personality from their handwriting derives from this.

Accordingly, when this technique reaches a certain degree of cultivation, it comes to connote ideals. But while the first technique mentioned above—namely, skill at expressing with clarity and precision our perception of an object—is not entirely unrelated to ideals, it is relatively independent of them. To put this in more easily understood terms, in depicting an object, even when we produce something very like the actual thing, the result at times fails to express the workings of our intellect, emotion, and will. There is something indifferent about it. It seems somehow mechanical. What I mean by "technique" here is this sort of technique. What I want to criticize here are those people who hope to become artists by relying only on this sort of technique. Of course, you gentlemen know better than to think that such technique alone is enough to make an artist. And yet, as you pursue your studies primarily as a matter of technique, as time passes you may, without realizing it, fall into the trap of this sort of bias. To return again to my basic point, art is that which expresses some ideal through the medium of some perceptual object. Therefore, in accord with this fundamental principle, if no ideal is made manifest to our perceptions, then art loses the meaning of its existence. Technique acquires value only as an expedient means for rendering palpable our ideals. A technician who lacks any sort of ideal can be called a show-off, a blustering hack of an artist. We call a painting that engages in self-aggrandizing flourishes vulgar because its surface manifests no ideals. Or if it does manifest them, it does so only in a shallow, narrow, and ignoble way and fails to touch on the essence of human life.

I have borrowed a phrase that has been much in vogue of late—the idea of touching on the essence of human life. What I mean in saying "touch on the essence of human life" is probably already apparent from the preceding discussion, but, as promised, let me explain this in schematic fashion, which should make it relatively simple and clear. At least it seems so to me. We desire for our consciousness to remain continuous. The particular form taken by this continuity and the transformation of its contents offer us a range of possible choices. This range of possible choices represents the ideals available to us. To actualize one of these ideals is to touch upon the essence of human life. Beyond this, there is no way to touch upon the essence of human life no matter how hard you may try. Moreover, these ideals can be divided into four types: truth, beauty, goodness, and the heroic. A person who can actualize these four ideals is to that extent a person who touches upon the essence of human life. A person who is able to express the ideal of truth possesses the same rights and importance as a person able to express the ideal of beauty, and is just as capable of touching upon the essence of human life. A person who is able to express the ideal of goodness possesses the same rights and importance as a person able to express the ideal of the heroic, and is just as capable of touching upon the essence of human life. No matter which ideal you manifest, you are equally able to touch upon that essence. To assert that only one type is capable of touching upon it, and that the others do not touch upon it, is to spout meaningless nonsense, as we have demonstrated logically here. Truth is an ideal of great depth and applicability. Yet to claim that truth alone can touch upon the essence of life, and that the other ideals cannot do so, is to be color-blind, unable to perceive that the world includes paths other than the truth. North, south, east, and west: paths lie in all four directions, all worth traveling and all important.

Each of the four ideals undergoes internal differentiation. These internal differentiations give rise to transformations. As they give rise to transformations, they present opportunities for progress. In this process of transformation a person who actualizes the newest ideal is a person who has recognized a new meaning in life. In this process of transformation the person who actualizes an ideal most deeply is the person who has touched most essentially the essence of life. (It goes without saying that "essential" here is an adjective that applies equally to the four ideals of truth, goodness, beauty, and the heroic. It is meaningless to claim that "essential" applies only to something like wretchedness or darkness.) In this process of transformation the person who actualizes an ideal in the broadest way is the person who has touched most broadly on the essence of life. The person who combines these three with an ability to actualize them using perfect technique is the ideal artist—a saint of the arts. A saint of the arts must, first of all, be a saint in general: only when technique is added to this does he or she become a saint of the arts. There is no unique ideal that distinguishes the saint from all others. A saint is simply one who has reached an understanding of the problem of how one should live.

When highly developed ideals and flawless technique come together, the literary arts reach a kind of perfection. (Therefore, it is, in fact, logical to interpret literary perfection as something that varies from age to age.) When literary art achieves perfection, those who come into contact with it will find themselves falling into perfect correspondence[15] with it—assuming the times are right for this. This perfect correspondence is the ultimate effect that the literary arts can bestow upon us. The times are right for this when the ideal manifested within a work of literary perfection is in agreement with our own ideal, or, again, when our own ideal finds itself being pulled along by the work toward something new, something deeper or more extensive, and thereby undergoes a moment of awakening, a moment of enlightenment. The difficulty for the ordinary masses to achieve enlightenment is not limited to the world of Buddhist law. One who is limited to an ideal of a different order will be unable to experience this effect, no matter how hard he may try.

The phrase "receptive affinity" may seem strange and hard to understand. Let me try to explain it more clearly. An artist uses as expedient means various words or colors to express the ideal that he has cultivated. Accordingly, the expressed ideal is nothing more than the exact depiction of a certain model of consciousness, a certain mode of continuity of consciousness. Therefore, to say a work produces pleasure is to say that one is in harmony with the continuity of consciousness expressed by the artist. We cannot experience this sort of pleasure if our own continuity of consciousness does not correspond to that of the artist. "Receptive affinity" is the phenomenon that occurs when this correspondence reaches its highest possible degree.

The meaning of correspondence here is perfectly clear. When a corresponding continuity of consciousness permeates our mind, the traces that it leaves even after we put down the work are what we call its affinity. This leaves only the word "receptive" requiring an explanation. In fact, this is already included within the word "correspondence." Correspondence means that my consciousness and his consciousness are matched, that—to speak from the position of how things appear before correspondence is achieved—these two have merged into one; once they come into correspondence, it is impossible to speak of either one or two. Once we enter this domain, we have left behind the ordinary human condition, transcending the world of self and objects. Moreover, with this transcending of the boundary between self and object, we return to the starting point of this lecture, the origin of all of our speculations. When we take up a literary work and lose ourselves in it, unconsciously (in the sense of being un-self-reflective) giving ourselves over to the enjoyment of it, then time and space no longer exist for us; all that exists, then, is a certain continuity of consciousness. In saying that neither time nor space exist, I do not mean that these do not exist for us within the work. Rather, I am referring to the time during which we take up and read the work, as well as to the space we occupy when we do so: we as good as forget how many hours it took us to read the work, just as we forget whether we read it in our study, somewhere at the edge of town, or lying in bed. In forgetting these things, we ordinarily surrender ourselves only for a little while to a state of corre-spondence with the author's continuity of consciousness—but then we step back from this, so that the self returns to the self, and the other to be-ing the other. When we are in that state of correspondence, if we happen to be bitten by a flea, we return immediately to ourselves, just as we do when the clock strikes the hour. Accordingly, we cannot immediately and completely lose ourselves in the pleasure that arises from this correspon-dence. When our own consciousness and that of the author are in this state of repeated merging and separation, we are unable to reach a realm that is purely one or the other—whether we are reading a book or looking at a picture. We call this being distracted, lacking purpose, or being scat-terbrained. Some people never once in their lives come within nodding distance of this realm transcending the self, never once wander in this domain of enchantment. Such a man is a prisoner of this world of things. When, for some reason, such a man suddenly happens to achieve a state of perfect correspondence, he becomes as happy as an ugly man who has won the love of a beautiful woman.

When, among the range of possible "continuities of consciousness," the ideal that is expressed relates primarily to the aspect of continuity, what usually results is a work of literature. When, on the other hand, the ideal that is manifested primarily concerns the content of consciousness, what usually results is a painting. The former ideal is expressed primarily through depiction of the fluctuation of consciousness. Therefore, works in which this mode of fluctuation takes an ideal form are the most apt to produce the effect of receptive affinity. This is the receptive affinity of mo-tion. The latter ideal is expressed primarily through the depiction of a fixed moment of consciousness. When this static mode is skillfully ren-dered, when consciousness finds something upon which it wishes to come to a halt and when this frozen moment is captured, the viewer is likely to achieve a state of receptive affinity. This is the receptive affinity of still-ness. However, this distinction between literature and painting holds only at the level of their primary tendencies; in reality the distinction is not so clear. To consider these two elements only in terms of literature, the mode of fluctuation can be thought of in terms of the problem of dynamics in literature, while the static mode should be thought of in terms of the prob-lem of literary subject matter. In the underdeveloped literary criticism that exists today, no one has yet taken up either topic, so there remains infinite room for future research. In my *Theory of Literature* I presented my own rather halting thoughts on this point, so please refer to it if you are interested. But this is really a matter of exploring uncharted territory, so my work will be of only limited help to you. If people should build on it, accumulating new knowledge, filling in the gaps and correcting my errors, it may yet be possible in the future to establish a true science of literary criticism. For various reasons I expect to devote myself primarily to composing creative works and thus don't expect to make many future contributions in this area. But I remain convinced that should a dedicated scholar emerge to pioneer this field in earnest, the scholarly world would profit enormously from his endeavors.

There is one final point I would like to make. By our nature we are imbued with a rather base desire to live—to live and nothing more. It is on the basis of this rather base motive that our distinction between subject and object rests. This, in turn, gave rise to the possibility of choosing what sort of continuity of consciousness we would like to live out, and as our range of possible choices expanded, it gave rise to certain ideal types. These ideal types branched out along several pathways: we have the philosopher (or scientist), the literary writer, and the man of action. The literary writer, in turn, created four ideal types, which branched off into various distinct paths, so that each carries on the process of actualizing that specific continuity of conscious that he or she individually desires. Which is to say that this is simply an instance that is already inferred from the more general problem of how we should exist, how we should live our lives. What one chooses to become, therefore, is never unrelated to the problem of actual profit or loss. The world at large calls artists and literary writers idlers and considers their work useless. But in truth there are any number of persons whose work is less valuable than that of artists and literary writers. Among those who have themselves run around in cars from morning to night are many whose work is less important than that of literary writers and artists. It doesn't change anything when they boast about how valuable their services are to the nation or bluster about busily as if they had a greater right to exist than ten ordinary men. What they mean by "valuable" or "useless" is utterly childish. I don't care if they become angry with me for saying this—it won't change anything. Their anger arises from their inability to understand reason. Rather than getting angry, they would be better off to come round with their heads bowed down in order to have some sense knocked into them. If they come with the right attitude, I'll be happy to teach them anytime.

Now, recently I quit my position at the university, and my friends all like to laugh at me because I lie on the verandah and take afternoon naps. In fact, it may not be laughter as much as it is envy. Well, yes, I do take the occasional afternoon nap. And that is not all: I take the occasional morning nap and evening nap, too. Yet if, while lying there, I devote myself to thinking about the way to realize some important ideal, then I may well be doing something more important than all those self-proclaimed national treasures who spend hours being carried around in their cars, racing with the streetcars. When I am lying down, I am not simply lying down. I am lying down in order to think about important matters. Unfortunately, I have not yet managed to reach any great conclusions. Yet I am no idler. Nor are you gentlemen idlers. Those who think of us as idlers are the real idlers—either that or they are fools. Literary writers may need idle time, but they are not idlers. An idler is someone who is unable to contribute to the world. It is someone who is unable to come up with some understanding of how we should live, unable to teach the significance of life to ordinary people. That sort of person is an idler, no matter how hard they may breathe when they work. A literary writer is not an idler, no matter how often he takes naps out on the verandah. The *idle time* of a literary writer should never be conflated with the *idle time* of lazy aristocrats or the careless rich. For a literary writer to think of himself as an idler is to abandon his true calling, it is to fly in the face of nature itself. We must insist that an artist is not an idler. No matter how often he may nap out on the verandah, we must insist that he is not an idler.

In order, however, to make this forthright assertion, we must possess the confidence of our convictions. In other words, we have to have the guts to come up with our own understanding of the question of how to live, so that no matter what anyone might say to us, we know our ideal is higher and so do not yield, calmly replying instead that those who know nothing about ideals or the significance of human life should not be so impertinent. If we are unable to do this, then no matter how much technique we can muster, what we write will fail to be noble. Nor could it possibly be. If a man takes up his writing brush with timidity, worried that what he writes may cause people to laugh or get angry at him, that fellow lacks guts and his ideals are half-baked; these flaws will be transparently reflected in his writings as well, so that they will seem lacking in self-confidence. No matter how skillful his technique, he will be unable to attract people, much less have an impact on them—to say nothing of eliciting receptive affinity. This sort of man of letters can properly be called an idler. Mr. Masaki's "show-offy spirit of the ordinary hack" can be applied to this sort of idle man of letters.

In sum, what we require are ideals—and ideals don't exist in writing or in paintings but rather in people. Accordingly, to borrow the power of artistic technique in order to render actual existence to some ideal is to realize a part of one's human character. By contrast, to write something that does not touch upon one's character, to scribble down phrases and string together sentences, to crank out writing superficially—this truly is the work of an idler and deserves to be called worthless. If you're going to produce something worthless, you might as well not bother since you'll still be an idler in the end. It is only when one has an ideal that is new, profound, or broad, only when one tries to realize that ideal in the world but finds the world foolishly prevents this—only then does technique become truly useful to the person in question. When the world prevents us from developing our ideal in real life, then the only avenue remaining is to use technique to realize that ideal in the form of a literary work. If one person in a hundred—even one in a thousand—should encounter this literary work and find themselves falling into correspondence with its continuity of consciousness; if they should go a step beyond this and carry forward into their future life some indelible trace that matches the truth, the good, the beautiful, and the heroic that flashed up from the depths of that literary work; if they should attain that rare domain of receptive affinity—if this should happen, then the literary writer's spirit and soul would be transformed into a kind of intangible heredity that influences the consciousness of society at large. The literary writer will then have obtained immortality in the history of human interiority, and he will at last have fulfilled his appointed task.

Translated by Michael K. Bourdaghs

"Preface" to *Literary Criticism*

Literary Criticism (Bungaku Hyōron) *was Sōseki 's second major volume of literary theory. Although it covers many of the issues discussed in* Theory of Literature, *here he focuses primarily on sociological and historical aspects in an attempt to situate eighteenth-century British literature and philosophy—David Hume, Daniel Defoe, Jonathan Swift, Alexander Pope, among many others—in their concrete historical moment. As with* Theory of Literature, *this book originated in a lecture course Sōseki taught at Tokyo Imperial University from September 1905 to March 1907 entitled "Eighteenth-century English Literature." It includes a discussion of methodology in literary history, provides a clearer statement on the position of literary criticism and theory in relation to the broader distinction he draws between literature and science, and a discussion of the disparities of "taste" across historical and cultural boundaries.*

N.B.: As Sōseki notes, the preface was actually delivered as a lecture during the previous semester. It is here translated in its entirety.

This year I intend to lecture on eighteenth-century English literature, but there are several things I must say before I do so. In order to address a topic as substantial as a century of literature, it is necessary to have a clear idea of how to address it. To arrive at this point requires a certain level of preparation. It is, of course, impossible to organize literary history by

From: *Bungaku hyōron* (1909)

means of pure fantasy and empty theory. To begin with, whatever methodology we choose to employ—whether it be criticism, comparison, or description—we must accumulate sufficient materials. "Materials" may sound simple, but it is certainly not easy to collect or organize them. It is difficult enough to go through all the materials that have already been collected. It is even more difficult to evaluate them based on one's own views after having gone through them. There are Chaucer specialists and scholars of Shakespeare. One writer alone provides enough material for a critic to conduct research over a lifetime. It is certainly no easy task clearly and accurately [lit. point to the palm of your hand] to evaluate the dozens or hundreds of writers who appeared within a span of one hundred years. Even among Western scholars, there are many who, beyond the confines of their own historical specialty, have yet to look at works that even ordinary people have read. What, then, can I say about myself, who am Japanese! On top of that, I cannot claim to have studied eighteenth-century literature extensively enough to call myself a specialist. For me to discuss eighteenth-century literature is thus quite unreasonable. In order for me stand before you and claim to be able to lecture on eighteenth-century literature, I should at least prepare for two or three years, read books that I have yet to read, and reread the books that I have read. However, the current academic year comes to an end in June, and I have to give a new lecture course starting in September. I won't be able to prepare as much as I'd like, and I won't be able to give a satisfactory lecture based on my current ability. That is why this lecture course will be a rather imperfect one. I will have to base any systematic criticism I offer on someone else's ideas. It is quite unpleasant for me, too.

Next, I'd like to point out that designations like "eighteenth-century literature" and "nineteenth-century literature" are merely customary designations and have no substantive meaning in and of themselves. Since history proceeds from one event to the next, the development and transformation of literature is natural. Just as it is difficult clearly to demarcate the difference between yesterday and today, the eighteenth century is not an independent entity. It is intimately connected to what came before and after. The eighteenth century naturally grew out of the seventeenth century and naturally flowed into the nineteenth. As a result, we can't tell where the eighteenth century ends and the nineteenth century begins. These are merely perfunctory names. Just because we artificially isolate the eighteenth century with such a perfunctory name doesn't mean we can artificially cut off the substance of its literature from what preceded and succeeded the eighteenth century. What people designate as eighteenth-century literature is merely based on convention and practicality—and, in fact, is actually inconvenient. At least it is not philosophical, nor is it scientific. As such, no one can characterize eighteenth-century literature in simple terms. Yet it is human nature to want to do so. People thus offer sweeping generalizations of complex literary phenomena that lie behind the perfunctory designation, treating them as something characterized by clearly defined features, and bestowing on them the name "eighteenth-century literature."

Needless to say, the eighteenth century lasted one hundred years. If we list the events as they happened from year 1 to year 100, we would have a thorough, continuous record of events. In this sense, eighteenth-century literature is history. It is a part of literary history. And as long as this lecture is on history—if it is at least possible to look at it as history—there is something else I must say before I proceed. Whether history is a form of literature or science depends on how one interprets "history." Past practices of history seem to contain elements of both, but history is undoubtedly a science if you consider how it analyzes and synthesizes social phenomena, how it attempts to clarify the complex, and how it painstakingly attempts to seek out causal relationships. Although no one has discovered an important principle like Newton's law of gravity in history, and although it is unlikely that anyone will ever discover such a reliable principle, it is quite safe to say that the methodology and approach to the study of history is scientific. As long as literary history bears the designation "history," it must, of course, be a part of history. If history is scientific, then literary history must also be scientific. However, some may claim that it is unscientific because, despite the designation "history," it is unlike any other history in that it takes literature as its material. Some may opine that it is not necessary to make literary history scientific. Others may think that literary history is by nature scientific, but since it takes literature as its material—which cannot easily be analyzed scientifically—it is not possible to evaluate it in strictly scientific terms. I'd like to say something on these issues.

It is our normal practice to employ literature and science as *opposite terms*.[1] We consider them to represent two primary forces of mental activity: When our intellectual and emotive activity are externalized, they take the forms of these two currents. There would, of course, be no limit to our discussion if we began rigorously to analyze this distinction. If we deliberately looked for similar aspects between these currents, I am certain that we would find close connections in unexpected places. New and interesting research could be conducted on this point, but from the perspective of common sense people do not have any objection to this distinction. For now, this will suffice. We don't need any additional knowledge or research on this matter for the purposes of this lecture. To convince you that commonsense perceptions are appropriate in this context, I need to refresh your memory concerning the approaches that scientists take.

Scientists interpret science in the following manner: science deals with the question of "how" and does not deal with the question of "why." Take, for example, the phenomenon where a blossom falls and then a fruit takes shape. Science describes in detail the process by which the blossom falls and the process by which the fruit takes shape. However, it ignores the question of *why* the blossom falls and why the fruit takes shape (why it necessarily does so). Once we begin to ask why, we can only arrive at explanations that require some agency or will: we may say it was "God's will" or that the tree wanted to, or that a human being forced it to. The law of nature as seen by the scientist is simply a given law. Scientists do not address the "why" questions that deal with whether or not God controls the universe or the universe evolves based on God's will. It is thus possible to say that science conducts research in a straightforward way.

By comparison, seeking out the "how" results in what we commonly perceive as cause and effect. However, as I suggested earlier, by "cause and effect" I mean that any given phenomenon is preceded by other phenomena, and that any given phenomenon is followed by other phenomena. It certainly does not mean that one *willed* the other to happen [which would answer the "why" question]. To seek out the cause and effect of a phenomenon, scientists dissect it.[2] Deciphering the "how" of a phenomenon is difficult; the more complex the phenomenon, the more difficult it is to decipher. Even when scientists think they understand it, they often make mistakes without sufficient dissection. This is why they dissect as much as they can, paying attention to the given moment as well as the historical context. Once they grasp the "how," they collect these facts and compare them. Scientists then begin searching for possible syntheses. Synthesis occurs when collected facts correspond with one another in their "how." Once synthesis is observed, a principle is produced. If, through the process of synthesis, scientists find that the numerous facts do not correspond in their "how," they classify them according to different categories. In schematic terms, this is what science is. Science, as everyone knows, is an intellectual activity whose foundation emerged out of a desire to possess a clear understanding of the phenomena of the universe and the principles of existence. "Clear understanding" here means clarifying through our intellect things that are not clear to our five senses. The myriad phenomena are thus reduced to categories, often making them abstract.

Insofar as science is like this, it goes without saying that literature—which is generally considered to be an expression of our emotions or an instrument that moves our emotions—is, by and large, different from science. However, if we further scrutinize this distinction, we run into the complications that I brought up earlier; the discussion may also overlap with the lecture I gave last year entitled "Theory of Literature." Let us avoid unprofitable repetition and pointless new research. I will proceed under the assumption that you acquiesce to the common notion that literature and science are opposite terms.

I believe that there is confusion in the ordinary laymen's understanding of literature precisely because they adhere firmly to this distinction. What I wanted to discuss briefly is this confusion. It derives from an understanding that, because literature and science are fundamentally different, literary criticism and literary history must also be different from science. Given the preoccupation with the designation "literature," it is assumed that everything related to literature is independent of science. This is a misunderstanding that must be corrected. Leaving the definition of literature aside, when asked what literature is, we most likely refer to literary products, that is, to the literary works themselves. Now, if we consider the process through which a given work is produced, it is (generally) different from science. However, literary works are, of course, not the same as their criticism or history. What distinguishes history and criticism is our stance [taido] vis-à-vis the finished work. Since we are not approaching a work from the perspective of creating verse or prose, we treat it as a material of objective research. As such, our stance can be equated with that of a scientist who takes a natural phenomenon as his research material. Because we see literary works as a given phenomenon, our stance differs greatly from that when we produce literary works.

But this discussion isn't enough. It is true that there is a great difference between creating a literary work and treating a literary work as research material, but even if everyone treats it as material or as a phenomenon, not everyone will address the work with the same stance. If we could sort out these stances, we could further untangle the misconception I mentioned earlier and better understand how to approach literary history.

In general terms, there are two types of stances with which we approach external things. One is based on one's own preference, that is, a stance based on whether one finds something interesting or boring. Let us call this "appreciative." The other is a stance entirely unrelated to preference, one that attempts to grasp the object's structure, system, and form; it is a very calm and collected stance. Let us call this "non-appreciative" or "critical." Now, let us assume that we are reading a literary work: For the writer literature is an expression of emotions. From the reader's perspective, it is a medium that transfers the writer's emotion to the reader or one that arouses unique emotions in the reader. From this perspective, our stance vis-à-vis a given verse or prose would be "Ah! That was interesting" or "Ah, that was boring," and that would be the end of it. This stance is thus "appreciative." In this regard, the state of mind of the writer and the reader are the same. In effect, there is no harm in conflating the reader's stance with that of the writer.

However, even if a literary work is a medium that arouses emotions, a reader is certainly not required to have an emotional reaction, and even if he does, it is possible to set it aside and approach the text with another stance. For example, it is like a medical doctor who examines excrement. He abandons his likes and dislikes and approaches it from another perspective. It is also like a school teacher who grades student exams. He sets aside his likes and dislikes of the students and looks at the exam papers. This stance can thus be called "non-appreciative" or "critical." It is possible to approach literary texts in a similar manner. We take a verse and look at its rhymes or count the number of lines without considering whether or not the verse is good.

Of these two stances, the second is scientific. It shows that it is possible to address literary works with a scientific stance. Our problem, however, isn't fully resolved yet. We need to further examine the appreciative stance. If someone asks me, "How is Shakespeare's *Hamlet*?" and I answer, "It's interesting," this manifests my view of *Hamlet* via the appreciative stance. But I wonder if the person would be satisfied by my answer. You may find a few individuals who would gladly go home after such a response, but most people won't be satisfied with it. They would add the question, "How so?" "How is it interesting?," they would ask. Now, what if I answer, "It is interesting because it is"? I wouldn't have deceived the person, but I wouldn't have satisfied him either. The person would understand that this fellow Natsume finds *Hamlet* interesting, but he would remain unclear as to why he found it interesting; and I, too, wouldn't be satisfied with the explanation.

The question arises: Could I really call this a criticism of *Hamlet*? I must have found *Hamlet* interesting when I read it and must have told people of that. However, this only means that I have described to people what I felt and have not explained the specific reasons why I felt it. Not only have I not explained it to others, but I haven't explained it to myself. It is appreciative, but there is nothing that answers "how." If the question "how" never came up, then it would be fine, but "how" appears everywhere, at least among thoughtful people, and especially among those with intellectual curiosity. Regardless of their personality, human beings are thoughtful and intellectually curious. That is why science has developed this far. In a response to my reaction to *Hamlet*, the "how" question will inevitably arise. As long as the question is raised, I cannot get by with a simple "it just is." Explaining it is a responsibility I have to myself and to the person who raises the question.

Needless to say, finding something interesting is a formless, odorless emotion. To explain something that is formless and odorless is beyond our capabilities. There is an old saying that "by drinking water, one becomes aware of heat and coldness"—in other words, emotions defy explanation. In order to ask the "how" question about something that defies explanation, we must reveal the intangible in some tangible form, we must translate the intangible into something tangible. For example, hot/cold is a type of perception, but it can be expressed in degrees shown on a thermometer. This is what we must do. Now, how can we explain, in tangible characters or signs, emotions aroused by literary works? This is the next question. Reflecting on our emotions in terms of the "how" question, it is clear that the literary text itself had aroused them. It is thus necessary to refer to the work to give form to our formless emotions. This may be trivial and may even be something that doesn't need to be stated, but it is nevertheless logical. The problem, however, is that it is logical but rather unsatisfying. We read a literary work, feel a certain emotion, ask ourselves "how," and then explain the emotion through the literary work. We may have been able to explain it logically, but we have inadvertently come back to where we started. Asked how we felt when reading *Hamlet*, we respond by saying that it was interesting. Asked "how," we point to *Hamlet* in response. We simply go in circles and don't get anywhere like this.

How, then, shall we proceed? Of course, we cannot leave the work itself behind as long as our feelings were prompted by the work, and as long as we use written characters and words to give form to formless emotions. However, a work is not made up of one character or a word; rather, it is a continuous string of characters and words. *Hamlet*, for example, has five acts. Each act is divided into several scenes. These are further subdivided into spoken lines by Hamlet, Ophelia, Laertes, and others. Although the title may be *Hamlet*, it is, in fact, a phenomenon made up of a continuous string of numerous words and characters. "It is interesting" is thus a response to these organized series of words and characters, which cannot be dismissed as a simple thing. It is an emotion well worth dissecting in our attempt to explain the work. The first step, then, is dissecting the emotions. They include those aroused by a vendetta against the parent's murderer, a broken heart, a massacre, the appearance of ghosts, the protagonist's emotions, ethics, a woman's guilty feeling toward her child for having killed her husband, and a person's loss of consciousness after committing a crime. Then there is the order, degree of strength, and distribution according to which these conditions, interacting with one another, affect our feelings. All these things combine to appeal to our heart and collaborate to make us feel emotion. In other words, if we dissect the emotion "it is interesting," we get various simpler emotions. These simple emotions can all be explained through corresponding tangible facts:

Emotion—interesting = (grief/sorrow + indignation + lamentation + etc.) + (their order, distribution, strength, tempo, development, ebbing and flowing)

Fact—Hamlet = (ghost + Hamlet's rank + love between Hamlet and Ophelia + etc.) + (their order, distribution, strength, tempo, development, ebbing and flowing)

When we dissect our emotions like this and simultaneously dissect the facts that provoke our emotions, we can make pairs between those that align with each other. The further we pursue this dissection, the more detailed our explanations become. If we can offer explanations, we satisfy our own curiosity as well as that of others.

Reflecting on our method here, we began the process of dissection with the emotion "it is interesting." In this sense, this constitutes an appreciative stance. But once we began the analysis, we pursued only dissection. This required us to adopt a critical stance. Hence the process itself is neither solely emotional nor solely rational but is a combination of both. We have designated the first approach as appreciative and the second as critical, but this third one is somewhere in between and can thus be named the "critico-appreciative stance."

Accordingly, we have three stances by which to approach literary production. The first one, the appreciative stance, has long been used by many critics, both from the East and West. This is particularly so for criticism of Chinese prose. This stance is more appropriate to an aficionado than a critic. For such a person it is enough to find a work interesting to enjoy it; they don't require any explanation beyond finding it interesting. However, if we want to satisfy our own curiosity or attempt to improve people's tastes, this is a most inconvenient and immature stance. Even in our time, there are people who simply say that a given work is elegant or fresh and think that this is a worthy criticism. Moreover, there are people who are satisfied by this. These people may have refined taste, but they cannot provide any reason or explanation. I must say that they are unfit to be critics.

The second stance is one that completely ignores taste and hence is a purely scientific approach. Using this approach, we never say something is well or badly done. If we are to evaluate a script, we say that the structure is such and such, the plot is such and such, the progress of the events and character development are such and such—but we never praise or criticize based on our taste. This is the polar opposite of the appreciative stance and is an approach that very few critics have adopted. In the rare cases it has been adopted, it seems to have been limited to dull people. Moreover, people generally do not fancy such an approach. They say that it lacks taste or that it is incomprehensible. But this is a different stance, and we must accept the fact that it features an objective attitude that precludes taste. We must also accept that such a stance is permissible in discussing literary works. In fact, leaving aside an analysis of a single work, this approach becomes especially useful in comparing two or more works, or comparing a series of works, which will become evident from what follows later.

The third stance is one that conventional critics have regularly adopted. When they become dissatisfied with the first stance, they all reach this stage, seeking to improve on it. It is, however, difficult to retain this stance and approach everything through it with confidence. As a result, critics commonly revert to the first stance when they find themselves in a precarious position. Some also repeat their predecessors' criticisms even when they themselves don't feel the same. Even if one strictly adheres to the third stance, it is not easy accurately to practice it in the way we are describing. First, dissecting emotions is extremely difficult. Even when the emotions can be dissected, it is very difficult to point to the specific incidents that provoke such emotional reactions. We tend to produce layers of distant associations even when we reflect on a single word or character. It is as if we are building a thick stack of paper by gluing together layers of thin paper. Just as it is difficult to peel off each individual paper, it is often difficult to dissect the emotions that derive from a single word or character.

I have been discussing these three types of stances in our approach to a single work. When comparing two or more works, the process of analysis becomes more complex but the stances themselves do not change. For example, take the first stance. It would suffice to say something like, "This work is more interesting than, or inferior to, the other." The second stance is much more tedious. We would first take the texts and divide them into categories, then select the similar elements and categorize them accordingly; the differing elements, too, would need to be included in their respective categories. The end product should clearly show the similarities and differences between the works. This constitutes the scientific approach through and through. For example, comparing two stage scripts, we would meticulously point out everything about them, ranging from their content to technical aspects, such as the number of acts and scenes. The comparison can be wide-ranging. We can discuss jealousy or love as a motive. We can examine the path along which a motive develops in a given work compared to that in another work. We can say the protagonist appears in all acts in one work but doesn't appear in the middle section in another work. We can also discuss whether or not two works correspond in their temporal setting.

With the third stance, we would first identify which work we like better and then begin our dissection in order to answer the "how" question. In the earlier example it was one work we found interesting. We could not have found a work interesting without an evaluative set of criteria by which we judged it so. In this instance the set of criteria itself was inside us, the mind of the critic. What we had previously found interesting in our reading or in the natural world subconsciously formed these criteria. Based on them, we had felt a text to be either interesting or boring and skillful or unrefined. In this sense, whether we take up one or two works does not make any difference. Yet when we externalize these mental criteria and use them to address two or more works, the comparison becomes even clearer and hence the degree of clarity stronger.

Logically speaking, if we adopt a given stance on two or more works and extend it across time, it becomes a stance with which we can approach the history of literature. In effect, our three stances can all be used to approach literature from a historical perspective. The first stance, however, is not suited to a lecture on literary history because one would simply take up each work and say it is either interesting or boring. In our society there are people who are well read and have refined tastes but are unable to explain anything when asked about the works. This is because they adopt this first stance to read literary works. In fact, this is an author's stance. It is sufficient for the author, but it proves insufficient for compiling history or critiquing a work. The differences between a critic and an author are too numerous to summarize in a word, but this is one of them. An author does not have to think about the "how"—I am not saying that he shouldn't—since he instinctively finds something interesting and writes about it. Readers, too, find it interesting. This fulfills the task of the author and he can let a critic take care of the "how." Someone callously said that one becomes a critic when one fails to become an author. People often still say this, but this isn't necessarily true. It is certainly not true that only those who fail to become authors become critics. And even if it were true, they differ in what they do, so the failure should not be considered a disgrace. Just because someone says that a man rides a bicycle because he failed to ride a horse, it does not blemish the reputation of the bicycle rider. Some people are suited to certain things and some to other things. It would be interesting to think further about the difference between an author and a critic, but since this isn't the place to do so, I'll just stop here in this introduction.

To return to the earlier discussion, the first stance is closer to that of an author and not that of a critic. It is thus not an appropriate stance to adopt when examining literature historically. That leaves only two to consider. Between them, the critico-appreciative stance never leaves our own likes and dislikes behind. Whatever work we examine, we begin our analysis with the feelings provoked by it. As such, the evaluative set of criteria is always within us, within our present selves. Thus, we evaluate works that appeared in history based on our present-day preferences. For example, let's say we feel that eighteenth-century English poetry is unnatural, pretentious, and boring. We then refer to specific verses and poems that are boring, highlight various poets, and show examples accordingly. We may then venture a historical comparison of works and say that the degree of unnaturalness is stronger in x than in y and provide evidence to back this up. For example, we may say that the unnaturalness diminished toward the end of the eighteenth century and outline our reasons for that. In such a manner, the taste we acquired in the present remains the sole criterion, always shaping our criticism.

The third stance is a purely critical one. This stance is not founded on taste but is one that studies literature from a historical perspective primarily to satisfy our intellectual curiosity. Through historical examination, it seeks clear and comprehensive understanding of the complex phenomenon called literature. Accordingly, if we are evaluating eighteenth-century verse, we do not show our own likes and dislikes. Just as a physicist examines the natural world, we bracket off our taste and dissect the works' characteristics and synthesize them. We then seek to gain knowledge of the conditions under which such characteristics appeared, whether they be social or political conditions or cultural preferences. There are various forms of "knowledge" that can be acquired. Some may seek to understand the writer through the work, while others may attempt to discern the historical conditions through the work. Some may put their effort into finding the cause and effect between two works, while still others may seek out the principles of cause and effect between a given work and its social conditions. Whatever we seek, the primary motive is the desire to know—to clarify the complex—and not whether we like or dislike a certain work. Approached from this stance, literature constitutes a social phenomenon; such criticism thus describes the importance of literature as a social factor.

Now let us reflect on the two stances. The starting point of the critico-appreciative stance may be our emotions, but the subsequent procedure is scientific. It won't be satisfactory if it is not carried out scientifically, so we can say that it ought to be scientific even if we don't have many successful cases. The critical stance is purely scientific. Even if the existing criticism is not scientific, ideally it, too, ought to be scientific.

Having come this far, I hope that I have largely dispelled whatever confusion you may have had concerning literature, literary criticism, and literary history. To summarize, the terms "literature" and "science" are generally used to denote two different human activities. Contrary to the common misunderstanding of the literary, not only do literary criticism and literary history involve many scientific elements, but literary history can be entirely scientific.

The reason why I am providing such a lengthy discussion on this issue is because I have encountered many people who say: "Literature is not science. There is no way one can study literature scientifically." This line of argument is like saying flowers are not science and hence there is no way to study flowers scientifically. Or it is like saying that birds are not science and therefore there is no way to study birds scientifically. Of course, flowers are not science, but botany is. Birds are not science, but zoology is. Literature is not science, but literary criticism and history are both science. At the very least, they must be approached, in part, scientifically. Whether or not one succeeds in doing so is, of course, entirely another issue.

As we have discussed, criticism and the historical study of literature can roughly be divided into two general approaches, which can be further subdivided in countless ways. The sheer number of approaches attests to the complexity of the endeavor. Strictly speaking, it gives the lie to any preposterous claims I might make about being able to explain something as daunting as eighteenth-century literature. To give my lecture after having raised these issues is like telling you in advance that I'm going to tell a tall tale; depending on how you look at it, it's rather comical. In fact, looking at works of literary historians and critics up to the present, there aren't any who have successfully carried out such a study. They have merely strung together what are nothing more than notes and memos. I am surprised that both the writers and readers have been satisfied with them. First, their stances are unclear. While one section offers a criticism based on the critico-appreciative stance, the following section provides purely appreciative remarks. Just when I think a section is purely critical, it moves on to the critico-appreciative stance. I can only suspect that the writer is offering disjointed comments to the reader. To take another case, one critic claims that we must focus on a work's characters, while another says that we should try to deduce the historical period from the work. No one explains which is more appropriate. Nor does anyone explain if both are good or both unreasonable. Even if both may be fine, there is no one who will offer descriptions of other possible methods to look at literature. They simply read a book and feel something. Then they read another book and feel yet another thing. But what remains ambiguous is the relationship between the two works, their relative importance, and where the works are situated within the whole field.

Looking at the existing scholarly works, we can say that critics have either critiqued literature in vague terms or have been so confused that they haven't been able to treat literature with clarity and precision. If that is the case for university-level specialists, it should come as no surprise that my lecture—given by such an unlearned man—lacks clarity, originality, or any coherent method. Not that I'm proud of it, but I feel like I need to say it. Therefore, I am certain that you will not be satisfied with my lecture course—nor will I. If I had five or ten years, I might be able to approach texts in ways that would give me relative satisfaction, but when I am pressed for time, as I am, and must begin right after the summer break, there is no way that I can write anything proper.

Now, what stance am I going to adopt in discussing eighteenth-century literature? No critic or literary historian has been able to answer this question with any clarity, and so my own stance will likewise be ambiguous. Just like my predecessors, I may take the appreciative stance in some cases, the critico-appreciative stance in others, and at times possibly even the purely critical stance. I wish there were some fixed principle that guided my shifts in stance in response to specific moments and situations, but I lack any fixed view or appropriate materials, and so I will shift when it seems necessary. This is all rather discouraging, but since the existing historians have done so based on similar circumstances, I hope you will forgive me for doing likewise.

There is one more thing I'd like to point out in relation to what I have said thus far. I don't think anyone discussing the history of foreign literature has said this before. I said earlier that I will not be able to offer originality in criticism or method in discussing eighteenth-century literature. If I don't have original ideas, I must offer secondhand ideas. In terms of what we have discussed thus far, I can offer secondhand ideas from the appreciative stance. I can offer secondhand ideas based on the critico-appreciative stance. Even based on the critical stance, it is possible to offer secondhand ideas. Offering secondhand ideas simply means regurgitating someone else's ideas, but there is an inherent contradiction in doing so with the critico-appreciative stance. Why is this so? Because, as I stated earlier, the starting point of the critico-appreciative stance is one's own taste; we then proceed scientifically to explicate this foundational taste. The criticism, in other words, is a validation of our taste, our own criteria. Just as I stated earlier, this taste resides in oneself, that is, in the present-day self. Thus, if hypothetically I were to say that I'll adopt this stance in lecturing on eighteenth-century literature, this also means that I am going to use my own present taste as the criteria by which to evaluate it. If I apply my taste, which is very specific to me, in my critique of eighteenth-century literature—whether it be Johnson, Pope, Fielding, or Sterne—and evaluate their work based on this criteria, it would be my criticism and not anyone else's. If my criticism is specific to me, it cannot be someone else's. I would be providing you with secondhand criticism if I take other critics, such as Dobson and Stephen, and introduce you to their criticism of eighteenth-century literature based on their own current tastes.[3] This, however, would not constitute a critico-appreciative stance on my part. It may comprise a critico-appreciative stance, but it is not my own because it merely replicates someone else's stance.

There is one instance in which this contradiction wouldn't be an issue. This is when the English critics' critico-appreciative stance and my own stance coincidentally correspond with one another, leading us to produce similar criticisms. As a matter of practice, this may still constitute second-hand criticism because the originator of the criticism is an Englishman. Even if another critic produced it by himself, as long as someone else has already publicly presented the idea, this critic cannot claim originality. From the public's point of view, this is secondhand criticism. Simultaneously, however, from my perspective it is in no way an imitation or a copy. The criticism is, after all, purely based on my own critico-appreciative stance. In this case my criticism would be both secondhand and original simultaneously.

If such correspondence is possible, we need to distinguish between two types. The first is coincidental correspondence. For example, let's say that there are two men—x and y—and they both get an upset stomach by eating soba noodles. Such correspondence occurs without any basis for correspondence. It is very rare precisely because there is no basis for it. The second is necessary correspondence. For example, if their own child were to die, x would feel grief and so would y. The same can be said of reading literature. There must be something that produces the same reaction in both Europeans and Asians. If their feelings naturally correspond for a reason, there is a necessary correspondence, one that is distinctly different from the first.

For us to assume that necessary correspondence is possible, we must also assume the universality of taste. Without the universality of taste, necessary correspondence cannot be conceived. Now, we cannot judge the value of this proposition without asking whether the universality of taste applies to all tastes, only to part of them, or to none of them. In fact, I was going to address this issue of universality in the lecture course I gave last year, but I ran out of time and didn't get around to it. It would be very convenient if I can use this time to go into detail, but since this lecture is not on the theory of literature, it is not the place for a detailed discussion. Instead, I'll simply mention several things that are on my mind. They are all rather commonplace, so it's not something that you need to pay close attention to. What is important is the conclusion, so do listen with that in mind.

To say that all tastes are universal is the view of a fool. This is easily seen merely by reflecting upon reality. To put it simply, there are those who are interested in living in a city and others who are attracted to life in the countryside. There is nothing that says you must like the city or that you must like the countryside. For one to find a place elegant or vulgar, lofty or low, is based on individual preferences. Even if such distinctions applied to the city and the countryside, in point of fact people don't necessarily prefer elegance. Vulgar and earthy are both a matter of taste. As long as there are people who like the vulgar, we cannot say that taste is universal in all aspects. However, this is not to say that tastes are all individually unique and that they do not partially overlap. This, too, can easily be seen by reflecting on reality. Here is another familiar example. Most people take pleasure in listening to a bird sing. Even if they are not moved by a singing bird, people no doubt feel pleased when they see a parent loving a child and feel pleasure seeing a husband and wife getting along with each other. This appears to be equally true in the West and in the East, as well as in the past and present. Of course, with the transformations brought about by time, the degree to which these events affect our feelings may differ. Even if our tastes for these things are not universal, there must be something that is. First of all, don't we correspond based on the fact that we are all human beings? We correspond based on the fact that men and women join together. We correspond based on the fact that it is the woman who gives birth. With all these correspondences, we won't simply be speculating if we assume that a partial correspondence exists, even if we can't claim that our tastes all correspond. Insofar as there is such a universal partial correspondence, our criticisms of a given work, based on the critico-appreciative stance, will arrive at the same conclusions. Here necessary correspondence must occur.

There is one other form of taste that is conducive to necessary correspondence. This is one that becomes especially important when studying foreign literature. Precisely because this form of taste is universal, we can, with reasonable conviction, expect to find a necessary correspondence with foreigners even as we make a relatively independent evaluation of works written in a foreign language. This taste responds to none other than the order, length, and structure of materials used in literary works. The taste I have been discussing until now responded to the content of the materials themselves, but that which I am discussing now responds to the relation and arrangement of materials. Let's take Delacroix's *Dante et Virgile* as an example. Dante and Virgil are standing on a boat, and we can see their well-proportioned profiles and facial expressions. The ghost and spirits, portrayed among what appear to be waves or flames, gather round them, and we see how they surround the two characters at the center. It is all very well balanced. If, at first glance, it appears complete and lacks nothing, arousing a satisfying sense that it is well constructed, then this painting appeals to our taste based on the arrangement of the materials. This taste is a universal one and is no different in the West and the East. It is universal because all it takes is a word of advice from a person of discernment and we are instantly enlightened as to its beauty. Even if there were a person who would stridently go against it, all we need do is ask him if he prefers an artistic work that lacks a center, one that is dispersed and lacking coherence, or one that is muddled. Go one step further and ask if he'd prefer a work that portrays things that are unnecessary or depicts the necessary in an incoherent manner. No one would answer in the affirmative. Of course, people don't necessarily agree on what is dispersed, tiresome, or unsatisfying. However, as long as a person is cultivated, in the majority of cases they will be persuaded if the man of good taste makes an effort to explain things. As such, there are ample grounds to claim that this is universal even if there might be a few exceptions.

However, within the Delacroix painting there lies among the ghosts a woman whose appearance is extremely unpleasant, even more distasteful than that of Kasane.[4] She lies there, beneath the boat, face up. If, in looking at this ghost, one feels that it's dreadful and that the painting would be better off without it, one's taste is responding to the material itself. (It goes without saying that such taste is also manifested in the beauty and ugliness, good and bad, truth and falsity, splendor and dullness of the materials, but it would be too tedious to provide examples for all, so I'll omit them.)

I suspect these two types of taste will become clearer once I discuss them with reference to literary works. Take Alexander Dumas's *Black Tulip*, for example.[5] If I say this work is bad—its structure is too contrived, almost like a cheap trick; it may be clever, but it is extremely artificial and unnatural—my taste is not responding to the materials themselves but to their order and arrangement. If I say that the characters' motives are not well developed, that they are too simplistically portrayed, my dissatisfaction derives from the characters in the work—hence the materials themselves. Here is another example. I take Maupassant's *Une Vie* and say it has no focus.[6] I cannot tell whether the main theme is the relationship between the husband and wife or the affection between a parent and child. They are both independent and do not properly combine with one another to produce a single work. Again, this is a criticism based not on my taste regarding the materials themselves but the way the materials are arranged.

I can cite other examples, but I'll stop here, assuming that people have understood. Tastes that respond to the arrangement of materials are, at least relatively speaking, unbound by local emotions and customs and hence universal. Individual tastes may differ in degree but they do not differ in kind. As long as you have a relatively cultivated taste—even as a Japanese—you can rely on your own taste as the standard criterion because there is no other kind, and you should be able to persuade a foreigner to agree with your views. Hence, this isn't merely about necessary correspondence. It is an important form of taste because, even if a foreigner and a Japanese should reach opposite conclusions, it allows each of us to claim validity and point out the other's mistake.

For these reasons, necessary correspondences occur in reading literary works, but because universality cannot be claimed for the whole range of taste—either because the realm of universality is not that large or because, even when there is universality, its degree varies, depending on historical period and nationality—necessary correspondence does not occur that easily or extensively. (This is especially the case with Western poetry, although not so much with novels.) Furthermore, there is one thing that interferes with this correspondence: Certain things in literature are constructed through simple elements. It is possible that those simple elements produce refined verse and prose. However, simple things tend to be lacking in variation. Without variation, people get tired of them. Moreover, social conditions and the human mind—the main source of materials for literature—become increasingly complex every day. Because of this, the literature of our latter-day world tends to become more complex, just as it tends to seek out variation, thereby leaving behind basic universal taste. Here's an example of something becoming complex. The phenomenon of a man and a woman falling in love is one that attracts all human beings universally. However, there can be many conditions surrounding the man and woman in love. For example, if a man loves a woman who has a husband, things become a little more complicated. If things become complicated, they may simultaneously lose universality. People in one country may find it interesting to see a man fall in love with a woman with a husband, but people in another country may not like the fact that she has a husband. And those in yet another country may feel that it is too banal and hence not worthy of literary production. Furthermore, let's say that a man and a woman are in love and war breaks out, and the man tries to stay with the woman instead of going off to war. In one historical period people may like the fact that he abandons war, while in another historical period they may not like it. In one period it may appear surprising, while in another it may be commonplace. We can also imagine an example in which the desire for variation leads away from universal taste. If a writer portrays a scene in which a character, astonished by the light of an electric lamp, jumps up and down in excitement and delight and says, "There is love, there is life, there is every emotion and every form of art in this light," the sense of this will certainly not be shared by the general public.

For these reasons, necessary correspondence based on universality of taste is quite rare (leaving aside those arising from the arrangement of materials). There is also one more hurdle besides this when we take up foreign literature as the object of criticism: it is language. By differences in language I do not mean that Japanese and English differ in structure or in grammar. Language has "delicate shades of meaning" as well as tone. Since this doesn't explain anything, I'll provide an easy example and discuss it further. As you know, in Japan there is a literary form called haiku, a poetic form composed of seventeen syllables. The issue at hand can be understood very easily with this form. Comparing two verses composed on the same topic, with the same materials, and using entirely the same design, it often happens that while one seems delightful, the other seems less so or, at times, even distasteful. If you analyze this carefully, it is possible to discover the reasons behind such reactions. I will proceed with my discussion under the assumption that this is true in haiku.

Looking at the two very similar verses, general readers, such as a hairdresser or a liquor store owner, might not recognize the difference. They would assume they are the same verse and think of them as equally worthy. Haiku, of course, is composed in Japanese. Even when they read verses on the same theme, composed in Japanese, Japanese people—people who use the Japanese language and read Japanese on a daily basis—can react in such a different manner. There is a reason for this. Some are perceptive to haiku language because they are familiar with it. As a result, they can make out the nuanced shades and tones that haiku language expresses. But others simply do not have the ability to discern them. For such a person "Ah! the clear moon" sounds the same as "Hey, the clear moon." Take another example. A person may say, "You are beautiful." Depending on context and tone, this statement can be taken seriously or as ridicule, a compliment or a simple joke. It can be said obnoxiously or even sincerely. Here's a better example. An actor plays the role of Hamlet. Leaving aside the overall interpretation, if he selects certain lines to show Hamlet's indignation, it is possible to express such indignation. If instead he uses them to show his humorous side, he can do so. The actor would not be changing any of the lines.

These issues help us to reassess our study of foreign literature. Japanese people do not have enough practice in English to make out the nuanced shades or tones. Thus, there will be times when a foreigner might say that a given expression is obnoxious, whereas we don't find it so. There will be times when we gloss over as a common phrase what is actually lofty and divine. Japanese people are not very perceptive about these things and hence are probably not as acute as those scholars in England. But this can lead to a bad habit. Somewhere at the back of their minds Japanese people believe that the English people's evaluation of the work is correct because they are taking up a work produced in England and offering a native evaluation of a native product. Evaluating a Japanese work is one thing, but they think that there can be no mistake in what the English say about English literature. It is like believing, without giving it a second thought, the words of a kimono shop clerk because one knows nothing about kimonos.

Without a doubt this problem arises from the difference in languages. You're unfamiliar with the language. You don't feel like saying something bold. It's also a little off-putting. Even if it doesn't put you off, you don't quite know where to start. It seems fuzzy, as if you're looking at someone's face through a silk cloth. You worry about making evaluations based on your own feelings. You would actually be a step ahead if you had feelings about it, but you often don't. That is why you want to believe as true the reading of a person who understands in clearer and more accurate terms. One who understands and sees clearly is not necessarily one who can clearly feel and decipher emotions accurately, but people generally leap to that mistaken conclusion without realizing it.

There is yet another mistaken supposition that arises from the difficulty of working in different languages. This is the common assumption that foreigners possess the standard by which to evaluate foreign literature, whereas we don't, and thus we must abide by their theory. When we believe this, not only do we adhere to the theories with which we agree, but also to those that seem rather unreasonable. This is what happens. Until now you thought a certain way about a given work, but, listening to the criticism of Mr. X—which is very different from yours and which appears rather forced to you—you conclude that what he feels must be correct since he is a native critic. You then think that what you felt before must have been a mistaken and vulgar feeling, and since it is a mistaken feeling, it must be corrected. Humans are strange creatures. You then begin to discard the feelings you had until then and move toward what you *think* is right. In effect, when you take up your study of foreign literature, your own feelings disappear and only those of the foreign critic remain. In fact, there are those whose feelings don't actually change but who pretend that they have. This is one pitfall that we easily encounter in studying foreign literature—which is, to some extent, understandable.

But if we think about this more closely, isn't this the same as assuming that the universality of taste applies to everything? If we can be sure that every aspect of our taste is universal, then there would be nothing wrong with thinking this way. As I mentioned earlier, however, universality of taste only applies to certain aspects of taste. When we try to apply it beyond them, we will end up falling into a fundamental fallacy. It is thus possible to say that the many people who are studying foreign literature, misled and confused by the language barrier, are forced to believe blindly that taste is entirely universal.

How, then, can we read foreign literature with the critico-appreciative stance? I believe there are two methods. The first is to analyze exactly how we feel about a given work without thinking of the language barrier, without worrying about clarity or ambiguity, without thinking about whether it corresponds to the Westerners' opinion. This is the most audacious and unabashed approach, and it produces a natural and honest criticism devoid of any falsehood. This criticism may at times be the polar opposite of that produced by Westerners. Just because your criticism contradicts a Westerner's, it does not mean that you are shallow-minded. This belief has become a widely held bad habit present among those who study foreign literature today. We ought to reflect deeply on this issue and correct it. When Aston wrote his *History of Japanese Literature* or Chamberlain analyzed Japanese rhetoric, they approached them from the English perspective and thereby produced legitimate criticism.[7] The language may be different, but the material content is literature. As long as literature remains the object of criticism, and as long as we use taste as the evaluative criterion, we must not relinquish our own taste and subject ourselves to someone else's. When we do so, we lose our own. If we lose our own taste, we lose the right to evaluate not only foreign literature but also the literature of our own country.

Taste, though universal in part, is primarily local. (We don't necessarily have to ask why; it is simply a fact that can't be denied.) What this means is that taste is shaped by the history, social legends, particular institutions, and customs belonging to a given society. If these varying factors comprise taste, and if these factors differ throughout the world, the tastes resulting from these different factors must also naturally differ. Of course, with the increase in world travel and the growth in human communication and interaction, taste is becoming unified. It is becoming universal. European countries like England, France, and Germany have undoubtedly been affected by this universalizing force. After Japan began interacting with foreign nations, it, too, has become affected by this universalizing force. Although Japan has undoubtedly begun to be affected by this force, it has yet to get through even the first stage of the process. Today there is still a chasm that separates us and them. For example, in the West the kiss is a common form of greeting between husband and wife, as well as between relatives, and the Westerners' taste is based on such a custom. In Japan, until the Restoration a kiss was equivalent to a man and a woman going to bed with one another. Even now kissing is not something that ought to be done in public, especially among the ranks of educated society. However, Japanese poets of *shintaishi*, discovering the word "kiss" in Western verses, use it without reservation in the Japanese context, where the general taste differs considerably.[8] The general public's sense of what this word signifies does not correspond to what the poets of *shintaishi* mean by it. As such, their verses seem unpleasant and deceptive. Even a trifling example such as this makes the current situation clear.

When we evaluate a work produced by people with different tastes, we still ought to apply the taste that we've acquired until now. Listening to our criticism, foreigners who think a kiss to be an innocent matter may well be surprised by our national character, but they will not consider our criticism to be immature. As such, we have ample reason to employ our own standard to evaluate foreign literature; even a Westerner cannot criticize our logic. Of course, if you take this method too far, without reading the text closely and rigorously, you could end up with sloppy criticism. Yet I think this is a risk worth taking. We ought to employ this method, especially under the current conditions that prevail in Japan. I am not sure whether I am up to the task, but I'd like to employ this method if possible.

For example, take the verses by Pope and his followers. Despite their popularity at the time of their production, the contemporary English public considers their verses to be artificial and quite unnatural. We therefore know that the contemporary English public does not have the taste for Pope's poetry. However, just because the contemporary English public says one thing, there is no reason why the contemporary Japanese public should say the same thing about Pope's verse. To say this is to apply uncritically the idea of the universality of taste to the verse of Pope and his followers. That Pope's verses enjoyed such popularity in the eighteenth century shows that they corresponded well with eighteenth-century taste. In other words, Pope's poetry seemed natural in the eighteenth century, though it may not have seemed so in the nineteenth. That Pope adhered to eighteenth- but not to nineteenth-century taste is a historical fact, but whether we Japanese will feel like the people in the eighteenth century or those in the nineteenth remains an open question. We may feel something unique, but nothing like the people in eighteenth- or nineteenth-century England. This, too, is still to be determined. In any case, we can't say anything until we examine our own feelings for the poetry, based on our own taste.

[*The Poems of*] *Ossian* was published at the end of the eighteenth century. People say that it's a fake by Macpherson, but it was extremely popular when it first came out.[9] Goethe and Napoleon both loved it. The English now take an interest in *Ossian* only as a historical phenomenon. There is even one critic who specifically noted that he couldn't bear to read it all the way through. *Ossian*, in other words, suited the popular consciousness of its contemporaries but not that of today. When we Japanese read *Ossian*, whether we would correspond to the taste of those in the eighteenth century or to those of today is yet to be determined. Just because its contemporaries lauded it, there is no reason for us to commend it. Just because those in the present disparage it, there is no reason for us to parrot that. We ought to evaluate it based on our own feelings (insofar as our feelings are actually provoked by it).

As I have said repeatedly, we have yet to evaluate foreign literature in a way that is honest to ourselves because of the language barrier and some other misunderstandings. We have either been too timid or have lacked enthusiasm. It is thus my hope that you will all be true to yourselves as you study foreign literature—and I, too, will try to remain as steadfast as possible. However, this is quite a tedious endeavor. We must read the works closely and thoroughly analyze the feelings evoked by them. As such, we can't possibly cover eighteenth-century literature within a year or two. We must proceed slowly. Please keep that in mind.

One other method possible under the critico-appreciative stance is to survey the works of Westerners—their feelings and their analyses of literary works of their own country—and to use them as a reference. These do not represent your own feelings but rather someone else's. The feelings provoked by the texts that they describe may not be your own, but they can help to cultivate yours and become a comparative reference point. Moreover, they are also an object of great curiosity. A work is produced under specific social conditions. We might ask: How did the people who lived within that society react to the work? How did they feel and analyze it? How do their feelings and analysis differ from our own? If they differ, in what respects do our tastes and theirs differ? From what social condition do such differences arise? To clarify these things is extremely beneficial in expanding our own perspective. In addition, if you introduce another criticism of the work produced fifty years later, showing how things changed over fifty years, it is possible to discern the change in taste within one nation. And if we can figure out why such differences occurred, we can discuss that as well.

When we look at transformation of taste this way, we see that taste undergoes a process of natural development, and that the taste of the earlier period is a necessary precondition for the present taste to take shape. In effect, if the taste of the earlier period had not been thus, the taste of the subsequent years might not be thus either. Since Japan has had a certain taste in the past, and since our present-day taste is a natural development of that, our contemporary taste will not necessarily correspond to contemporary English taste. Just because they don't correspond, there is no need to be embarrassed by it. This is something we can begin to understand as we survey the works of Western critics. Thus, although this method may appear to be a simple introduction of the secondhand critico-appreciative stance, one that does not derive from one's own feelings, if carried out competently it can constitute a method of great interest. As long as my meager knowledge permits—and as long as time permits—I would like to try this method as well. It is a misconception to say that it is too routine or dull simply to survey other people's theories. To survey a large body of work and to introduce it in clear terms is a skill in itself. If this is merely routine, then descriptive sciences that simply categorize natural phenomena are equally routine. Lecturing on literature is similar. A routine lecture is often valuable, but it is hard to produce a valuable lecture given the way I approach things, so please keep that in mind, too.

Translated by Atsuko Ueda

THE MERITS AND FLAWS OF -ISMS

This brief essay, first published in the Asahi *newspaper on July 23, 1910, constitutes one of Sōseki's most direct responses to the literary theories of the Naturalist* (shizenshugi) *school of fiction, which held sway in Japanese literary circles at the time. While Naturalists advocated a confessional literature that sought to represent even the ugliest truths about human existence, Sōseki here advocates a more fluid view of literary value.*

Generally what we call -isms or doctrines refer to something that a man of meticulous character has conjured up by sorting through an infinite number of facts, thereby making it easier for us to abstract them and store them neatly in the drawers of our minds. Because they are tightly bound and nicely tucked away, it is rather tedious to take them apart and tiresome to pull them out; as such, they often prove useless when needed. In this respect, most -isms are unlike the compass chariots that provide direct guidance in our daily lives and instead are mere filing cabinets created to satisfy our intellectual curiosity.[1] They are not so much a composition as an index to one.

Simultaneously, many -isms take shape when a number of arbitrary yet similar examples are filtered through a relatively sophisticated mind and

---

"Izumu no kōka" (Tokyo *Asahi* Newspaper, 1910)

are further condensed by it. It isn't exactly a form but more like the contours of one. It has no substance. We preserve only the contours of things and discard their substance for the same reason we carry paper money instead of coins—it is convenient for small human beings.

In this sense, -isms are like a company's financial statement or, for that matter, like a student's report card. Behind the single column of figures, behind the two rows of final grades there lies hidden the passage of time, a time in which many people experienced many things—their strivings, joys, and griefs; their successes and failures—all of which can never be repeated.

Therefore, -isms are founded upon events that have passed. They capture and consolidate the past, simplifying the history of experience. They are the contours or patterns of known facts. To address the future with these patterns is like anticipating all the events that will ever occur under the heavens and trying to fit them all into a man-made receptacle. Perhaps, for convenience's sake, it is possible to apply such patterns to mechanical phenomena that exist in the natural world, especially to the simple ones that are prone to repetition. This is why scientists' study can be projected into the future. However, if our mental lives were to fall under the sway of some -ism, that predetermined pattern would immediately cause us to feel constrained in our existence. To exist as the vehicle for some predetermined pattern is to perform a mechanical function for the sake of a lifeless shell. We would feel rage at the shame of being unable to develop mentally according to our own natural principles, at being unable to follow our own true contours.

When our minds feel this sort of shame, we experience a premonition that the past contours of things are about to crumble. We see the transgression of trying to project into the future recklessly and blindly and use that which simply cannot be projected into the future.

To assume that these -isms should govern us in the future because they have done so in the past and make decisions based on them because they appeared to work for a short period of time is simply reckless, like measuring height or length with a measuring cup.

It has been five or six years since the advent of Naturalism. I am sure that its advocates have their reasons for supporting it. As far as I know—and as far as I understand it (leaving aside the discussions that I do not understand)—not everything about it necessarily warrants criticism. However, Naturalism is an -ism. Whether it be in life or in art, it took a slice of history that developed for various reasons in the West, reduced it to a certain contour, and brought it over on a boat. It goes without saying that we do not live our lives to substantiate these contours. Naturalism is meaningful only when the substance of our activities naturally happens to conform with these contours.

The general public detests Naturalism. Naturalists make their doctrine sound like an eternal truth and attempt forcefully to apply it to every aspect of our lives. If the Naturalists pursued their ways a little more cautiously and with a little more patience, they would realize that they are accelerating their own demise. Rather than trying to sketch out a large enough circle to accommodate every aspect of human life and then trying to corral the future into it, I suspect it would be wiser for them to firmly hold on to one small particle within it and instead try to win recognition of the permanence of Naturalism through it.

Translated by Atsuko Ueda

My Individualism

This is one of Sōseki's most celebrated philosophical lectures. In it he defines his own ethical stance and provides his critical analysis of the position of Japanese society—in particular its elite segments—at the beginning of the Taishō era (1912–26). It is also of particular interest because he reflects back on the period of his life in which he produced his Theory of Literature. *Together with another late lecture entitled* "The Civilization of Modern-Day Japan" (Gendai Nihon no kaika, 1911),[1] *it is the closest version we possess of the final form of the ten-year project Sōseki had set for himself during his 1900–1902 stay in London: to theorize literature in all of its psychological and sociological ramifications.*

This is my first visit to the famous Gakushūin. I had always imagined the campus to be out here somewhere, but I was never quite sure until today.

As Mr. Okada mentioned in his introduction, he originally asked me to speak to you last spring.[2] I was unable to oblige him at the time—exactly why this was so Mr. Okada seems to remember better than I, and I trust that his explanation has been sufficient. In any case, I had to refuse. However, rather than simply decline the invitation, I volunteered to deliver the next lecture in the series and learned that it was scheduled for October. After some calculating, I concluded that I should be able to pull something together, what with so many months left to go, and I accepted.

Watakushi no Kojinshugi (1914)

Unfortunately—or perhaps fortunately—I became ill and spent the entire month of September in bed.[3] I was up and around by October, it is true, but I was still too unsteady for lecturing. On the other hand, I could hardly ignore my promise, and the thought that they were going to be after me any day now was a constant source of anxiety.

Soon the unsteadiness went away, but the end of October arrived with no communication from Gakūshuin. I had not sent word of my illness, but a few of the newspapers had apparently carried the news, which led me to the comforting belief that the Gakūshuin people had realized the problem and had asked someone else to give the lecture instead. Then, all of a sudden, Mr. Okada showed up again—in boots, no less. Of course, the fact that it was raining that day may have had something to do with it. But there he was, having trekked in his rain boots all the way to my house in Waseda to announce that the lecture had been postponed until the end of November, at which time he hoped I would make good on my promise. Meanwhile, I had assumed that I had evaded my responsibility, and I was more than a little taken aback. But there was still over a month left and I thought I should be able to manage something. Again I agreed to give a talk.

One would think that from the spring to October, or from the end of October to the twenty-fifth of November, I could have found plenty of time to organize a lecture of some kind. But I was not feeling well, and just thinking about a talk became burdensome. No, I decided, I simply wouldn't bother with the talk until the twenty-fifth of November, and then let it go day after day. At last, with barely three days left, I began to feel that I had better think of something to talk about, but it was still such an unpleasant prospect that I spent the day painting.

Now, please don't think that I really know how to paint. I simply dashed off this little thing, stuck it to the wall, and then spent two or three days alone, staring vacantly at what I had done. Yesterday, I believe, a friend came by and said he thought my picture was very good—no, not that the painting itself was good but rather that it looked like something I must have done when I was in a very good mood. I told him he was wrong: I had done the painting not because I was feeling good but because I was feeling bad. And I went on to explain my mood to him. Just as there are those who channel their happiness into paintings or calligraphy or books, there are others who take up the brush to create paintings or literature as a way to attain happiness. And when we see the results that spring from these two very different psychological states, oddly enough they are often identical. I won't go any deeper into this subject. It is just something I wanted to mention and has nothing to do with the main idea of my talk.

At any rate, there I was, passing the time looking at this funny painting and doing nothing to organize my lecture. And so the twenty-fifth arrived—today—the day I must appear to give my talk whether I liked it or not. I spent some time this morning trying to organize my thoughts, but it seems I am inadequately prepared. I must ask you to bear with me and not expect too much.

I do not know how long your club has been in existence,[4] but I see nothing wrong with your practice of bringing in outsiders and having them lecture. On the other hand, it seems to me that you are not likely to hear the kind of entertaining lectures you would like, no matter whom you bring in. I suspect that what interests you is the novelty of someone from the outside.

Here is an ironic tale I heard from a *rakugo* storyteller.[5] Once two feudal lords were enjoying falconry near Meguro. After they had been galloping around for several hours, they became famished, but they had brought no food with them and had strayed from their retainers. All they could do was demand something to eat at a nearby peasant's shack. Taking pity on them, the old farmer and his wife broiled some mackerel they happened to have on hand and served this with barley rice—crude fare for such grand warriors. The lords enjoyed the meal enormously—so much so that the aroma of the fish lingered in their nostrils the next day, and they could hardly stop thinking about the wonderful favor. One of the lords invited the other for a mackerel dinner, much to the surprise of his retainers. There was no gainsaying the commands of the lord, however. The retainers ordered the cook to remove all of the mackerel's slender bones, marinate the fish in sweet sake, and roast it exactly so before serving it to the lord and his guest. This time, of course, the two men were not famished, and the ridiculous care with which the cook had prepared this odd dish had long since expunged any flavor of mackerel. After a few perfunctory pokes with their chopsticks, the two lords looked at each other and said, "If you want mackerel, you've got to go to Meguro."[6]

As I see it, your inviting me to speak to you, your willingness to listen after having been kept waiting from spring to late autumn—despite the fact that you are at the excellent Gakushūin and in constant contact with excellent teachers—exactly resembles the case of the two lords who, satiated with the finest delicacies, long to taste that mackerel from Meguro.

I see Professor Ōmori is here today.[7] Professor Ōmori and I graduated from the university at about the same time. Once, I recall, he complained to me that the students were not really listening to his lectures, that they were lacking in seriousness. He was not talking about Gakushūin students, I believe, but students at a private college. In any case, my reply to him then was rather impolite. Although I am embarrassed to repeat it here, I said, "There's not a student anywhere in the world who would come running to hear *your* lectures." Professor Ōmori may well have misunderstood what I meant by that, so let me take this opportunity to correct any misunderstanding. When we were your age, or perhaps a little older, we were far less well behaved. It would not be too much of an exaggeration to say that we never listened to lectures. I speak from my own experience and observations, of course, and what I have to say may not apply to anyone outside my immediate acquaintance, but, looking back now, I can't help thinking that my impression is quite accurate. Certainly in my own case I looked docile enough, but I was not the type to pay attention to lectures. I did nothing but loaf. With memories like these, I can't find it in me to criticize the earnest young men I see in school today, and it was merely this idea that I sought to convey to Professor Ōmori when I spoke to him so rashly. My purpose in coming here today was not to apologize to Professor Ōmori, but now, in your presence, let me take the opportunity to do so.

Having strayed so far from my subject, I will now try to return to it.

You are all students at an excellent school under the constant guidance of excellent teachers, whose lectures—both specialized and general—you attend every day. As I said earlier, I would imagine that you have bothered to invite me here for a talk much as the two lords enjoyed the mackerel from Meguro: you want to take a bite out of something new. However, I am sure the lectures of the professors you see every day, the men employed by Gakushūin, are of far greater value and interest than anything I might have to say. You know as well as I do that if I were a professor here, there would not be so many of you in the audience today, and the enthusiasm and curiosity with which you are listening to me now would not have been forthcoming.

I mention this only because many years ago I tried to become a Gakushūin instructor myself. No, I did not come looking for a job; a friend of mine here recommended me. Back then I was the kind of dull-witted fellow who still didn't know what he wanted to do to make a living right up to the moment of graduation. Once you go out into the world, of course, the rent money does not come in while you wait with arms folded. I had to find a position for myself. And so, without considering whether I was, in fact, qualified to become an educator, I did as my friend advised and began to jockey for an opening here. There was a rival applicant, but my friend assured me that I had nothing to worry about. Deciding that I was as good as hired, I went so far as to ask him how instructors were expected to dress. A morning coat would be essential, he told me. So, before anything was decided, I had myself fitted for a morning coat—this, mind you, while I still had only the vaguest notion of where Gakushūin was located!

Well, the coat was finished soon enough, but I failed to receive the appointment I was counting on. The other man was chosen to fill the post of instructor of English. I can't seem to recall his name—probably because I was not especially chagrined at the loss—but apparently he had just come back from studying in America. If, by some fluke, they had hired me instead, and if I had continued teaching here all these years, then I might never have received your courteous invitation or been given the opportunity to speak to you from on high like this. Indeed, look how long you have waited for me: this in itself is proof that you see me as a delicious Meguro mackerel only because I failed in my bid for a job here at Gakushūin![8]

I would now like to say a few words about what has happened to me since my failure to enter Gakushūin—not simply because it follows logically from what I have been saying but because it is an essential part of my talk today.

I was turned down here, but I still had my morning coat. And I wore it because I had nothing else to wear. And where do you suppose I wore it? Finding a job was a very simple matter in those days, unlike the situation today. There was a shortage of people, and you could be sure of finding a fair number of openings no matter where you looked. Even I had almost simultaneous offers from the First National Higher School and the Higher Normal School. I more or less told the faculty member who was negotiating for me with the First National Higher School, who had been a former teacher of mine, that I would accept their offer. Meanwhile, I was still giving noncommittal answers to the Higher Normal School. As a result, I got myself into a very difficult situation. I suppose this was just what I deserved for such youthful irresponsibility, but the fact remains that I felt terrible. My former higher school professor, who was negotiating for me, called me in and scolded me for putting him in such an awkward position.

With a foolishly short temper to match my youth, I decided to turn down both offers, and I set about doing so.

But then a note arrived from President Kuhara of the First National Higher School asking me to come and see him.[9] I hurried over to find there the president of the Higher Normal School, Kanō Jigorō, and my former First National Higher School professor.[10] Everything had been decided, they said. I need feel no obligation toward the First National Higher School and should take the Higher Normal School job. I had no choice but to accept the post. Secretly, however, I was greatly annoyed at the way things had turned out, for I did not think very highly of the Higher Normal School, an opinion I know now to have been unjustified. I even attempted to convince President Kanō of my unworthiness. I insisted that if what he had said were true—that as a teacher I must be a model for the students—I was unfit to teach at the Higher Normal School. But he went me one better. Hearing me decline with such simple honesty, he said, made him want me all the more. He refused to let me go. It had never crossed my mind to be so greedy as to hold both jobs at once, but in my immaturity I had nevertheless managed to cause everyone concerned a lot of needless bother. And so I ended up taking the job at the Higher Normal School.

The fact remained, however, that I had never been qualified to make anything of myself as an educator, and now I found myself in an exceedingly uncomfortable position. Perhaps I could have shirked my duties if I had been cleverer; Mr Kanō had complained that I was *too* simple and honest. But I could not escape the feeling that I was in the wrong place. I felt like a fish seller working in a pastry shop.

A year later I finally went to work in a provincial middle school. This was in Matsuyama.[11] I see this amuses you. No doubt you have read my novel *Botchan*. When I wrote *Botchan*, many people asked me who the model for the character nicknamed "Redshirt" might have been. It so happens that I was the only one in Matsuyama Middle School at the time to have a university degree, so if you're going to try to find living models for each of the characters, then Redshirt must be me—a cheering thought indeed![12]

I remained at Matsuyama for just one year. The prefectural governor asked me not to leave, but I had made an arrangement with another school, the Fifth National Higher School in Kumamoto. My teaching experience thus progressed from middle to higher school, and then on to university. The only places in which I haven't taught are elementary school and girls' school.

My stay in Kumamoto was a long one. After I had been there several years, a confidential inquiry suddenly arrived from the Ministry of Education inviting me to go to England to study. At first I thought of declining. After all, I reasoned, how would it serve the nation for someone like me to go abroad with no clear-cut objective? However, my superior, who had relayed the ministry's inquiry, would have none of this. "The ministry knows why it has chosen you," he said. "There is no need for self-appraisal on your part. Just go." Having no good reason to refuse, I followed the government's orders and went to England. But, sure enough, when I got there I had nothing to do.

This requires some explanation, for which I will have to speak about my life and experiences up to the time I went abroad. You may assume that we have come to an important part of today's talk.

At the university I majored in English literature. What, exactly, *is* English literature, you may well ask. I myself did not know the answer to that after three years of intensive study. Our instructor in those days was Professor Dixon.[13] He would make us read poetry aloud, read prose passages to him, do composition. He would scold us for dropping articles and explode when we mispronounced things. His exam questions were always of one kind: give the dates of Wordsworth's birth and death; give the number of Shakespeare's folios; list the works of Scott in chronological order. Even as young as you are, surely you can see what I mean. Can *this* be English literature? Is *this* any way to instill an understanding of what literature is, English or otherwise? All right, you say, forge ahead on your own. But this is like the proverbial blind man peeking through the fence.[14] I would wander about in the library searching for something that would get me started. But there was nothing. This was not simply because I lacked motivation. The field was represented by the most meager collection of books. For three years I studied, and at the end I still did not know what literature was. This was the root cause of my agony.

It was with this ambivalent attitude that I emerged from school to take my place in the world. I became—or, rather, was made into—a teacher. Questionable as my language ability was, I knew enough to get along and managed to squeak by each day. Deep inside, however, I knew only emptiness. No. Perhaps if it had been emptiness, I could have resigned myself more completely, but there was something continually bothering me, some vague, disagreeable, half-formed thing that would not leave me in peace. To make matters worse, I felt not the slightest interest in my work as a teacher. I had known from the start that I was no educator, but I saw it was hopeless when just teaching English classes seemed like an enormous burden. I was always in a crouch, ready to spring into my true calling as soon as the slightest opening should present itself. Yet this "true calling" of mine was something that seemed to be there and, at the same time, was not. No matter where I turned, I could not bring myself to make the plunge.

Having been born into the world, I had to find something to do. But what that something was I had no idea. I stood paralyzed, alone and shut in by a fog, hoping that a single ray of sunlight would shine through, hoping even more that I could turn a searchlight outward and find a lighted path ahead, however narrow. But wherever I looked, there was only obscurity, a formless blur. I felt as if I had been sealed in a sack, unable to escape. If only I had something sharp, I thought, I could tear a hole in the sack. I struggled frantically, but no one handed me what I needed, nor could I find it for myself. There was nothing for me to do but spend day after day in a pall of gloom that I concealed from others even as I kept asking myself, "What will become of me?"

I graduated from the university clutching this anxiety to my breast. I took it with me to Matsuyama and from Matsuyama to Kumamoto. And when, at last, I journeyed to England, the anxiety was still there, deep within me.

Given the opportunity to study abroad, anyone would feel some new sense of responsibility. I worked hard. I strove to accomplish something. But none of the books I read helped me tear my way through the sack. I could search from one end of London to the other, I felt, and never find what I needed. I stayed in my room, thinking how absurd this all was. No amount of reading was going to fill this emptiness in the pit of my stomach. And when I resigned myself to the hopelessness of my task, I could no longer see any point in my reading books.

It was then that I realized that my only hope for salvation lay in fashioning for myself a conception of what literature is, working from the ground up and relying on nothing but my own efforts. At long last I saw that I had been no better than a rootless, floating weed, drifting aimlessly and wholly centered on others—"other-centered" [tanin hon'i] in the sense of an imitator, a man who has someone else drink his liquor for him, who asks the other fellow's opinion of it and makes that opinion his own without question. Yes, it sounds foolish when I put it like this, and you may well doubt that there are people who imitate others in this manner. But, in fact, there are. Why do you think you hear so much about Bergson these days, or Eucken?[15] Simply because Japanese see what is being talked about abroad and, in imitation, they begin shouting about it at home.

In my day it was even worse. Attribute something—anything—to a Westerner and people would follow it blindly, all the while acting as though it made them very important. Everywhere there were men who thought themselves extremely clever because they could pepper their speech with foreign names. Practically everybody was doing it. I say this not in condemnation of others, however. I myself was one of those men. For example, I might read one European's critique of another European's book. Then, never considering the merits of the critique—and without, in fact, understanding it—I would spout it as my own. This piece of mechanically acquired information, this alien thing that I had swallowed whole, which was neither possession nor blood nor flesh of mine, I would regurgitate in the guise of personal opinion. And the times being what they were, everyone would applaud.

No amount of applause, however, could still my anxiety, for I myself knew that I was showing off borrowed clothes, preening with glued-on peacock feathers. I began to see that I must abandon this empty display and move toward something more genuine. Until I did, that anxiety in the pit of my stomach would never go away.

A Westerner, for example, might say a poem was very fine, or its tone extremely good, but this was his view, his Western view. While certainly not irrelevant, it was nothing that I had to repeat if I could not agree with it. I was an independent Japanese, not a slave to England, and it was incumbent upon me *as* a Japanese to possess at least this degree of self-respect. A respect for honesty as well, the ethical precept shared by all nations, forbade me to alter my opinion.

However, the fact remained that as a specialist in English literature, it made me terribly uneasy to find that my ideas clashed with those of native English critics. Whence, indeed, did this clash arise? From differences in habits? Mores? Customs? Surely, if you traced it back far enough, national character was a source. But the average scholar, confounding literature with science, mistakenly concludes that what pleases country A must of necessity win the admiration of country B. This, I was forced to recognize, was where I had made my mistake. All right, then, perhaps it *was* impossible to reconcile the contradiction between the English critics' views and my own. But if it could not be reconciled, at least it could be explained, and that explanation could cast a ray of light on the world of letters here.

It embarrasses me to confess that I was realizing such obvious notions for the first time so late in life, but I have no intention of concealing the truth from you.

My next step was to strengthen—perhaps I should say to build anew— the foundations upon which my study of literature rested. To this end, I began to read books that had nothing whatever to do with literature. If earlier I had been other-centered, it occurred to me that now I must become self-centered [*jiko hon'i*]. I became absorbed in scientific studies, philosophical speculation, anything that would support this position. Now the times are different and the need for self-centeredness should be clear to anyone who has done some thinking, but I was immature then, and the world around me was still not very advanced. There was really no other way for me to proceed.

Once I had grasped this idea of self-centeredness, it became for me an enormous fount of strength, even defiance. Who did these Westerners think they were anyway? I had been feeling lost, in a daze, when the idea of ego-centeredness [*jiga hon'i*] told me where to stand and showed me the road I must take.

I confess that self-centeredness became for me a new beginning, and it helped me to find what I thought would be my lifework. I resolved to write books, to tell people that they need not imitate Westerners, that running blindly after others as they were doing would only cause them great anxiety. If I could spell this out for them with unshakable proof, it would give me pleasure and make them happy as well. This was what I hoped to accomplish.

My anxiety disappeared without a trace. I looked out on London's gloom with a happy heart. I felt that after years of agony my pick had at last struck a vein of ore. A ray of light had broken through the fog and illuminated my way.

At the time that I experienced this enlightenment, I had been in England for more than a year. There was no hope of my accomplishing the task I had set for myself while I was in a foreign country. I decided to collect all the materials I could find and to complete my work after returning to Japan. As it happened, I would return to Japan with a strength I had not possessed when I left for England.

No sooner was I back in Japan, however, than I was obliged to chase about in order to make a living. I taught at the First National Higher School in Tokyo. I taught at the university. Later—my income was still insufficient to make ends meet—I took another job with a private college. On top of all this, I experienced nervous exhaustion. I finally ended up having to write stories for magazines.[16] Circumstances compelled me to give up my contemplated task long before it was completed. My *Theory of Literature* is thus not so much a memorial to my projected "lifework" as its corpse—and a deformed corpse at that. It lies like the ruins of a city street that has been destroyed by an earthquake in the midst of its construction.

However, the idea that came to me at the time—the idea of self-centeredness—has stayed with me. Indeed, it has grown stronger with the passing of each year. My projected work ended in failure, but I found a belief that I could get my hands on, the conviction that I was the single most important person in my life, while others were only secondary. This has given me enormous confidence and peace of mind, and I feel that it will continue to make it possible for me to live. Its strength may well be what enables me to be standing up here like this lecturing to young men like yourselves.

In my talk thus far I have tried to give you a rough idea of what my experience has been, my only motive being a solicitous hope that it will be of some relevance to your own situation. All of you will leave school and go out into the world. For many of you, this will not happen for some time yet. Others will be active in the real world before long. But I suspect that all of you are likely to relive the agony—perhaps a different kind of agony—that I once experienced. There must be those among you who desperately want to break through to something but cannot, as I once did, who want to get a firm hold on something but meet with as maddeningly little success as you would in trying to grasp a slippery, hairless pate. Those of you who may already have carved out a way for yourselves are certainly the exception.

There may be some who are satisfied to travel the old, proven routes behind others—and I do not say you are wrong in doing so *if* it gives you genuine, unshakable peace of mind and self-confidence. If it does not, however, you must continue to dig ahead with your very own pick until you strike that vein of ore. I repeat, you *must* do it, for anyone who fails to strike ore will be unhappy for life, straying through the world in an endless, uneasy crouch. I urge you on so emphatically because I want to help you avoid such a predicament. I have absolutely no intention of suggesting that you take me as a model and emulate me. I know that I have succeeded in making my own way, and however unimpressive it may appear to you, that is entirely a matter of your observation and critical judgment and does me no injury at all. I am satisfied with the route I have taken, but let there be no misunderstanding: it may have given *me* confidence and peace of mind, but I do not for a moment believe that it can, for that reason, serve as a model for you.

In any case, I would suspect that the kind of anguish I experienced lies in store for many of you. And if, indeed, it does, then I hope you will see the necessity for men such as yourselves, engaged in learning and education, to forge ahead until you collide with something, whether you must work at it for ten years, twenty years—or a lifetime. "I have found my way at last! I have broken through at last!" Only when this exclamation echoes from the bottom of your heart will you find peace. And with that shout an indestructible self-confidence will arise within you. Perhaps a goodly number of you have already reached that stage, but if there are any of you now suffering the anguish of being trapped somewhere in a fog, I believe that you should forge ahead until you know that you have struck ore, whatever the sacrifice. I urge you to accomplish this *not* for the nation's sake, nor even for the sake of your families, but because it is absolutely necessary for your own personal happiness. If you have already taken a route similar to mine, then what I have to say here will be of little use to you, but if there is something holding you back, you must press on until you have trampled it to dust. Of course, simply pressing on will not in itself reveal to you the direction you must take: all you can do is go forward until you collide with something.

I do not mean to stand up here and preach to you, but I cannot keep silent when I know that a part of your future happiness is at stake. I speak out because it seems to me that you would hate it if you were always in some amorphous state of mind, if deep down inside you there was nothing but some half-formed, inconclusive, jellyfish sort of thing. If you insist that it does not bother you to feel like that, there is nothing I can say. If you insist that you have surmounted such unhappiness, that is splendid too. It is everything I wish for you. But I myself was unable to surmount that unhappiness even after I had left school—indeed, until I was over thirty. It was, to be sure, a dull ache that afflicted me, but one that persisted year after year. That is why I want so badly for you—any of you who have caught the disease that I once had—to forge bravely onward. I ask you to do this because I believe that you will be able to find the place where you belong and that you will attain peace of mind and self-confidence to last a lifetime.

This concludes the first part of my lecture, and I shall now move on to the second part.

Gakushūin is generally thought of as—and, in fact, it surely is—a school for young men of good social position. If, as I suspect, the sons of the upper classes gather here to the exclusion of the genuinely poor, then foremost among the many things that will accrue to you in the years to come must be power. In other words, when you go out into the world, you will have a good deal more power at your disposal than would a poor man.

I did say earlier that you must forge ahead in your work until you break through in order to attain happiness and peace of mind, but what is it that brings that happiness and peace of mind? You make peace with yourself when the individuality with which you were born arrives where it belongs. And when you have settled on the track and move steadily forward, that individuality of yours proceeds to grow and develop. Only when your individuality and your work are in perfect harmony can you claim to have found the place where you belong.

Having understood this, let us consider what is meant by the word "power." Power is a tool by means of which one forces one's individuality on others. If this sounds too arbitrary, let us say that power *can be used* as such a tool.

After power comes money. This, too, is something that you will have more of at your disposal than would a poor man. Seen in the context in which I have viewed power, money—financial power—can be an exceedingly useful tool for aggrandizing one's individuality through the temptation of others.

Thus, we would have to characterize power and money as enormously convenient implements, for with them one is able to impose one's individuality on other men or to entice them in any direction, as a poor man never could. A man with this kind of power seems very important. In fact, he is very dangerous.

Earlier I spoke primarily with reference to education, literature, and culture when I said that individuality could develop only when one has reached the place where one belongs. But individuality functions in areas well beyond the confines of the liberal arts. I know two brothers, the younger of whom likes to stay at home reading, while the elder is fanatically devoted to fishing. The elder is disgusted with his brother's reclusive ways, his habit of staying bottled up in the house all day long. He's decided that his brother has turned into a world-weary misanthrope because he doesn't go fishing, and he does all he can to drag him along. The younger brother hates the idea, but the elder loads him down with fishing gear and demands that he accompany him to the pond. The younger brother grits his teeth and goes along, hoping he won't catch anything. But luck is against him: he spends the day pulling in disgusting, fat carp. And what is the upshot of all this? Does the elder's plan work? Does his brother's personality change for the better? No, of course not. He ends up hating fishing all the more. We might say that fishing and the elder brother's personality are a perfect match; they ft together without the smallest gap in between. It is strictly a matter of *his* personality, however, and has nothing to do with his brother's nature.

What I have tried to do here is explain how power is used to coerce others. The elder's individuality oppresses the younger and forces him to go fishing against his will. Granted, there are situations where such oppressive methods are unavoidable—say, in the classroom or the army, or in the kind of dormitory that stresses military discipline. But all I have in mind in this instance is the situation that will prevail when you become independent and go out into the world.

So, let us suppose you are fortunate enough to collide with something you think is good, something you like, something that matches your personality. You go on to develop your individuality, all the while forgetting the distinction between yourself and others, and you decide that you are going to get this fellow or that fellow into your camp even if it means dragging him into it. If you have power, then you end up with a strange relationship like that of the two brothers. If you have money, you spread it around, trying to make the other fellow over in your own image. You use the money as a tool of enticement, and with its seductive power you try to change the other fellow into something that pleases you more. Either way, you are very dangerous.

And so it is that my ideas on the subject have come down to this: First, that you will be unhappy for life unless you press on to the point where you discover work that suits you perfectly and enables you to develop your individuality. Second, that if society is going to permit you to respect your own individuality, it only makes sense for you to recognize the individuality of others and respect their inclinations. To me this seems not only necessary but proper. I think it is wrong for you to blame the other fellow for facing left simply because you, by nature, face right. Of course, when it comes to complex questions of good and evil, right and wrong, some fairly detailed examination of the facts may be called for. But where no such questions are involved, or where the questions are not particularly difficult, I can only believe that so long as others grant us liberty, we must grant equal liberty to them and treat them as equals.

There has been a good deal of talk about the "ego" and "self-awareness" these days as a justification for unrestrained self-assertion. You should be on your guard against those who spout such nonsense, for while they hold their own egos in the highest esteem, they make no allowance whatever for other people's egos. I firmly believe that if one has any sense of fairness, if one has any idea of justice, one must grant others the freedom to develop their individuality for the sake of their personal happiness, even as one secures it for oneself. Unless we have a very good reason, we must not be allowed to obstruct others from developing their individuality as they please for the sake of their own happiness. I speak of "obstruction" because one day many of you here will surely be in positions from which you will be able to obstruct others; one day many among you will be able to exploit your power and your money.

Properly speaking, there should be no such thing as power that is unaccompanied by obligation. As long as I reserve the right to stand up here looking down at you and to keep you listening quietly to what I have to say for an hour or more, I should be saying something worthy of keeping you quiet. Or at least if I am going to bore you with a mediocre talk like this one, I had better make certain that my manner and appearance have the dignity to command your respect. Oh, I suppose we could say that you have to behave yourselves because you are the hosts and I am the guest, but that is quite beside the point. It stops short at superficial etiquette—convention—and has nothing whatever to do with the spirit.

Let me give you another example. I am certain you all know what it is like to be scolded by your teachers. But if in this world there is a teacher who does nothing but scold, that teacher is simply unqualified to teach. A teacher who is going to scold must give himself entirely to his teaching, for a teacher who has a right to scold also has a duty to teach. Teachers, as you know, make full use of the right they are given to maintain order and discipline. But there is a duty inseparable from that right, and if they do not discharge it, they cannot live up to the functions implicit in their profession.

The same holds true for money. As I see it, there should be no financially powerful man in this world who does not understand responsibility. Let me explain what I mean. Money is exceptionally handy to have around. It can be used for anything with the utmost flexibility. Let's say I make a hundred thousand yen on the stock market. With that money I can build a house, I can buy books, I can even have a good time in the pleasure quarters. Money can take any form at all. But I think you will agree when I say that the most frightening thing money can do is buy men's minds. This means throwing it down as bait and buying off a man's moral sense, making it a tool to corrupt his soul. Now, assuming that the money I've made on the stock market can have a great ethical and moral impact, we would have to conclude that this is an improper application of money—or so it would seem. And yet this is how money functions; this is a fact we must live with. The only way to prevent it from corrupting the human heart is for those who have money to have a sense of decency and to use their money wisely so that it will do no moral damage. This is why money must always be accompanied by responsibility. One must cultivate sufficient discrimination to appreciate the influence one's money will have in any given situation, and one must manage one's money as responsibly as one's discrimination demands. To do less is to wrong not only the world at large but to wrong oneself.

Everything I have said thus far comes down to these three points. First, if you want to carry out the development of your individuality, you must respect the individuality of others. Second, if you intend to utilize the power in your possession, you must be fully cognizant of the duty that accompanies it. Third, if you wish to demonstrate your financial power, you must respect its concomitant responsibilities.

To put this another way, unless a man has attained some degree of ethical culture, there is no value in his developing his individuality, no value in his using his power or wealth. Or, yet again, in order for him to enjoy these three privileges, he must submit to the control imposed by the character that should accompany such privileges. When a man is devoid of character, everything he does poses a threat. When he seeks to develop his individuality without restraint, he obstructs others. When he attempts to use power, he merely abuses it. When he tries to use money, he corrupts society. Someday you will be in a position where you can do all of these things quite easily. That is why you must not fail to become upstanding men of character.

Let me change the subject for a moment. England, as you know, is a country that cherishes liberty. There is not another country in the world that so cherishes liberty while maintaining the degree of order that England does. I am not very fond of England, to tell you the truth. As much as I dislike the country, however, the fact remains that no nation anywhere is so free and, at the same time, so very orderly. Japan cannnot begin to compare with her. But the English are not merely free. From the time they are children they are taught to respect the freedom of others as they cherish their own. "Freedom" for them is never unaccompanied by the concept of duty. Nelson's famous declaration "England expects every man to do his duty" was by no means limited to that particular wartime situation. It is a deep-rooted ideology that developed as an inseparable concomitant of liberty. They are like two sides of a single coin.

When the English have some complaint, they often stage protest demonstrations. The government, however, never interferes but takes an attitude of silent disinterest. The demonstrators, meanwhile, are fully appreciative of this and never engage in reckless activities that will embarrass the government. We see headlines nowadays about "suffragettes" committing violence, but these women are the exception. One might object that there are too many of them to be dismissed as an exception, but I think that is the only way we can view them. I don't know what it is with these "suffragettes"—perhaps they can't find husbands or they can't find jobs; maybe they are taking advantage of the long-ingrained ethos of respect for women. In any case, this is not the way the English have always behaved. Destroying famous paintings; going on hunger strikes in prison, making life miserable for their jailers; tying themselves to benches in Parliament and shouting in order to drown out the proceedings—perhaps these women go through these unimaginable contortions because they know the men will employ restraint in dealing with them. Whatever their reasons, they are the exception to the rule. In general, the English temperament cherishes liberty that does not depart from the concept of duty.

I am not suggesting that we take England as a model. I simply believe that freedom without a sense of duty is not true freedom, for such self-indulgent freedom cannot exist in society. And if, for a moment, it did, it would quickly be expelled, stamped out by others. I sincerely wish for all of you to be free. At the same time I want to make very certain that you understand what we mean by "duty." I believe in and practice individualism in this sense, and I do not hesitate to declare this before you now.

There must be no misunderstanding in what I mean by "individualism." I ask your undivided attention on this point, for it would be particularly unforgivable of me to instill misunderstanding in young men such as yourselves. Time is running out, so let me explain individualism as simply as I can. Individual liberty is indispensable for the development of individuality about which I spoke earlier. And the development of your individuality will have a great bearing on your happiness. Thus, it would seem to me that we must keep for ourselves and grant to others a degree of liberty such that I can turn left while you turn right, each of us equally unhindered so long as what we do has no effect on others. This is what I mean when I speak of individualism.

The same is true of power and money. What will happen if people abuse these things, if they exploit their wealth and power to attack men they happen not to like? This will surely destroy individuality and give rise to human misery. For example, what if the police commissioner had his men surround my house for no better reason than that the government did not take a fancy to me? The commissioner may actually have that much power, but decency will not permit him to use it in this manner. Or, again, what if one of the great magnates—Mitsui, say, or Iwasaki—were to bribe our maid and have her oppose me in everything? If these individuals have the slightest bit of what we call character behind their money, it would never occur to them to commit such an injustice.

All such evils arise because people like that are incapable of understanding ethical individualism. Instead, they try to aggrandize themselves at the expense of the general public, to use their power—be it financial or otherwise—to further their own selfish ends. Thus it is that individualism—the individualism I am describing here—in no way resembles the danger to the nation that ignorant people imagine it to be. As I see it, individualism involves respecting the existence of others at the same time that one respects one's own existence. I find that a most worthy philosophy.

Simply stated, individualism is a philosophy that replaces cliquism with values based on personal judgment of right and wrong. An individualist is not forever running with the group, forming cliques that thrash around blindly in the interests of power and money. That is why there lurks beneath the surface of his philosophy a loneliness unknown to others. As soon as we deny our little groups, then I simply go my way and I let the other man go his, unhindered. Sometimes, in some instances, we cannot avoid becoming scattered. That is what is lonely.

Back when I was in charge of the literary column of the *Asahi Shimbun*, we ran an article with an unflattering remark about Miyake Setsurei. It was a critical commentary, of course, not a personal attack, and it consisted of a mere line or two. I don't remember exactly when it was printed—perhaps while I was sick, or possibly I *was* the one who gave the go-ahead—but in any case this bit of criticism appeared in the *Asahi* literary column, which made them very angry over at Setsurei's magazine, *Nihon oyobi Nihonjin* [Japan and the Japanese]. They didn't deal directly with me but instead approached a subordinate of mine to demand a retraction. Setsurei himself, of course, had nothing to do with this. It was something that a few of his henchmen took it upon themselves to do. (Perhaps I should call them his "colleagues." "Henchmen" makes them sound like a bunch of thugs.)[17] Well, these "colleagues" of his insisted on a retraction. We would have been happy to oblige them, of course, if it had been a question of factual error, but this was a critique, after all, and there was nothing we could do but insist on our right to publish what we wanted. Their demand was surprising enough in itself, but then some of these men at *Nihon oyobi Nihonjin* started writing negative comments about me in every issue, which truly came as a shock. I never dealt with them directly, but when I heard what was going on, it made me feel very odd. While I was acting out of individualism, they seemed to be functioning strictly as a clique. At times I had gone so far as to publish negative reviews of my own novels in the literary column that I myself controlled, so it shocked me and made me feel very strange to see these "colleagues" of Setsurei angered by a little criticism.[18] I know this will sound disrespectful, but I could not help feeling that they were living in the wrong century. They were like something out of the feudal era.

But even as I reached this conclusion about Setsurei's men, I myself could not deny a sense of loneliness. Differences of opinion, I realize, are bound to arise between the closest of friends. That is why I may have given advice to the many young men who frequent my home but have never—unless it was for some other substantial reason—tried to keep any of them from expressing their views. I acknowledge the existence of others. I grant them this degree of freedom. Thus, I can never hope for another man to support me against his will, however wronged by someone I may feel. Herein lies the loneliness of individualism. Before the individualist will take a stand based on what others are doing, he chooses a course of action based on the merits of the case. As a result, he will sometimes find himself quite alone. He will miss the comfort of having allies. And that is as it should be: even matchsticks feel secure in a bundle.

I would like to add just one other word to avoid any misunderstanding. Many people seem to think of individualism as something opposed to—or even destructive of—nationalism. But individualism in no way justifies such a misguided, illogical interpretation. (Actually, I don't like these labels I've been using. People cannot be neatly defined by any single "-ism." For clarity's sake, however, I am forced to discuss a variety of subjects under one heading.) Nowadays some people are spreading the idea—and they believe it—that Japan cannot survive unless she is entirely nationalistic. Many go so far as to assert that our nation will perish unless this terrible "individualism" is stamped out. What utter nonsense! All of us, in fact, are nationalists *and* internationalists *and* individualists as well.

Freedom is the essential substance of individualism, which, in turn, serves as the foundation of individual happiness. However, each man's share of freedom rises and falls like a thermometer in accordance with the relative security or insecurity of the nation. This is not so much an abstract theory as a generalization determined by the facts; it is the way things happen in the natural course of events. The individual's liberty contracts when the country is threatened and expands when the nation is at peace. This is all obvious. No man of character is going to aim solely at the development of his individuality when the very survival of the nation is at stake. On the other hand, do be sure you see that the individualism I am talking about implies a warning against becoming the kind of fellow who insists on keeping his helmet on even after the fire is out, the man who wants to keep in lockstep when that is no longer necessary.

Here is another example. When I was a student in the First National Higher School, some of the other students organized a club. I've forgotten now what they called it and just what its aims were, but the club was a particularly severe advocate of nationalism.[19] Of course, there was nothing wrong with this club. It had plenty of support, including that of the school president, Kinoshita Hirotsugu.[20] All of the members wore badges on their chests. I did not intend to wear any badges, but I was nevertheless made a member. Not being one of the club's originators, I knew that many of my opinions were at odds with theirs, but I joined because I had no good reason not to. When it came time for the inaugural meeting in the big lecture hall, one of the students apparently decided that the occasion deserved a speech. I was, to be sure, a member of the club, but there was much in it that conflicted with my opinions and I recall having strongly attacked its aims. Yet here, at the opening meeting, everything this fellow had to say was a rebuttal of what I had said! I had no idea if he was doing this on purpose or by coincidence, but in any case I was going to have to answer him, and when he was through I stepped to the podium. I suppose I handled myself very badly, but at least I said what was on my mind. My remarks were quite simple, and they went something like this:

> The nation may well be important, but we cannot possibly concern ourselves with the nation from morning to night, as though possessed by it. There may be those who insist that we think of nothing but the nation twenty-four hours a day, but, in fact, no one can go on thinking only of one single thing so incessantly. The bean curd seller does not go around selling bean curd for the nation's sake. He does it to earn a living. Whatever his immediate motives might be, he does contribute something necessary to society and in that sense, perhaps, the nation benefits indirectly. The same might be said of the fact that I had three bowls of rice today for lunch and four for supper. I took a larger serving not for the nation's sake but, frankly, to suit my stomach. These things might be said to have some very indirect influence on the country—indeed, from certain points of view they might bear some relation to the entire drift of world affairs. But what a horror if we had to take that into account and eat for the nation, wash our faces for the nation, go to the toilet for the nation! There is nothing wrong with encouraging nationalism, but to pretend that you are doing all of these impossible things for the nation is simply a lie.

This was more or less what I said.

No one—and I do mean no one—is going to be unconcerned about the nation's safety when one's country is in danger. But when the country is strong and the risk of war small, when there is no threat of being attacked from without, then nationalism should diminish accordingly and individualism enter to fill the vacuum. This only stands to reason. We are all aware that Japan today is not entirely secure. Japan is a poor country—and small. Anything could happen at any time. In that sense all of us must maintain our concern for the nation. But this country of ours is in no danger of suddenly collapsing; we are not about to suffer annihilation. And as long as this is true, there should be no need for all the commotion on behalf of the country. It is like running through the streets dressed in fire-fighting gear, full of self-sacrifice, before any fire has even broken out.

Finally, however, this is all a matter of degree. When war does break out, when a crisis involving the nation's survival does arise, anyone with a mind that can think—anyone who has cultivated sufficient character such that he cannot help but think—will naturally turn his attention to it. Nature itself will see to it that he gives his all for the nation, even if this means placing restrictions on his individual liberty and cutting back on personal activity. Thus, I do not for a moment believe that nationalism and individualism are irreconcilable opposites engaged in a constant state of internecine warfare.

I would like to say more on the subject, but time does not permit, so I will limit myself to these remarks. There is just one other point that I would like to bring to your attention, namely, that a nationalistic morality comes out a very poor second when compared with an individualistic morality. Nations have always been most punctilious concerning the niceties of diplomatic language but not with respect to the morality of their actions. They swindle and cheat and trick each other every chaotic step of the way. That is why you will have to content yourself with a pretty cheap grade of morality when you make the nation your standard, when you conceive of the nation as an indivisible monolith. Approach life from a foundation of individualism, however, and you arrive at a far loftier morality. The difference between the two deserves a good deal of thought. To me, therefore, it seems obvious that in a time of tranquility for the nation, we should place the greater emphasis on individualism, with its lofty moral sense. I am afraid I have no time to say anything further on this subject today.

I want to thank you for inviting me. I have tried my best to explain how necessary individualism will be for young men such as yourselves, who will have the opportunity to live lives of individual fulfillment, and I have done so in the hope that it might be of some use to you once you have gone out into the world. Whether or not I have, in fact, made myself understood I obviously cannot know, but if there should be points that are still unclear to you, it is because I have expressed myself insufficiently or poorly. If you do find that something I have said remains vague, please do not assign some random meaning to my words but instead come to see me at home whenever you wish and I will do my best to explain. Of course, nothing could give me greater satisfaction than to have gained your understanding of my true meaning without this extra effort.[21]

And now I shall step down, lest I overstay my welcome.

Translated by Jay Rubin

Introduction: Natsume Sōseki and the Ten-Year Project

1. Natsume Sōseki, *Sanshirō*, trans. Jay Rubin (Tokyo: University of Tokyo Press, 1977), 30.

2. Extended English-language sources on Sōseki's life include: Beongcheon Yu, *Natsume Sōseki* (New York: Twayne, 1969); and Edwin McClelland, *Two Japanese Novelists: Sōseki and Tōson* (Chicago: University of Chicago Press, 1969). Two standard biographies in Japanese are: Komiya Toyotaka, *Natsume Sōseki*, 3 vols. (Tokyo: Iwanami Shoten, 1953); and Etō Jun, *Sōseki to sono jidai*, 5 vols. (Tokyo: Shinchōsha, 1970–99).

3. Karatani Kōjin, *Origins of Modern Japanese Literature*, trans. ed. Brett de Bary (Durham, N.C.: Duke University Press, 1993), 12.

4. On the connection between Sōseki's London journey and the Sino-Japanese War, see Komori Yōichi, *Sōseki wo yominaosu* (Tokyo: Chikuma Shobō, 1995), esp. 57–86. James Fujii makes the point that while Sōseki's travel to London is often celebrated as a key to his career, his connections to Japanese imperialism in Asia—including his 1909 journey to Manchuria and Korea, commemorated in his travelogue *Here and There in Manchuria and Korea* (*Man-Kan tokorodokoro*, 1909)—are often effaced from Sōseki studies. See James A. Fujii, "Writing Out Asia: Modernity, Canon, and Natsume Sōseki's Kokoro," *positions* 1, no. 1 (1993): 194–223.

5. The text of the lecture can be found in *Science* 14, no. 351 (September 1901): 425–43. Interestingly, the article following Rücker's address is "A Notable Factor of Social Degeneration," by Amos Butler (444–53), which is followed by a review of the book *Anatomy of the Cat*, by Reigherd and Jennings (453–54).

6. "The Civilization of Modern-Day Japan" is available in an English translation by Jay Rubin in Natsume Sōseki, *Kokoro: A Novel and Selected Essays* (Lanham, Md.: Mádison Books, 1992). It is reprinted in J. Thomas Rimer and Van C. Gessel, eds., *The Columbia Anthology of Modern Japanese Literature*, 2 vols. (New York: Columbia University Press, 2005), 1:315–22.

7. Nagayama Yasuo, *Ōgai no okaruto, Sōseki no kagaku* (Tokyo: Shinchōsha, 1999), 11.

8. Joseph A. Murphy, *Metaphorical Circuit: Negotiations Between Literature and Science in Twentieth-Century Japan*, Cornell East Asia Series (Ithaca, N.Y.: Cornell East Asia Series, 2004), 24–54.

9. Karatani, *Origins of Modern Japanese Literature*, 11–17.

10. Quoted in Komiya Toyotaka, "Kaisetsu," afterword to *Bungakuron*, in *Sōseki Zenshū*, 19 vols. (Tokyo: Iwanami Shoten, 1966), 9:523. Ikeda would later become famous for the isolation and patenting of the flavor compound monosodium glutamate, the commercial exploitation of which by the Ajinomoto company brought him great wealth See James Bartholomew, *The Formation of Science in Japan* (New Haven, Conn.: Yale University Press: 1989), 180–81.

11. Quoted in Komiya, "Kaisetsu," 527.

12. Ibid., 525–28.

13. John H. D'Arms, "Funding Trends in the Academic Humanities, 1970–1995: Reflections on the Stability of the System," in *What's Happened to the Humanities?*, ed. Alvin Kernan (Princeton, N.J.: Princeton University Press: 1997), 54.

14. While "cognition" may appear anachronistic, the terminology used in translating psychological terms in the more scientific early parts of Sōseki's *Theory of Literature* pose a difficult problem. The terms "consciousness" and "cognition" cover a wide range of ideas and problems, and their relation in the specialists' literature today is far from settled. For example, there are active controversies over whether "affect" is or is not part of cognition, whether, in fact, there is a question of consciousness outside the question of neurophysiology and cognitive science, and whether that would be a physical problem or some larger psycho-physical proposition For the former see Richard Lane and Lynn Nadel, *Cognitive Neuroscience of Emotion* (New York: Oxford University Press, 2000), 3–10; for the latter two see David Chalmers, *The Conscious Mind: In Search of a Fundamental Theory* (New York: Oxford University Press, 1996). Thus, while Sōseki does not use the word himself, part of the collective point of this volume is that he was trying to express things for which a vocabulary had not yet been invented. Hence the use of the term "cognition" in this volume is intentionally anachronistic at times and is meant to mark Sōseki's use of psychology as distinct from the behaviorism that shortly follows and is dominant in the twentieth century. For a detailed consideration of the appropriateness of the term with regard to Sōseki, see Joseph Murphy, "Separation of Cognition and Affect in *Bungakuron*." *Japan Forum* 20, no. 1 (2008): 103–26.

15. Komori Yōichi, "Bungaku to kagaku," in *Natsume Sōseki wo yomu*, Iwanami bukkuretto, no. 325 (Tokyo: Iwanami Shoten, 1993), 30–42.

16. Some of the material discussed in this section previously appeared in Michael K. Bourdaghs, "Property and Sociological Knowledge: Natsume Sōseki and the Gift of Narrative," *Japan Forum*, 20, no. 1 (2008): 79–101.

17. Takayoshi Matsuo, "A Note on the Political Thought of Natsume Sōseki in His Later Years," in Bernard S. Silberman and H.D. Harootunian, eds., *Japan in Crisis: Essays on Taisho Democracy* (Princeton, N.J.: Princeton University Press, 1974), 67–85.

18. Nozomu Kawamura, *Sociology and Society of Japan* (London: Kegan Paul, 1994), 40–77.

19. John Dower, *War Without Mercy: Race and Power in the Pacific War* (New York: Pantheon, 1986), 204.

20. Charles Letourneau, *Property: Its Origin and Development* (London: Walter Scott, 1892), 170. Sōseki's personal library is housed at Tōhoku University in Sendai, Japan.

21. Charles Letourneau, *The Evolution of Marriage and of the Family* (London: Walter Scott, 1891), 157.

22. John Beattie Crozier, *History of Intellectual Development: On the Lines of Modern Evolution*, 2 vols. (London: Longman, Green, 1897), 1:119

23. Satō Yūko, *Sōseki no seorii: Bungakuron kaidoku* (Tokyo: Ōfūsha, 2005), 8.

24. Mark Anderson, "On Sōseki's *Bungakuron*" (paper presented at Workshop on Natsume Sōseki's *Theory of Literature*, Princeton University, March 17, 2006).

25. Thomas Lamarre, "Expanded Empiricism: Natsume Sōseki with William James," *Japan Forum* 20, no. 1 (2008), 47–77.

26. Sakuta Keiichi, *Kojinshugi no unmei: kindai shōsetsu to shakaigaku* (Tokyo: Iwanami Shoten, 1981), esp. 131–47.

27. Terada Torahiko, "On the Passing of My Teacher, Natsume Sōseki" (Natsume Sōseki sensei no tsuioku), quoted in Nagayama, *Ōgai no okaruto, Sōseki no kagaku*, 11.

28. Komori, *Natsume Sōseki wo yomu*, 31–32.

29. Miyake Yūjirō [Setsurei], "The Introduction of Western Philosophy," in *Fifty Years of New Japan*, ed. Okuma Shigenobu and Marcus Huish, 2 vols. (New York: E. P. Dutton, 1909), 2:230.

30. Masumitsu Keiko, *Natsume Sōseki ron: Sōseki bungaku ni okeru 'ishiki'* (Tokyo: Izumi Shoin, 2004), 99–101.

31. William James, *The Principles of Psychology*, Great Books of the Western World, vol. 53 (Chicago: Encyclopaedia Britannica, 1952), 120.

32. James, *Principles of Psychology*, xiii.

33. James, *Principles of Psychology*, 121.

34. Komiya, "Kaisetsu."

35. Richard Feynman, *The Pleasure of Finding Things Out* (Cambridge, Mass.: Da Capo Press, 2000), 202.

36. Sōseki, "The Civilization of Modern-Day Japan," 274–75.

37. In the lecture these are figured as physical series: from walking, to rickshaw, to automobile, to airplane; from verbal message, to letter, to telegraph, to telephone; and so forth.

38. Takeuchi Yoshimi, "Hōhō toshite no Ajia," in Takeuchi, *Nihon to Ajia* (Tokyo: Chikuma Shobō, 1993), 53–82. The essay is available in English translation as "Asia as Method," in Takeuchi, *What Is Modernity? Writings of Takeuchi Yoshimi*, ed. Richard F. Calichman (New York: Columbia University Press, 2005), 149–65.

39. See Rene Wellek, *The Rise of English Literary History* (New York: McGraw-Hill, 1966).

40. Franklin E. Court, *Institutionalizing English Literature: The Culture and Politics of Literary Study 1750–1900* (Stanford, Calif.: Stanford University Press, 1992), 18. See also Robert Crawford, *Devolving English Literature* (Oxford: Oxford University Press, 1992) and the introduction to James L. Golden and Edward P. J. Corbett, *The Rhetoric of Blair, Campbell, and Whately* (Carbondale and Edwardsville: Southern Illinois University Press, 1990), 1–17.

41. Court, *Institutionalizing English Literature*, 18. See also Crawford, *Devolving English Literature*, 42.

42. See Wellek, *The Rise of English Literary History*, 49.

43. Hippolyte Taine, *History of English Literature*, trans.Henri Van Laun, 4 vols. (New York: Worthington Co., 1889), 1:1.

44. Ibid., 2.

45. Ibid., 4–5.

46. Tsukamoto Toshiaki, "Natsume Sōseki," in Nakajima Takezō et al., eds., *Nihon kindai shōsetsu—hikaku bungakuteki ni mita, Hikaku bungaku kōza III* (Tokyo: Shimizu Kōbundō, 1971), 69–70.

47. Tsukamoto Toshiaki, "'Bungakuron' no hikaku bungakuteki kenkyū," *Nihon bungaku*, vol. 16 (Tokyo: Miraisha, 1967), 16.

48. Nakayama Akihiko, "Chinmoku no rikigakuken—riron=hanriron to shite no Bungakuron," *Hihyō kūkan*, vol. 9 (Tokyo: Fukutake Shoten, 1993).

49. Kamei Hideo, "Sōseki no shinkei suijaku to kyōki," *Kokubungaku kaishaku to kyōzai no kenkyū* 35, no. 5 (April 1989): 80–85; idem, '*Shōsetsu' ron* (Tokyo: Iwanami Shoten, 1999).

50. Atsuko Ueda "*Bungakuron* and 'Literature' in the Making," *Japan Forum* 20, no. 1 (2008): 25–46.

51. Tomiyama Takao, *Popai no kage ni* (Tokyo: Misuzu shobō, 1996).

52. Those arguing for continuity include: Senuma Shigeki, *Natsume Sōseki* (Tokyo: Tokyō Daigaku Shuppankai, 1962); Shigematsu Yasuo, "Bungakuron no ichi—sono mikansei no mondai ni sokushite," in *Kokubungaku* 33, no. 13 (November 1968): 58–64; Shibundō, 1968); Komori Yōichi, *Sōseki o yominaosu* (Tokyo: Chikuma Shobō, 1995); and

Ishihara Chiaki, *Tekusuto wa machigawanai* (Tokyo: Chikuma Shobō, 2004). Those arguing for discontinuity include: Etō Jun, *Natsume Sōseki* (Tokyo: Tōkyō Raifusha, 1956); Ino Kenji, "Sōseki sono joshō," *Iwanami kōza: Nihon bungakushi*, 15 (Tokyo: Iwanami Shoten, 1959); and Yamashiki Kazuo, "Sōseki to kanbungaku—Bungakuron jo o megutte," *Nihon bungaku* 15, no. 4 (April 1966): 19–26.

53. This applies to the academic world as well. In 2004 Ishihara Chiaki counted approximately 450 scholarly articles published on *Kokoro*, 200 of which were published after 1985. See Ishihara Chiaki, *Tekusuto wa machigawanai: Shōsetsu to dokusha no shigoto* (Tokyo: Chikuma Shobō, 2004), 34.

54. This is apparently a postwar trend. During the prewar era Sōseki's first three works were included more often than his later works. See Ishihara Chiaki, *Sōseki to san'nin no dokusha* (Tokyo: Kōdansha Gendai Shinsho, 2004).

55. This is a trend that can be traced back to Komiya Toyotaka's *Sōseki no geijutsu* (Tokyo: Iwanami Shoten, 1942).

56. Takano Mikio, "Sōseki no bungaku riron no kōzō to sono isō," *Nihon kindai bungaku* 28 (1981): 38–51.

57. Karatani, *Origins of Modern Japanese Literature*.

58. Komori Yōichi, *Seikimatsu no yogensha: Natsume Sōseki* (Tokyo: Kōdansha, 1999).

59. Nakayama Akihiko, "Chinmoku no rikigakuken—riron=hanriron to shite no Bungakuron" *Hihyō kūkan* vol. 9 (Tokyo: Fukutake Shoten, 1993).

60. Ogura Shūzō, *Natsume Sōseki Wiriamu Jēmusu juyō no shūhen* (Tokyo: Yūseidō, 1980); idem, "Monoconscious Theory to Bungakuron—Roido Mōgan Hikaku shinrigaku no eikyō" *Kokubungaku nōto* 30 (March 1993):85–103.

61. Masumitsu, *Natsume Sōseki ron*.

62. Shigematsu Yasuo, "Bungakuron kara 'Bungei no tetsugakuteki kiso' 'Sō-sakuka no taido'—Wiriamu Jēmusu to no kanren ni oite," in Uchida Michio and Kubota Yoshitarō eds., *Natsume Sōseki: Sakuhinron*, (Tokyo: Sōbunsha Shuppan, 1976): 361–82.

63. Tomiyama Takao, "Sōseki no yomanakatta hon," *Popai no kage ni* (Tokyo: Misuzu shobō, 1996): 145–84.

64. Karatani Kōjin, *Sōsekiron shūsei* (Tokyo: Daisan Bunmeisha, 1992).

65. Michael Bourdaghs "Eigoken ni okeru Bungakuron no igi—riron, kagaku, shoyū," *Kokubungaku kaishaku to kyōzai no kenkyū* 51, no. 3 (March 2006): 137–47.

66. Murphy, *Metaphorical Circuit*.

67. Matsui Sakuko, *Natsume Sōseki as a Critic of English Literature* (Tokyo: Centre for East Asian Cultural Studies, Tōyō Bunko, 1975).

68. Natsume Sōseki, letter to Morita Sōhei, October 21, 1906, in *Sōseki zenshū*, 29 vols. (Tokyo: Iwanami Shoten, 1993–95), 22:591–93.

69. Karatani, *Origins of Modern Japanese Literature*, 11.

Part One
Excerpts from *Theory of Literature* (*Bungakuron*, 1907)

Preface

1. Ueda Kazutoshi (1867–1937) is widely regarded as the founder of modern Japanese linguistics. He was also, incidentally, the father of novelist Enchi Fumiko (1905–1986).

2. At the beginning of the twentieth century, "literature" (*bungaku*) had yet to emerge as a well-defined discipline at universities, either in Japan or the West. In Japan the word *bungaku* still preserved a much broader definition that had long been current in the Chinese classical tradition, referring to the sorts of intellectual texts that an educated person should know—including philosophical essays, official histories, and canonical poetry, but excluding virtually all works of fiction, which were considered vulgar. The modern notion of *bungaku* as a field consisting of aesthetically distinguished writings from the realms of fiction, poetry, and theater had begun to emerge (see Sōseki's later references to students of "pure literature" [*jun bungaku*]), but in 1907 it was still subordinate to the older and broader definition. This difference in meanings is one of the problems that Sōseki tries to resolve in the present work.

3. *Sa-koku-shi-kan*: four classical Chinese histories, namely, *Spring and Autumn Annals* (*Chunqiu*), *Legends of the States* (*Guoyu*), *Records of the Scribe* (*Shiji*), and *The History of the Former Han Dynasty* (*Hanshu*).

4. After graduating from Tokyo Imperial University in 1893, Sōseki accepted a teaching position at Ehime Prefecture Middle School in Matsuyama. In 1896 he moved to the Fifth Higher School in Kumamoto, where he taught until leaving for London in late 1900. Both cities are far removed from Tokyo, the cultural and intellectual center of the nation—and Sōseki's hometown.

5. Ōtsuka Yasuji (1868–1931) was a professor of aesthetics at Tokyo Imperial University. In accepting the position at the university, Sōseki replaced Lafcadio Hearn as the primary lecturer in English literature.

6. Nakagawa Yoshitarō (1882–1939) was a student of Sōseki's at Tokyo Imperial University.

7. This refers to Sōseki's first three published books of fiction: the novel *I Am a Cat* (*Wagahai wa neko de aru*, 1905–6), the short-story collection *Drifting in Space* (*Yōkyoshū*, 1906), and *Quail Cage* (*Uzurakago*, 1907), which comprises three novellas he had previously serialized: *The Young Master* (*Botchan*); *Grass Pillow*, also known as *The Three-Cornered World* (*Kusamakura*); and *The Two Hundred Tenth Day* (*Nihyaku Tōka*).

Book 1. Classification of Literary Substance

1. Théodule Armand Ribot (1839–1916), French psychologist, lecturer in experimental psychology at the University of Paris, and professor of clinical and comparative psychology at the Sorbonne and the College de France. His principal publications include: *Psychology of the Contemporary English* (1870); *Hereditary Psychology* (1873; and *Psychology of Emotions* (1896). Ribot published *The Logic of Emotions* in 1905, but this was likely too recent to have been incorporated into Sōseki's work.

2. "Wave of consciousness" is a fundamental conception that weaves throughout *Theory of Literature* and will be illustrated repeatedly, in various forms, in Sōseki's work from this point on. In the later lectures "The Philosophical Foundation of the Literary Arts" (Bungei no tetsugakuteki kiso, 1907) and "The Attitude of the Creative Artist" (Sōsakuka no taido, 1908), the concept is taken up in more approachable language. Furthermore, Sōseki's strong interest in psychological phenomena related to the movement of consciousness and the unconscious would reveal itself in various forms in his literary works and his philosophy of life. Here Sōseki seeks to explicate the fundamental shape of this development of consciousness by appropriating the explanation of empirical psychologists.

3. Conwyn Lloyd Morgan (1852–1936), English zoologist and psychologist who investigated animal psychology in the light of evolutionary theory and was a forerunner of comparative psychology. His most representative work is *An Introduction to Comparative Psychology* (Hikaku shinrigaku, 1894).

4. Edward Wheeler Scripture (1864–1943), American psychologist who taught at Yale University and advanced a finely detailed theory of experimental psychology in such works as *The New Psychology* (Shin shinrigaku, 1897). When Sōseki refers to "chapter 4" he most likely means part 4.

5. Sōseki cites the phrase "Iwaku ten nari to kotae, Inochi nari to yobu," roughly translated as "Answer Heaven, and I call back Life." The purport of the following discussion of "using x to explain y" refers to using one relatively poorly understood or delineated concept to explain another relatively poorly understood concept (versus, for example, metaphor, which uses a relatively clearly delineated concept to explore a relatively poorly understood one). Here this seems to refer both to the attempt to explicate the relatively difficult-to-grasp concept *ikioi* with the equally difficult-to-grasp concept *ten* and *inochi*, and the attempt to explicate the idea of *shūgōteki F* (cumulative F) with *ikioi*. Here Sōseki finds himself at the limits of explanation.

6. Matthew Arnold (1822–1888), English critic and poet who resisted the current of utilitarianism and science worship of the nineteenth century and instead argued for the kind of cultivation of character and richness of possibility he found in the Greek and Roman classics. His essay "Sweetness and Light" was collected in the volume *Culture and Anarchy* (1869). Here he argued that the two characteristics that should be

pursued by cultivation, i.e., the pursuit of human perfection, are "sweetness" (beauty) and "light" (wisdom).

7. Karl Groos (1861–1946), German psychologist and aesthetician who studied the faculty of imitation through the play of animals and children and adapted this to the various aspects of human artistic activity. He is well regarded for his research into the psychological and physiological dimensions of artistic creativity. *Die Spiele der Menschen* (1899) was translated into English as *The Play of Man* (1901).

8. Sōseki systematically provides such a section ("Chōwa no hō") in book 4 and specifies these rules as harmony, balance, integration, etc.

9. "ikkōsennen yūmōseishin gyōjūzaga."

10. William Bowles (1762–1850), British poet and critic.

11. The original can be found at the following Web site: http://www.fullbooks. com/Selections-from-the-Prose-Works-of-Matthew4.html

Book 2. Quantitative Change in Literary Substance

1. Jeremy O' Brien, "Precision without Entanglement," *Science* 318 (2007): 1393–94.

2. J. Laplanche and J. B. Pontalis, *The Language of Psychoanalysis*, trans. Donald Nicholson-Smith (New York: Norton, 1973), 127.

3. See Richard D. Lane and Lynn Nadel, introduction to *Cognitive Neuroscience of Emotion* (London: Oxford University Press, 2000), 3–12; see also Jaak Panksepp, "Gray Zones at the Emotion-Cognition Interface," *Cognition and Emotion* 4 (1990): 289–302

4. There is a scene in chapter 7 of Sōseki's *Grass Pillow*, also known as *Three-Cornered World* (*Kusamakura*, 1906), in which the narrator, the sole guest at a remote hot springs resort, falls into a reverie while taking the waters and wonders: "Wasn't there some poem by Swinburne where a woman sinks to the bottom of the sea and experiences a kind of elation?" This may refer to Swinburne's "Triumph of Time," though the subject of that poem is a drowning man.

5. This story is from the Chinese classic *Records of the Scribe* (*Shiji*).

Book 3. The Particular Character of Literary Substance

1. Miyake Yūjirō, "The Introduction of Western Philosophy," in Okuma Shig-enobu, ed., *Fifty Years of New Japan*, 2 vols. (London: Smith, Elder, 1909), 2:226–42. This quote appears on page 231. Subsequent citations from this source are identified parenthetically in the text.

2. See Etō Jun, *Sōseki to Sono Jidai*, (Tokyo: Shinchōsha, 1970); and Komiya Toyo-taka, "Kaisetsu" (Afterword) to *Bungakuron*, in *Sōseki Zenshū*, 16 volumes (Tokyo: Iwanami Shoten: 1966), 9:523–545.

3. The purport of this is obscure and the term "conceptual discontinuity of bodies," which is in English in the original, does not appear to remain in the specialized literature. It seems to refer to debates in solid mechanics over whether elasticity in solids is similar to fluids, and the bearing of this on the atomic thesis, which was still unsettled at this point. Sōseki retained an accurate and fairly current view of contemporary debates in physics, both through his sense of the problem residing in a field of knowledge and his long acquaintance with his pupil Terada Torahiko, a research physicist at Tokyo Imperial University.

4. Adolf Zeising (1810–1876), German aesthetician. He was mistakenly identified as Fechner in the original lecture. Sōseki groups philosophy with science in its impulse to analyze.

5. Cf. Plato's *Republic*, book 10: "The poet is like a painter who, as we have already observed, will make a likeness of a cobbler though he understands nothing of cobbling; and his picture is good enough for those who know no more than he does, and judge only by colours and figures" (trans.Benjamin Jowett [Oxford: Clarendon Press, 1908], 600).

6. The first painting is conjectured to be *The Fighting Téméraire* (1839); while the second is *Rain, Steam and Speed* (1844), again referenced in Sōseki's *Grass Pillow* (*Kusamakura*, 1906).

Book 4. Interrelations Between Literary Substances

1. This chart is reproduced from Tsukamoto Toshiaki, "Bungakuron no hikaku bungakuteki kenkyū: sono hassōhō ni tsuite," in *Nihon bungaku*, vol. 16 (Tokyo: Miraisha, 1967).

2. Karatani Kōjin, *Origins of Modern Japanese Literature*, trans. ed. Brett de Bary (Durham, N.C.: Duke University Press, 1993). A similar and perhaps more accessible argument is made in Sōseki's lecture "The Attitude of the Creative Artist" (Sōsakuka no taido, 1908).

3. Pronounced "large F prime" plus "small f prime."

4. Shunkan (1143–1179), a Late Heian priest of the Shingon sect who plotted to overthrow the Taira in 1177 and was exiled to an island together with other members of the Fujiwara family. A general pardon issued shortly thereafter excluded Shunkan, who was made to remain on the island. The story became the subject of early Noh repertoire in the fifteenth century and has been retold in many formats.

5. Sōseki uses the rakugo expression "kumo wo kasumi to nigesaru."

6. George Crabbe (1754–1832), a poet who lived and wrote in poverty for many years until he was befriended by Edmund Burke. He published numerous long poems in the manner of Pope on such subjects as the evils of drink, destitution, and reflections on books and reading. His poem "The Village" (1783) contains a grim, minutely

observed picture of rural poverty and blight. Crabbe was a particular favorite of Jane Austen's, whom Sōseki discusses at length later on.

7. Both poems are quoted in book 1, chapter 2, on sense modalities.

8. "Peter Grimes" is Letter 22, "Strolling Players" is Letter 12, and "The Smoking Club" is Letter 10—all taken from Crabbe's long narrative poem *The Borough* (1810).

9. "Yūjōken no jijitsu." With the idea of a reality based on conditions Sōseki seems to be aiming at an Aristotelian sense of plausibility. In this sense the strategy of definition through character status anticipates parts of Northrop Frye's taxonomy of genre in *Anatomy of Criticism* (Princeton, N.J.: Princeton University Press, 1957). Recall also the qualifications about "psychological realism" in the initial reference to Shakespeare's characters.

10. In an 1815 review Sir Walter Scott praised her work, referring to "that exquisite touch which renders ordinary commonplace things and characters interesting." For a concise discussion of the history of Austen's reception, see the *Oxford Companion to English Literature,* 6th ed., ed. Margaret Drabble (New York: Oxford University Press, 2000), 51–52.

11. Charles Reade (1814–1884), British novelist and playwright.

12. *Zōsui,* a thin soup of rice and vegetables. Cf. chicken soup.

13. Note this is not the same as (F + f). What is at issue here is a difference (a) between certain expressive techniques where f and f′ reinforce each other and certain where they do not or are not defined, and (b) between expressive techniques and thematic techniques. The argument concerning realism and romanticism plays out over these distinctions.

14. Presumably Sōseki is here referring to celsius.

15. Sōseki has eluded the technical requirement to define what is being made susceptible to increase, decrease, and equivalence by designating this quantification "relative" (*hireiteki*). However, the inadequacy of this for quantitative analysis is clear when one poses the question of "equal to ?".

Book 5. Group F

1. René is the protagonist of François-Auguste-René de Chateaubriand's novel *René* (1805).

2. The Heike, or Taira clan, was a powerful warrior family whose defeat in 1185 at the hands of the Genji, or Minamoto clan, was recounted in many classical literary works.

3. Zhuang Zi writes of a monkey trainer who tried to cut his monkeys' food by giving them three acorns in the morning and four at night. The monkeys protested, whereupon he offered them four in the morning and three at night. The foolish mon-

keys accepted. See *Chuang Tzu: Basic Writings*, trans. Burton Watson (New York: Columbia University Press, 1964), 36.

4. Yosa Buson (1716–1783), a celebrated Japanese poet.

5. James Mark Baldwin (1861–1934), American pioneer in developmental psychology; Cesare Lombroso (1836–1909), Italian psychologist known for his studies of criminal behavior; Gustave Le Bon (1841–1931), French scholar of social psychology.

6. Nichiren (1222–1282), founder of a major sect of Japanese Buddhism who narrowly escaped being assassinated by political opponents in 1271.

7. Ruler of the Xia Dynasty (ca. 2100–1600 B.C.) in China who is said to have collected copper throughout his realm to cast nine tripods symbolizing the unity of his country. They became a standard figure of speech used to refer to something very heavy.

8. Henry Marshall (1852–1927), American architect who also wrote widely on philosophy and psychology.

9. Fujii Chikugai (1807–1866), poet best known for his Chinese-style poetry.

10. Mori Sosen (1747–1821), painter in the Kanō School style best known for his depictions of animals—especially monkeys.

11. Thomas Carlyle (1795–1887), famous Scottish essayist and historian.

12. George Meredith (1828–1909), respected British novelist during Sōseki's lifetime.

13. Edward Dowden (1843–1913), British literary critic.

14. Sōseki does not use ellipses here, although he skips several lines in the original text.

15. See William Martin Conway, *The Domain of Art* (London: John Murray, 1901), 139–42.

Part Two
Other Writings on Literary Theory, 1907–14

Statement on Joining the *Asahi*

1. Sōseki's good friend Masaoka Shiki had also retired from his university post to join the newspaper *Nihon*. Sōseki describes Masaoka Shiki as a "newspaper man" (*shinbunya*) in *Miyako ni tsukeru yū* ("Evening Arrival at the Capital"). See Natsume Sōseki, *Sōseki zenshū*, 29 vols. (Tokyo: Iwanami Shoten, 1993–95), 16:675 n. 60.3.

2. Sōseki is referring to the time he spent teaching English after graduating from university.

3. Under Meiji constitutional law, the term "imperial appointee" (*chokuninkan*) indicated a senior governmental official from the second class or higher, who had

been invested by imperial command. The *chokuninkan* ranked directly above the *sōninkan*, who ranked above the *hanninkan*. At Tokyo Imperial University, the college president was an imperial appointee (*chokuninkan*) and faculty members were either *sōninkan* or *chokuninkan*. See *Sōseki zenshū*, 16:675 n. 60.8.

4. This is a reference to the famous main gate at Tokyo Imperial University.

5. Tsuboi Kumezō (1858–1936) was a doctor of literature.

6. Sōseki also taught at the First Higher School and Meiji University.

7. This is an allusion to the Chinese classic *Shunjū Sashi-den* (The Spring and Autumn Annals): "Undoubtedly I will meet my untimely death by means of exhaustion from ceaseless activity." Sōseki is punning on the literal meaning of the characters that make up his pen name, which signify one who hates to admit defeat. See *Sōseki zenshū*, 16:676 n.62.12.

Philosophical Foundations of the Literary Arts

1. A *ken* is a unit of length slightly less than six feet. A *tsubo* is a unit of area approximately four yards square.

2. An allusion to Tobari Chikufū (1873–1955), a literary critic and scholar of German literature. He was one of the first to introduce Nietzsche's philosophy to Japan.

3. This alludes to a passage from the *Analects* of Confucius.

4. A reference to the four hereditary status groups, derived from Confucian thought, used to organize Japanese society during the Tokugawa era (1600–1867).

5. Kusunoki Masashige (?–1336), a warrior renowned for his loyalty and devotion to the Emperor Go-Daigo during the turbulent days of the Northern and Southern Courts, when two rival branches of the imperial family both claimed the throne.

6. Unkei (?–1223), Japanese sculptor best known for Buddhist works carved from wood.

7. A reference to the painting *L'Angélus* (1859) by the French artist Jean-François Millet (1814–1875).

8. Sōseki's implict target here is the Naturalism school of writers and critics. See also his essay "The Merits and Flaws of –isms" elsewhere in this volume.

9. Sōseki uses the English word "heroism" here.

10. *Chūshutsuhō*: alternately, "the law of extraction." This concept is also discussed in Sōseki's *Theory of Literature*.

11. Sōseki is here referring to "A Vagabond" (Le Vagabond,1887), a short story by the French writer Guy de Maupassant (1850–1893).

12. Kobe and Yokohama were the first Japanese treaty ports opened to foreigners in the 1850s and remained active centers of the import and export trade in Japan at the time of this lecture.

13. "The Necklace" (La Parure, 1884), a short story by Maupassant.

14. Sōseki gives the two quotations in English. The first is from Shakespeare's *Henry IV, Part 2* (act 2, sc. 3). The second is from the opening chapter of Defoe's *Robinson Crusoe*.

15. Depending on the context, *kangenteki kanka* can also be translated as "receptive affinity" (see next paragraph).

"Preface" to *Literary Criticism*

1. Sōseki uses English here alongside the Japanese "tairitsu aihan no gengo."

2. In his notes Sōseki himself translates *bunkai* as "decomposition."

3. Henry Austin Dobson (1840–1921), English poet, essayist, and biographer. Leslie Stephen (1832–1904), English philosopher and critic; the father of Virginia Woolf.

4. Kasane, whose name is synonymous with ugliness, is the female protagonist of a famous ghost story often taken up in Kabuki and *jōruri* puppet plays.

5. Alexander Dumas père (1802–1870) published *The Black Tulip* in 1850. A historical novel and political allegory set in seventeenth-century Holland, it deals with love and murder.

6. Guy de Maupassant (1850–1893), French author and representative writer of the Naturalist school. *Une Vie* (A Woman's Life), his first novel, was published in 1883.

7. William Aston (1841–1911) served in the British Consular Service in Japan and Korea. His renowned *History of Japanese Literature* (1899) was arguably the first literary history of Japan published in English. Basil Hall Chamberlain (1850–1935), professor of Japanese and philology at Tokyo Imperial University, pioneered the "scientific" study of the Japanese language and rhetoric.

8. *Shintaishi*, literally "poetry of new style," refers to a genre of poetic composition that developed in Japan in the 1880s in response to Western poetry.

9. James Macpherson (1736–1796), Scottish poet who claimed to have translated *The Poems of Ossian* from an ancient Gaelic document. Its authenticity was immediately challenged and a long controversy ensued. It is now believed that Macpherson wrote the work himself, albeit basing it on Scottish folklore.

The Merits and Flaws of –isms

1. Compass chariots (*shinansha*) were carts used in ancient China that came equipped with a device that always pointed south. They were used as a figure of speech to mean something that provides instruction or guidance.

My Individualism

1. "The Civilization of Modern-Day Japan," trans. Jay Rubin, in Natsume Sōseki, *Kokoro: A Novel and Selected Essays* (Lanham, Md.: Madison Books, 1992), 257–83. It has been reprinted in J. Thomas Rimer and Van C. Gessel, eds., *The Columbia Anthology of Modern Japanese Literature*, 2 vols. (New York: Columbia University Press, 2005), 1:315–22.

2. Okada Masayuki (1864–1927), professor of literature and head of the debating club.

3. This was Sōseki's fourth serious bout with stomach ulcers, the illness that finally killed him on December 9, 1916.

4. Sōseki had been invited to speak by the Hojinkai, the group that produced *Hojinkai Zasshi*, in which appeared not only "Watakushi no Kojinshugi" but also, in later years, the juvenilia of such Gakushūin Higher School literary types as the Shirakaba group and Mishima Yukio.

5. *Rakugo* is a traditional form of comic storytelling in which a single performer speaks the parts of all the characters and ties the threads of the tale together at the end in a startling punch line.

6. One version of this story, "Meguro no Sanma," can be found in Imamura Nobuo, ed., *Rakugo Zenshū*, 3 vols. (Tokyo: Kin'ensha, 1969), I:915–36. In my translation "mackerel" is a somewhat arbitrary rendering of *sanma*, *Cololabis saira*, or mackerel (or saury) pike, a saltwater fish that the sheltered lords are convinced can be found only in the woods of Meguro.

7. Ōmori Kingorō (1867–1963), a professor of history at Gakushūin.

8. Sōseki graduated from—and entered the graduate school of—Tokyo Imperial University in July 1893 at the age of twenty-six. By August it was clear that he would not be teaching at Gakushūin, and by October he had settled on the job at the Higher Normal School, as described later on. The man who secured the Gakushūin post, Shigemi Shūkichi, held degrees in science and medicine from Yale University.

9. By the time of Sōseki's lecture, Kuhara Mitsuru (1855–1919) had become president of Kyoto Imperial University.

10. Kanō Jigorō (1860–1938), judo expert and founder of the Kōdōkan.

11. In April 1895 Soseki left graduate school and his part-time post at the Higher Normal School for a full-time position as an English teacher in Matsuyama.

12. A conniving hypocrite, Redshirt receives a sound thrashing at the end of the novel.

13. James Main Dixon (1856–1933), a Scotsman, taught English literature at the university from 1886 to 1892.

14. The original Japanese is "Mekura no kakinozoki." There are several such expressions for pointless activity (e.g., "Tsunbo no tachigiki," a deaf man's eavesdropping).

15. Rudolph Eucken (1846–1926), German philosopher and winner of the 1908 Nobel Prize in literature.

16. Thus, inauspiciously, did his literary career begin in 1905 with the publication of "Wagahai wa Neko de Aru" (I Am a Cat) in the journal *Hototogisu*. In response to popular demand, the story was expanded into a novel.

17. "Henchmen" here is the usual underworld term for an underling (*kobun*, lit. "having the characteristics of a child"). Sōseki is sardonically pointing to the familial organization shared by underworld gangs, intellectual cliques, and most other groups in Japan despite the use of such egalitarian-sounding terms as *dōjin* (same-[aspiration]-people), here translated as "colleague." For more information on the clash between Setsurei's "henchmen" and Sōseki's assistants, see Natsume Sōseki, *Kokoro: A Novel and Selected Essays*, 315–18.

18. Abe Jirō's critique of *And Then . . .* (*Sore kara . . .*,1909) filled the column for three issues on June 18, 20, 21, 1910. While it paid due respect to the richness of the novel's philosophical content and praised Sōseki as the only novelist of his day capable of handling such grandiose themes, the essay pointed out an unwelcome artificiality and abstractness that marred crucial events in the novel. It also lamented the fact that the portrayal of the central love relationship was particularly unsatisfactory for this reason.

19. The club was probably the one known as the Dōtoku-kai (Moral Society). It was founded in 1889 amid the new wave of intense nationalism (*kokusuishugi*) that had been marked by such events as the assassination of Mori Arinori, the minister of education, on February 11, 1889, for supposed offenses against the national gods, and the founding in 1888 of Miyake Setsurei's new magazine, *Nihonjin* (later called *Nihon oyobi Nihonjin*), devoted to the preservation of the "national essence" (*kokusui*).

20. Kinoshita Hirotsugu (1851–1910) later became president of Seoul Imperial University.

21. In *Within My Glass Doors* (*Garasudo no Naka*, 1915), Sōseki tells of three young men who came to see him shortly after the lecture. One of them did indeed ask for further clarification, but the other two had specific domestic difficulties and asked how they might apply Sōseki's ideas to these practical problems. One of the Gakushū-in students who helped arrange the lecture claimed to have known four or five students who visited Sōseki seeking clarification.

INDEX